BOLLINGEN SERIES LXXX

The Divine Comedy

Paradiso

1: Italian Text and Translation

DANTE ALIGHIERI

The Divine Comedy

TRANSLATED, WITH A COMMENTARY, BY

CHARLES S. SINGLETON

Paradiso

1: Italian Text and Translation

BOLLINGEN SERIES LXXX

PRINCETON UNIVERSITY PRESS

THIS IS VOLUME III OF

THE DIVINE COMEDY OF DANTE ALIGHIERI

CONSTITUTING NUMBER LXXX IN BOLLINGEN SERIES

SPONSORED BY BOLLINGEN FOUNDATION.

THIS VOLUME, PARADISO,

IS IN TWO PARTS: ITALIAN TEXT AND TRANSLATION,

AND COMMENTARY

Library of Congress Catalogue card number 68-57090

ISBN 0-691-09888-3

Printed in the United States of America

by Princeton University Press, Princeton, New Jersey

Second printing, with corrections, 1977

CONTENTS

Paradiso

Italian Text and Translation

PARADISO

LA GLORIA di colui che tutto move
  per l'universo penetra, e risplende
  in una parte più e meno altrove.   *3*
Nel ciel che più de la sua luce prende
  fu' io, e vidi cose che ridire
  né sa né può chi di là sù discende;   *6*
perché appressando sé al suo disire,
  nostro intelletto si profonda tanto,
  che dietro la memoria non può ire.   *9*
Veramente quant' io del regno santo
  ne la mia mente potei far tesoro,
  sarà ora materia del mio canto.   *12*
O buono Appollo, a l'ultimo lavoro
  fammi del tuo valor sì fatto vaso,
  come dimandi a dar l'amato alloro.   *15*
Infino a qui l'un giogo di Parnaso
  assai mi fu; ma or con amendue
  m'è uopo intrar ne l'aringo rimaso.   *18*

CANTO I

THE GLORY of the All-Mover penetrates
through the universe and reglows in one part
more, and in another less. I have been in the
heaven that most receives of His light, and
have seen things which whoso descends from
up there has neither the knowledge nor the
power to relate, because, as it draws near to
its desire, our intellect enters so deep that
memory cannot go back upon the track.
Nevertheless, so much of the holy kingdom
as I could treasure up in my mind shall now
be the matter of my song.

   O good Apollo, for this last labor make me
such a vessel of your worth as you require
for granting your beloved laurel. Thus far
the one peak of Parnassus has sufficed me, but
now I have need of both, as I enter the arena
that remains.

Entra nel petto mio, e spira tue
   sì come quando Marsïa traesti
   de la vagina de le membra sue.   21
O divina virtù, se mi ti presti
   tanto che l'ombra del beato regno
   segnata nel mio capo io manifesti,   24
vedra'mi al piè del tuo diletto legno
   venire, e coronarmi de le foglie
   che la materia e tu mi farai degno.   27
Sì rade volte, padre, se ne coglie
   per trïunfare o cesare o poeta,
   colpa e vergogna de l'umane voglie,   30
che parturir letizia in su la lieta
   delfica deïtà dovria la fronda
   peneia, quando alcun di sé asseta.   33
Poca favilla gran fiamma seconda:
   forse di retro a me con miglior voci
   si pregherà perché Cirra risponda.   36
Surge ai mortali per diverse foci
   la lucerna del mondo; ma da quella
   che quattro cerchi giugne con tre croci,   39
con miglior corso e con migliore stella
   esce congiunta, e la mondana cera
   più a suo modo tempera e suggella.   42
Fatto avea di là mane e di qua sera
   tal foce quasi; e tutto era là bianco
   quello emisperio, e l'altra parte nera,   45
quando Beatrice in sul sinistro fianco
   vidi rivolta e riguardar nel sole:
   aguglia sì non li s'affisse unquanco.   48

4

Enter into my breast and breathe there as when you drew Marsyas from the sheath of his limbs. O divine Power, if you do so lend yourself to me that I may show forth the image of the blessed realm which is imprinted in my mind, you shall see me come to your beloved tree and crown me with those leaves of which the matter and you shall make me worthy. So rarely, father, are they gathered, for triumph of caesar or of poet—fault and shame of human wills—that the Peneian frond ought to beget gladness in the glad Delphic deity whenever it causes anyone to long for it. A great flame follows a little spark: perhaps, after me, prayer shall be offered with better voices, that Cyrrha may respond.

The lamp of the world rises to mortals through different passages; but through that which joins four circles with three crosses it issues with a better course and conjoined with better stars, and tempers and stamps the wax of the world more after its own fashion. Almost such an outlet had made morning there and evening here, and all the hemisphere there was white, and the other dark, when I saw Beatrice turned to her left side and looking at the sun: never did eagle so fix his gaze thereon.

E sì come secondo raggio suole
  uscir del primo e risalire in suso,
  pur come pelegrin che tornar vuole,   *51*
così de l'atto suo, per li occhi infuso
  ne l'imagine mia, il mio si fece,
  e fissi li occhi al sole oltre nostr' uso.   *54*
Molto è licito là, che qui non lece
  a le nostre virtù, mercé del loco
  fatto per proprio de l'umana spece.   *57*
Io nol soffersi molto, né sì poco,
  ch'io nol vedessi sfavillar dintorno,
  com' ferro che bogliente esce del foco;   *60*
e di sùbito parve giorno a giorno
  essere aggiunto, come quei che puote
  avesse il ciel d'un altro sole addorno.   *63*
Beatrice tutta ne l'etterne rote
  fissa con li occhi stava; e io in lei
  le lùci fissi, di là sù rimote.   *66*
Nel suo aspetto tal dentro mi fei,
  qual si fé Glauco nel gustar de l'erba
  che 'l fé consorto in mar de li altri dèi.   *69*
Trasumanar significar *per verba*
  non si poria; però l'essemplo basti
  a cui esperïenza grazia serba.   *72*
S'i' era sol di me quel che creasti
  novellamente, amor che 'l ciel governi,
  tu 'l sai, che col tuo lume mi levasti.   *75*
Quando la rota che tu sempiterni
  desiderato, a sé mi fece atteso
  con l'armonia che temperi e discerni,   *78*

And even as a second ray is wont to issue from the first, and mount upwards again, like a pilgrim who would return home: thus of her action, infused through the eyes into my imagination, mine was made, and I fixed my eyes on the sun beyond our wont. Much is granted to our faculties there that is not granted here, by virtue of the place made for humankind as its proper abode. I did not endure it long, nor so little that I did not see it sparkle round about, like iron that comes molten from the fire. And suddenly day seemed added to day, as if He who has the power had adorned heaven with another sun.

Beatrice was standing with her eyes all fixed upon the eternal wheels, and I fixed mine on her, withdrawn from there above. Gazing upon her I became within me such as Glaucus became on tasting of the grass that made him sea-fellow of the other gods. The passing beyond humanity may not be set forth in words: therefore let the example suffice any for whom grace reserves that experience.

Whether I was but that part of me which Thou didst create last, O Love that rulest the heavens, Thou knowest, who with Thy light didst lift me. When the revolution which Thou, by being desired, makest eternal turned my attention unto itself by the harmony which Thou dost temper and distinguish,

7

parvemi tanto allor del cielo acceso
  de la fiamma del sol, che pioggia o fiume
  lago non fece alcun tanto disteso.   *81*
La novità del suono e 'l grande lume
  di lor cagion m'accesero un disio
  mai non sentito di cotanto acume.   *84*
Ond' ella, che vedea me sì com' io,
  a quïetarmi l'animo commosso,
  pria ch'io a dimandar, la bocca aprio   *87*
e cominciò: "Tu stesso ti fai grosso
  col falso imaginar, sì che non vedi
  ciò che vedresti se l'avessi scosso.   *90*
Tu non se' in terra, sì come tu credi;
  ma folgore, fuggendo il proprio sito,
  non corse come tu ch'ad esso riedi."   *93*
S'io fui del primo dubbio disvestito
  per le sorrise parolette brevi,
  dentro ad un nuovo più fu' inretito   *96*
e dissi: "Già contento *requïevi*
  di grande ammirazion; ma ora ammiro
  com' io trascenda questi corpi levi."   *99*
Ond' ella, appresso d'un pïo sospiro,
  li occhi drizzò ver' me con quel sembiante
  che madre fa sovra figlio deliro,   *102*
e cominciò: "Le cose tutte quante
  hanno ordine tra loro, e questo è forma
  che l'universo a Dio fa simigliante.   *105*
Qui veggion l'alte creature l'orma
  de l'etterno valore, il qual è fine
  al quale è fatta la toccata norma.   *108*

so much of the heaven seemed to me then to be kindled by the sun's flame that rain or river never made a lake so wide. The novelty of the sound and the great light kindled in me a desire to know their cause, never before felt with such keenness. Whereupon she who saw me as I saw myself, to quiet my perturbed mind, opened her lips before I opened mine to ask, and began, "You make yourself dull with false imagining, so that you do not see what you would see had you cast it off. You are not on earth, as you believe; but lightning, fleeing its proper site, never darted so fast as you are returning to yours."

If by these brief words which she smiled to me I was freed from my first perplexity, within a new one I became the more enmeshed; and I said, "I was already content concerning one great wonder; but now I marvel how it can be that I should pass through these light bodies."

Whereupon, after a pitying sigh, she turned her eyes on me with the look that a mother casts on her delirious child. And she began, "All things have order among themselves, and this is the form that makes the universe like God. Herein the high creatures behold the imprint of the Eternal Worth, which is the end wherefor the aforesaid ordinance is made.

9

Ne l'ordine ch'io dico sono accline
   tutte nature, per diverse sorti,
   più al principio loro e men vicine;   *111*
onde si muovono a diversi porti
   per lo gran mar de l'essere, e ciascuna
   con istinto a lei dato che la porti.   *114*
Questi ne porta il foco inver' la luna;
   questi ne' cor mortali è permotore;
   questi la terra in sé stringe e aduna;   *117*
né pur le creature che son fore
   d'intelligenza quest' arco saetta,
   ma quelle c'hanno intelletto e amore.   *120*
La provedenza, che cotanto assetta,
   del suo lume fa 'l ciel sempre quïeto
   nel qual si volge quel c'ha maggior fretta;   *123*
e ora lì, come a sito decreto,
   cen porta la virtù di quella corda
   che ciò che scocca drizza in segno lieto.   *126*
Vero è che, come forma non s'accorda
   molte fïate a l'intenzion de l'arte,
   perch' a risponder la materia è sorda,   *129*
così da questo corso si diparte
   talor la creatura, c'ha podere
   di piegar, così pinta, in altra parte;   *132*
e sì come veder si può cadere
   foco di nube, sì l'impeto primo
   l'atterra torto da falso piacere.   *135*
Non dei più ammirar, se bene stimo,
   lo tuo salir, se non come d'un rivo
   se d'alto monte scende giuso ad imo.   *138*

In the order whereof I speak all natures are
inclined by different lots, nearer and less near
unto their principle; wherefore they move to
different ports over the great sea of being,
each with an instinct given it to bear it on:
this bears fire upwards toward the moon; this
is the motive force in mortal creatures; this
binds together and unites the earth. And not
only does this bow shoot those creatures that
lack intelligence, but also those that have in-
tellect and love. The Providence which or-
dains all this, with Its light makes ever quiet
that heaven within which revolves the sphere
that has the greatest speed; and thither now,
as to a place decreed, the virtue of that bow-
string bears us on, which aims at a joyful
target whatsoever it shoots.

"To be sure, even as a shape often does not
accord with the intention of the art, because
the material is deaf to respond, so the creature
sometimes departs from this course, having
the power, thus impelled, to swerve toward
some other part; and even as the fire from a
cloud may be seen to fall downwards, so the
primal impulse, diverted by false pleasure, is
turned toward earth. You should not wonder
more at your rising, if I deem aright, than at
a stream that falls from a mountain top to the
base.

Maraviglia sarebbe in te se, privo
   d'impedimento, giù ti fossi assiso,
   com' a terra quïete in foco vivo."
Quinci rivolse inver' lo cielo il viso.   *142*

It would be a marvel if you, being freed from hindrance, had settled down below, even as stillness would be in living fire on earth."

Then she turned her gaze heavenwards again.

PARADISO

O VOI CHE siete in piccioletta barca,
  desiderosi d'ascoltar, seguiti
  dietro al mio legno che cantando varca,   *3*
tornate a riveder li vostri liti:
  non vi mettete in pelago, ché forse,
  perdendo me, rimarreste smarriti.   *6*
L'acqua ch'io prendo già mai non si corse;
  Minerva spira, e conducemi Appollo,
  e nove Muse mi dimostran l'Orse.   *9*
Voialtri pochi che drizzaste il collo
  per tempo al pan de li angeli, del quale
  vivesi qui ma non sen vien satollo,   *12*
metter potete ben per l'alto sale
  vostro navigio, servando mio solco
  dinanzi a l'acqua che ritorna equale.   *15*
Que' glorïosi che passaro al Colco
  non s'ammiraron come voi farete,
  quando Iasón vider fatto bifolco.   *18*

CANTO II

O you that are in your little bark, eager to hear, following behind my ship that singing makes her way, turn back to see again your shores. Do not commit yourselves to the open sea, for perchance, if you lost me, you would remain astray. The water which I take was never coursed before. Minerva breathes and Apollo guides me, and nine Muses point out to me the Bears.

You other few who lifted up your necks betimes for bread of angels, on which men here subsist but never become sated of it, you may indeed commit your vessel to the deep brine, holding to my furrow ahead of the water that turns smooth again. Those glorious ones who crossed the sea to Colchis, when they saw Jason turned plowman, were not as amazed as you shall be.

La concreata e perpetüa sete
  del deïforme regno cen portava
  veloci quasi come 'l ciel vedete.   *21*
Beatrice in suso, e io in lei guardava;
  e forse in tanto in quanto un quadrel posa
  e vola e da la noce si dischiava,   *24*
giunto mi vidi ove mirabil cosa
  mi torse il viso a sé; e però quella
  cui non potea mia cura essere ascosa,   *27*
volta ver' me, sì lieta come bella,
  "Drizza la mente in Dio grata," mi disse,
  "che n'ha congiunti con la prima stella."   *30*
Parev' a me che nube ne coprisse
  lucida, spessa, solida e pulita,
  quasi adamante che lo sol ferisse.   *33*
Per entro sé l'etterna margarita
  ne ricevette, com' acqua recepe
  raggio di luce permanendo unita.   *36*
S'io era corpo, e qui non si concepe
  com' una dimensione altra patio,
  ch'esser convien se corpo in corpo repe,   *39*
accender ne dovria più il disio
  di veder quella essenza in che si vede
  come nostra natura e Dio s'unio.   *42*
Lì si vedrà ciò che tenem per fede,
  non dimostrato, ma fia per sé noto
  a guisa del ver primo che l'uom crede.   *45*
Io rispuosi: "Madonna, sì devoto
  com' esser posso più, ringrazio lui
  lo qual dal mortal mondo m'ha remoto.   *48*

The inborn and perpetual thirst for the dei-
form realm bore us away, swift almost as you
see the heavens. Beatrice was gazing upward,
and I on her; and perhaps in that time that a
bolt strikes, flies, and from the catch is re-
leased, I saw myself arrived where a wondrous
thing drew my sight to it. She, therefore, from
whom my thoughts could not be hidden,
turned toward me, as glad as she was fair, and
"Direct your mind to God in gratitude," she
said, "who has united us with the first star."

It seemed to me that a cloud had enveloped
us, shining, dense, solid and polished, like a
diamond smitten by the sun. Within itself the
eternal pearl received us, as water receives a
ray of light, itself remaining uncleft. If I was
body (and if here we conceive not how one
bulk could brook another, which must be if
body enters body), the more should longing
enkindle us to see that Essence wherein we
behold how our nature and God united them-
selves. There that which we hold by faith
shall be seen, not demonstrated, but known of
itself, like the first truth that man believes.

I answered, "My Lady, devoutly as I most
may, I do thank Him who has removed me
from the mortal world.

17

Ma ditemi: che son li segni bui
   di questo corpo, che là giuso in terra
   fan di Cain favoleggiare altrui?"   *51*
Ella sorrise alquanto, e poi "S'elli erra
   l'oppinïon," mi disse, "d'i mortali
   dove chiave di senso non diserra,   *54*
certo non ti dovrien punger li strali
   d'ammirazione omai, poi dietro ai sensi
   vedi che la ragione ha corte l'ali.   *57*
Ma dimmi quel che tu da te ne pensi."
   E io: "Ciò che n'appar qua sù diverso
   credo che fanno i corpi rari e densi."   *60*
Ed ella: "Certo assai vedrai sommerso
   nel falso il creder tuo, se bene ascolti
   l'argomentar ch'io li farò avverso.   *63*
La spera ottava vi dimostra molti
   lumi, li quali e nel quale e nel quanto
   notar si posson di diversi volti.   *66*
Se raro e denso ciò facesser tanto,
   una sola virtù sarebbe in tutti,
   più e men distribuita e altrettanto.   *69*
Virtù diverse esser convegnon frutti
   di princìpi formali, e quei, for ch'uno,
   seguiterieno a tua ragion distrutti.   *72*
Ancor, se raro fosse di quel bruno
   cagion che tu dimandi, o d'oltre in parte
   fora di sua materia sì digiuno   *75*
esto pianeto, o, sì come comparte
   lo grasso e 'l magro un corpo, così questo
   nel suo volume cangerebbe carte.   *78*

But tell me, what are the dusky marks of this body which there below on earth cause folk to tell the tale of Cain?"

She smiled a little, and then said to me, "If the judgment of mortals errs where the key of sense does not unlock, truly the shafts of wonder should not prick you henceforth, since even when following after the senses you see that reason's wings are short. But tell me what you yourself think of it."

And I, "That which appears to us diverse here above I suppose to be produced by rare and dense matter."

And she, "Verily you shall see that your belief is plunged deep in error, if you listen well to the argument I shall make against it.

"The eighth sphere displays to you many lights which both in quality and in magnitude can be seen to be of diverse countenances. If rarity and density alone produced this thing, one single virtue, more or less or equally distributed, would be in all. Different virtues must needs be fruits of formal principles, the which, save only one, would be destroyed, according to your reckoning. Further, were rarity the cause of that darkness whereof you make question, either this planet would thus be lacking in its matter quite through and through, or else, just as fat and lean are distributed in a body, it would alternate the pages in its volume.

Se 'l primo fosse, fora manifesto
  ne l'eclissi del sol, per trasparere
  lo lume come in altro raro ingesto.   *81*
Questo non è: però è da vedere
  de l'altro; e s'elli avvien ch'io l'altro cassi,
  falsificato fia lo tuo parere.   *84*
S'elli è che questo raro non trapassi,
  esser conviene un termine da onde
  lo suo contrario più passar non lassi;   *87*
e indi l'altrui raggio si rifonde
  così come color torna per vetro
  lo qual di retro a sé piombo nasconde.   *90*
Or dirai tu ch'el si dimostra tetro
  ivi lo raggio più che in altre parti,
  per esser lì refratto più a retro.   *93*
Da questa instanza può deliberarti
  esperïenza, se già mai la provi,
  ch'esser suol fonte ai rivi di vostr' arti.   *96*
Tre specchi prenderai; e i due rimovi
  da te d'un modo, e l'altro, più rimosso,
  tr'ambo li primi li occhi tuoi ritrovi.   *99*
Rivolto ad essi, fa che dopo il dosso
  ti stea un lume che i tre specchi accenda
  e torni a te da tutti ripercosso.   *102*
Ben che nel quanto tanto non si stenda
  la vista più lontana, lì vedrai
  come convien ch'igualmente risplenda.   *105*
Or, come ai colpi de li caldi rai
  de la neve riman nudo il suggetto
  e dal colore e dal freddo primai,   *108*

If the first were the case, this would be mani-
fest in the eclipse of the sun, by the shining
through of the light, as it does when it is
poured upon any rare matter. This is not so;
therefore we must look at the other supposi-
tion, and if it chance that I quash that, your
opinion will be refuted.

"If it be that this rarity does not pass
throughout, needs must there be a limit at
which its contrary intercepts its passing far-
ther, and thence that other's ray would be
cast back, just as color returns from the glass
that hides lead behind itself. Now you will
say that the ray shows itself dimmer there
than in other parts, because it is reflected there
from further back. From this objection experi
ment, which is wont to be the fountain to the
streams of your arts, may deliver you, if ever
you try it. You shall take three mirrors, and set
two of them equally remote from you, and let
the other, even more remote, meet your eyes
between the first two. Turning toward them,
cause a light to be placed behind your back
which may shine in the three mirrors and
return to you reflected from all three. Al-
though the more distant image may not reach
you so great in quantity, you will there see it
must needs be of equal brightness with the
others.

"Now—as beneath the blows of the warm
rays the substrate of the snow is left stripped
both of the color and the coldness which it
had—

così rimaso te ne l'intelletto
  voglio informar di luce sì vivace,
  che ti tremolerà nel suo aspetto.   *111*
Dentro dal ciel de la divina pace
  si gira un corpo ne la cui virtute
  l'esser di tutto suo contento giace.   *114*
Lo ciel seguente, c'ha tante vedute,
  quell' esser parte per diverse essenze,
  da lui distratte e da lui contenute.   *117*
Li altri giron per varie differenze
  le distinzion che dentro da sé hanno
  dispongono a lor fini e lor semenze.   *120*
Questi organi del mondo così vanno,
  come tu vedi omai, di grado in grado,
  che di sù prendono e di sotto fanno.   *123*
Riguarda bene omai sì com' io vado
  per questo loco al vero che disiri,
  sì che poi sappi sol tener lo guado.   *126*
Lo moto e la virtù d'i santi giri,
  come dal fabbro l'arte del martello,
  da' beati motor convien che spiri;   *129*
e 'l ciel cui tanti lumi fanno bello,
  de la mente profonda che lui volve
  prende l'image e fassene suggello.   *132*
E come l'alma dentro a vostra polve
  per differenti membra e conformate
  a diverse potenze si risolve,   *135*
così l'intelligenza sua bontate
  multiplicata per le stelle spiega,
  girando sé sovra sua unitate.   *138*

you, left thus stripped in your intellect, will I inform with light so living that it shall quiver as you look on it.

"Within the heaven of the divine peace revolves a body in whose power lies the being of all that it contains. The following heaven, which has so many things to show, distributes this being through diverse essences, distinct from it and contained by it. The other circles, by various differentiatings, dispose the distinctions which they have within themselves unto their ends and their sowings. These organs of the universe proceed, as you now see, from grade to grade, for they receive from above and operate downwards. Observe well now how I advance through this pass to the truth which you seek, so that hereafter you may know how to take the ford alone. The motion and the virtue of the holy spheres, even as the hammer's art by the smith, must needs be inspired by the blessed movers; and the heaven which so many lights make beautiful takes its stamp from the profound mind that turns it, and of that stamp makes itself the seal. And as the soul within your dust is diffused through different members and conformed to different potencies, so does the Intelligence deploy its goodness, multiplied through the stars, itself circling upon its own unity.

Virtù diversa fa diversa lega
  col prezïoso corpo ch'ella avviva,
  nel qual, sì come vita in voi, si lega.   *141*
Per la natura lieta onde deriva,
  la virtù mista per lo corpo luce
  come letizia per pupilla viva.   *144*
Da essa vien ciò che da luce a luce
  par differente, non da denso e raro;
  essa è formal principio che produce,
conforme a sua bontà, lo turbo e 'l chiaro."   *148*

Divers virtues make divers alloy with the precious body it quickens, wherein, even as life in you, it is bound. Because of the glad nature whence it flows, the mingled virtue shines through the body, as gladness does through a living pupil. Thence comes what seems different between light and light, not from density and rarity. This is the formal principle which produces, conformably with its own excellence, the dark and the bright."

PARADISO

Quel sol che pria d'amor mi scaldò 'l petto,
  di bella verità m'avea scoverto,
  provando e riprovando, il dolce aspetto;   *3*
e io, per confessar corretto e certo
  me stesso, tanto quanto si convenne
  leva' il capo a proferer più erto;   *6*
ma visïone apparve che ritenne
  a sé me tanto stretto, per vedersi,
  che di mia confession non mi sovvenne.   *9*
Quali per vetri trasparenti e tersi,
  o ver per acque nitide e tranquille,
  non sì profonde che i fondi sien persi,   *12*
tornan d'i nostri visi le postille
  debili sì, che perla in bianca fronte
  non vien men forte a le nostre pupille;   *15*
tali vid' io più facce a parlar pronte;
  per ch'io dentro a l'error contrario corsi
  a quel ch'accese amor tra l'omo e 'l fonte.   *18*

CANTO III

THAT SUN which first had heated my breast
with love, proving and refuting had un-
covered to me the sweet aspect of fair truth,
and, to confess me corrected and assured, I
raised my head more erect to speak, in meas-
ure as was meet; but a sight appeared which
held me so fast to itself, to look on it, that I
bethought me not of my confession.

As through smooth and transparent glass,
or through clear and tranquil waters, yet not
so deep that the bottom be lost, the outlines
of our faces return so faint that a pearl on a
white brow comes not less boldly to our eyes,
so did I behold many a countenance eager to
speak; wherefore I fell into the contrary
error to that which kindled love between the
man and the fountain.

Sùbito sì com' io di lor m'accorsi,
   quelle stimando specchiati sembianti,
   per veder di cui fosser, li occhi torsi;   *21*
e nulla vidi, e ritorsili avanti
   dritti nel lume de la dolce guida,
   che, sorridendo, ardea ne li occhi santi.   *24*
"Non ti maravigliar perch' io sorrida,"
   mi disse, "appresso il tuo püeril coto,
   poi sopra 'l vero ancor lo piè non fida,   *27*
ma te rivolve, come suole, a vòto:
   vere sustanze son ciò che tu vedi,
   qui rilegate per manco di voto.   *30*
Però parla con esse e odi e credi;
   ché la verace luce che le appaga
   da sé non lascia lor torcer li piedi."   *33*
E io a l'ombra che parea più vaga
   di ragionar, drizza'mi, e cominciai,
   quasi com' uom cui troppa voglia smaga: *36*
"O ben creato spirito, che a' rai
   di vita etterna la dolcezza senti
   che, non gustata, non s'intende mai,   *39*
grazïoso mi fia se mi contenti
   del nome tuo e de la vostra sorte."
    Ond' ella, pronta e con occhi ridenti: *42*
"La nostra carità non serra porte
   a giusta voglia, se non come quella
   che vuol simile a sé tutta sua corte.   *45*
I' fui nel mondo vergine sorella;
   e se la mente tua ben sé riguarda,
   non mi ti celerà l'esser più bella,   *48*

No sooner was I aware of them than, taking them for mirrored faces, I turned round my eyes to see of whom they were, and saw nothing; and I turned them forward again, straight into the light of the sweet guide, whose holy eyes were glowing as she smiled.

"Do not wonder," she said to me, "that I smile at your childish thought, since it does not yet trust itself upon the truth, but turns you, after its wont, to vacancy. These that you see are real substances, assigned here for failure in their vows. Wherefore speak with them and hear and believe, for the true light that satisfies them does not suffer them to turn their steps aside from it."

And I directed myself to the shade who seemed most eager to speak, and I began like a man whom excessive desire confuses, "O well-created spirit, who in the rays of life eternal do taste the sweetness which, if not tasted, is never understood, it would be a kindness to me if you satisfied me with your name and with your lot."

Whereon she, eager and with smiling eyes, "Our charity does not shut the doors against right will any more than that which wills that all Its court be like Itself. In the world I was a virgin sister, and if your memory be searched well, my being more beautiful will not conceal me from you,

ma riconoscerai ch'i' son Piccarda,
   che, posta qui con questi altri beati,
   beata sono in la spera più tarda.   *51*
Li nostri affetti, che solo infiammati
   son nel piacer de lo Spirito Santo,
   letizian del suo ordine formati.   *54*
E questa sorte che par giù cotanto,
   però n'è data, perché fuor negletti
   li nostri voti, e vòti in alcun canto."   *57*
Ond' io a lei: "Ne' mirabili aspetti
   vostri risplende non so che divino
   che vi trasmuta da' primi concetti: *60*
però non fui a rimembrar festino;
   ma or m'aiuta ciò che tu mi dici,
   sì che raffigurar m'è più latino.   *63*
Ma dimmi: voi che siete qui felici,
   disiderate voi più alto loco
   per più vedere e per più farvi amici?"   *66*
Con quelle altr' ombre pria sorrise un poco;
   da indi mi rispuose tanto lieta,
   ch'arder parea d'amor nel primo foco: *69*
"Frate, la nostra volontà quïeta
   virtù di carità, che fa volerne
   sol quel ch'avemo, e d'altro non ci asseta.   *72*
Se disïassimo esser più superne,
   foran discordi li nostri disiri
   dal voler di colui che qui ne cerne;   *75*
che vedrai non capere in questi giri,
   s'essere in carità è qui *necesse*,
   e se la sua natura ben rimiri.   *78*

but you will recognize that I am Piccarda, who, placed here with these other blessèd ones, am blessèd in the slowest sphere. Our affections, which are kindled solely in the pleasure of the Holy Ghost, rejoice in being conformed to His order. And this lot, which appears so lowly, is given to us because our vows were neglected and void in some particular."

Whereon I said to her, "In your wondrous aspects a something divine shines forth that transmutes you from recollection of former times; therefore I was not quick in calling you to mind, but now that which you tell me helps me so that I more clearly recall your features. But tell me, you who are happy here, do you desire a more exalted place, to see more, and to make yourselves more dear?"

With those other shades she first smiled a little, then answered me so glad that she seemed to burn in the first fire of love, "Brother, the power of love quiets our will and makes us wish only for that which we have and gives us no other thirst. Did we desire to be more aloft, our longings would be discordant with His will who assigns us here: which you will see is not possible in these circles if to exist in charity here is of necessity, and if you well consider what is love's nature.

Anzi è formale ad esto beato *esse*
   tenersi dentro a la divina voglia,
   per ch'una fansi nostre voglie stesse;   *81*
sì che, come noi sem di soglia in soglia
   per questo regno, a tutto il regno piace
   com' a lo re che 'n suo voler ne 'nvoglia.   *84*
E 'n la sua volontade è nostra pace:
   ell' è quel mare al qual tutto si move
   ciò ch'ella crïa o che natura face."   *87*
Chiaro mi fu allor come ogne dove
   in cielo è paradiso, *etsi* la grazia
   del sommo ben d'un modo non vi piove.   *90*
Ma sì com' elli avvien, s'un cibo sazia
   e d'un altro rimane ancor la gola,
   che quel si chere e di quel si ringrazia,   *93*
così fec' io con atto e con parola,
   per apprender da lei qual fu la tela
   onde non trasse infino a co la spuola.   *96*
"Perfetta vita e alto merto inciela
   donna più sù," mi disse, "a la cui norma
   nel vostro mondo giù si veste e vela,   *99*
perché fino al morir si vegghi e dorma
   con quello sposo ch'ogne voto accetta
   che caritate a suo piacer conforma.   *102*
Dal mondo, per seguirla, giovinetta
   fuggi'mi, e nel suo abito mi chiusi
   e promisi la via de la sua setta.   *105*
Uomini poi, a mal più ch'a bene usi,
   fuor mi rapiron de la dolce chiostra:
   Iddio si sa qual poi mia vita fusi.   *108*

Nay, it is the essence of this blessed existence
to keep itself within the divine will, whereby
our wills themselves are made one; so that
our being thus from threshold to threshold
throughout this realm is a joy to all the realm
as to the King, who draws our wills to what
He wills; and in His will is our peace. It is
that sea to which all moves, both what It
creates and what nature makes."

Then was it clear to me how everywhere in
Heaven is Paradise, even if the grace of the
Supreme Good does not there rain down in
one same measure. But as it happens when of
one food we have enough and the appetite
for another still remains, that this is asked for
and thanks are returned for that, so I did with
gesture and with speech, to learn from her
what was the web through which she had not
drawn the shuttle to the end.

"Perfect life and high merit enheaven a
lady more aloft," she said to me, "according
to whose rule, in your world below, are those
who take the robe and veil themselves that
they, even till death, may wake and sleep
with that Spouse who accepts every vow
which love conforms unto His pleasure. From
the world, to follow her, I fled while yet a
girl, and in her habit I clothed me and prom-
ised myself to the way of her order. Then
men, more used to evil than to good, snatched
me from the sweet cloister: and God knows
what then my life became.

E quest' altro splendor che ti si mostra
   da la mia destra parte e che s'accende
   di tutto il lume de la spera nostra,   *111*
ciò ch'io dico di me, di sé intende;
   sorella fu, e così le fu tolta
   di capo l'ombra de le sacre bende.   *114*
Ma poi che pur al mondo fu rivolta
   contra suo grado e contra buona usanza,
   non fu dal vel del cor già mai disciolta.   *117*
Quest' è la luce de la gran Costanza
   che del secondo vento di Soave
   generò 'l terzo e l'ultima possanza."   *120*
Così parlommi, e poi cominciò "*Ave,*
   Maria" cantando, e cantando vanio
   come per acqua cupa cosa grave.   *123*
La vista mia, che tanto lei seguio
   quanto possibil fu, poi che la perse,
   volsesi al segno di maggior disio,   *126*
e a Beatrice tutta si converse;
   ma quella folgorò nel mïo sguardo
   sì che da prima il viso non sofferse;
e ciò mi fece a dimandar più tardo.   *130*

"And this other splendor which shows itself to you at my right side, and which is enkindled with all the light of our sphere, understands of herself that which I say of me. She was a sister, and from her head in like manner was taken the shadow of the sacred veil. Yet, turned back as she was into the world, against her will and against right custom, from her heart's veil she was never loosed. This is the light of the great Constance, who bore to the second blast of Swabia the third and final power."

Thus did she speak to me, and then began to sing *Ave Maria*, and, singing, vanished, as through deep water some heavy thing. My sight, which followed her so far as was possible, after it lost her, turned to the mark of greater desire and wholly reverted to Beatrice; but she so flashed upon my gaze that at first my sight endured it not; and this made me the slower with my questioning.

PARADISO

Intra due cibi, distanti e moventi
   d'un modo, prima si morria di fame,
   che liber' omo l'un recasse ai denti;   *3*
sì si starebbe un agno intra due brame
   di fieri lupi, igualmente temendo;
   sì si starebbe un cane intra due dame: *6*
per che s'i' mi tacea, me non riprendo,
   da li miei dubbi d'un modo sospinto,
   poi ch'era necessario, né commendo.   *9*
Io mi tacea, ma 'l mio disir dipinto
   m'era nel viso, e 'l dimandar con ello,
   più caldo assai che per parlar distinto.   *12*
Fé sì Beatrice qual fé Danïello,
   Nabuccodonosor levando d'ira,
   che l'avea fatto ingiustamente fello;   *15*
e disse: "Io veggio ben come ti tira
   uno e altro disio, sì che tua cura
   sé stessa lega sì che fuor non spira.   *18*

CANTO IV

Bᴇᴛᴡᴇᴇɴ ᴛᴡᴏ foods, distant and appetizing
in equal measure, a free man would die of
hunger before he would bring one of them to
his teeth. So would a lamb stand between two
cravings of fierce wolves, in equal fear of
both; so would a hound stand still between
two hinds. Wherefore, if I was silent, urged in
equal measure by my doubts, I neither blame
nor commend myself, since it was of necessity.

I was silent, but my desire was depicted on
my face, and my questioning with it, in
warmer colors far than by distinct speech.
Beatrice did what Daniel did, when he lifted
Nebuchadnezzar out of the wrath that had
made him unjustly cruel, and she said, "I see
well how one and another desire so draw you
on that your eagerness entangles its own self
and therefore breathes not forth.

Tu argomenti: 'Se 'l buon voler dura,
    la vïolenza altrui per qual ragione
    di meritar mi scema la misura?'   *21*
Ancor di dubitar ti dà cagione
    parer tornarsi l'anime a le stelle,
    secondo la sentenza di Platone.   *24*
Queste son le question che nel tuo *velle*
    pontano igualmente; e però pria
    tratterò quella che più ha di felle.   *27*
D'i Serafin colui che più s'india,
    Moïsè, Samuel, e quel Giovanni
    che prender vuoli, io dico, non Maria,   *30*
non hanno in altro cielo i loro scanni
    che questi spirti che mo t'appariro,
    né hanno a l'esser lor più o meno anni;   *33*
ma tutti fanno bello il primo giro,
    e differentemente han dolce vita
    per sentir più e men l'etterno spiro.   *36*
Qui si mostraro, non perché sortita
    sia questa spera lor, ma per far segno
    de la celestïal c'ha men salita.   *39*
Così parlar conviensi al vostro ingegno,
    però che solo da sensato apprende
    ciò che fa poscia d'intelletto degno.   *42*
Per questo la Scrittura condescende
    a vostra facultate, e piedi e mano
    attribuisce a Dio e altro intende;   *45*
e Santa Chiesa con aspetto umano
    Gabrïel e Michel vi rappresenta,
    e l'altro che Tobia rifece sano.   *48*

You reason, 'If right will endures, by what justice can another's violence lessen the measure of my desert?' Further, that the souls appear to return to the stars, in accordance with Plato's teaching, gives you occasion for doubt. These are the questions that thrust equally upon your will. And therefore I will first treat that which has the most venom.

"Of the Seraphim he who is most in God, Moses, Samuel, and whichever John you will —I say, even Mary—have not their seats in any other heaven than these spirits which have now appeared to you, nor have they more or fewer years for their existence; but all make the first circle beautiful, and have sweet life in different measure, by feeling more and less the eternal breath. These showed themselves here, not because this sphere is allotted to them, but to afford sign of the celestial grade that is least exalted. It is needful to speak thus to your faculty, since only through sense perception does it apprehend that which it afterwards makes fit for the intellect. For this reason Scripture condescends to your capacity, and attributes hands and feet to God, having other meaning; and Holy Church represents to you with human aspect Gabriel and Michael and the other who made Tobit whole again.

Quel che Timeo de l'anime argomenta
   non è simile a ciò che qui si vede,
   però che, come dice, par che senta.   *51*
Dice che l'alma a la sua stella riede,
   credendo quella quindi esser decisa
   quando natura per forma la diede;   *54*
e forse sua sentenza è d'altra guisa
   che la voce non suona, ed esser puote
   con intenzion da non esser derisa.   *57*
S'elli intende tornare a queste ruote
   l'onor de la influenza e 'l biasmo, forse
   in alcun vero suo arco percuote.   *60*
Questo principio, male inteso, torse
   già tutto il mondo quasi, sì che Giove,
   Mercurio e Marte a nominar trascorse.   *63*
L'altra dubitazion che ti commove
   ha men velen, però che sua malizia
   non ti poria menar da me altrove.   *66*
Parere ingiusta la nostra giustizia
   ne li occhi d'i mortali, è argomento
   di fede e non d'eretica nequizia.   *69*
Ma perché puote vostro accorgimento
   ben penetrare a questa veritate,
   come disiri, ti farò contento.   *72*
Se vïolenza è quando quel che pate
   nïente conferisce a quel che sforza,
   non fuor quest' alme per essa scusate: *75*
ché volontà, se non vuol, non s'ammorza,
   ma fa come natura face in foco,
   se mille volte vïolenza il torza.   *78*

What Timaeus argues about the souls is not like this which is seen here, for seemingly he holds what he says for the truth. He says the soul returns to its own star, believing it to have been severed thence when nature gave it for a form. But perhaps his opinion is other than his words sound, and may be of a meaning not to be derided. If he means that the honor of their influence and the blame returns to these wheels, perhaps his bow hits some truth. This principle, ill-understood, once misled almost the entire world, so that it ran astray in naming Jove and Mercury and Mars.

"The other perplexity that troubles you has less of poison, for its malice could not lead you away from me elsewhere. For our justice to seem unjust in mortal eyes is argument of faith, not of heretical iniquity. But since your understanding can well penetrate to this truth, I will make you content as you desire.

"If it be violence when he who suffers contributes nothing to what forces him, these souls would not be excused on that account. For will, if it will not, is not quenched, but does as nature does in fire, though violence wrest it aside a thousand times.

Per che, s'ella si piega assai o poco,
    segue la forza; e così queste fero
    possendo rifuggir nel santo loco.   *81*
Se fosse stato lor volere intero,
    come tenne Lorenzo in su la grada,
    e fece Muzio a la sua man severo,   *84*
così l'avria ripinte per la strada
    ond' eran tratte, come fuoro sciolte;
    ma così salda voglia è troppo rada.   *87*
E per queste parole, se ricolte
    l'hai come dei, è l'argomento casso
    che t'avria fatto noia ancor più volte.   *90*
Ma or ti s'attraversa un altro passo
    dinanzi a li occhi, tal che per te stesso
    non usciresti: pria saresti lasso.   *93*
Io t'ho per certo ne la mente messo
    ch'alma beata non poria mentire,
    però ch'è sempre al primo vero appresso;   *96*
e poi potesti da Piccarda udire
    che l'affezion del vel Costanza tenne;
    sì ch'ella par qui meco contradire.   *99*
Molte fïate già, frate, addivenne
    che, per fuggir periglio, contra grato
    si fé di quel che far non si convenne;   *102*
come Almeone, che, di ciò pregato
    dal padre suo, la propria madre spense,
    per non perder pietà si fé spietato.   *105*
A questo punto voglio che tu pense
    che la forza al voler si mischia, e fanno
    sì che scusar non si posson l'offense.   *108*

For should it bend itself much or little, it follows force: and thus did these when they had power to return to the holy place. If their will had remained whole, such as held Lawrence on the grid and made Mucius severe to his own hand, it would have urged them back, so soon as they were loosed, by the road along which they had been dragged—but such sound will is all too rare. And by these words, if you have gathered them up as you should, is the argument quashed that would have troubled you yet many times.

"But now across your path another strait confronts your eyes, such that you would not get through it by yourself before you would be exhausted. I have put it in your mind for certain that a soul in bliss cannot lie, since it is always near the Primal Truth; and then you could hear from Piccarda that Constance kept her love for the veil, so that here she seems to contradict me. Many a time ere now, brother, has it happened that unwillingly, in order to escape from danger, that was done which ought not to have been done; even as Alcmeon who, urged thereto by his father, slew his own mother, and, so as not to fail in piety, became pitiless. At this point I would have you realize that force mixes with the will, and they so act that the offenses cannot be excused.

43

Voglia assoluta non consente al danno;
   ma consentevi in tanto in quanto teme,
   se si ritrae, cadere in più affanno.   *111*
Però, quando Piccarda quello spreme,
   de la voglia assoluta intende, e io
   de l'altra; sì che ver diciamo insieme."   *114*
Cotal fu l'ondeggiar del santo rio
   ch'uscì del fonte ond' ogne ver deriva;
   tal puose in pace uno e altro disio.   *117*
"O amanza del primo amante, o diva,"
   diss' io appresso, "il cui parlar m'inonda
   e scalda sì, che più e più m'avviva,   *120*
non è l'affezion mia tanto profonda,
   che basti a render voi grazia per grazia;
   ma quei che vede e puote a ciò risponda.   *123*
Io veggio ben che già mai non si sazia
   nostro intelletto, se 'l ver non lo illustra
   di fuor dal qual nessun vero si spazia.   *126*
Posasi in esso, come fera in lustra,
   tosto che giunto l'ha; e giugner puollo:
   se non, ciascun disio sarebbe *frustra*.   *129*
Nasce per quello, a guisa di rampollo,
   a piè del vero il dubbio; ed è natura
   ch'al sommo pinge noi di collo in collo.   *132*
Questo m'invita, questo m'assicura
   con reverenza, donna, a dimandarvi
   d'un'altra verità che m'è oscura.   *135*
Io vo' saper se l'uom può sodisfarvi
   ai voti manchi sì con altri beni,
   ch'a la vostra statera non sien parvi."   *138*

Absolute will does not consent to the wrong, but the will consents thereto in so far as it fears, by drawing back, to fall into greater trouble. Therefore, when Piccarda says this, she means it of the absolute will, and I of the other; so that we both speak truth together."

Such was the rippling of the holy stream which issued forth from the Fount from which springs every truth, and such it set at rest one and the other desire.

"O beloved of the First Lover, O divine one," said I then, "whose speech overflows me and warms me so that it quickens me more and more, not all the depth of my affection is sufficient to render to you grace for grace; but may He who sees and can answer thereto. Well do I see that never can our intellect be wholly satisfied unless that Truth shine on it, beyond which no truth has range. Therein it rests, as a wild beast in his lair, so soon as it has reached it; and reach it it can, else every desire would be in vain. Because of this, questioning springs up like a shoot, at the foot of the truth; and this is nature which urges us to the summit, from height to height. It is this, Lady, that invites and emboldens me to question you with reverence of another truth which is obscure to me. I wish to know if man can so satisfy you for broken vows, with other goods, as not to weigh too short upon your scales."

45

Beatrice mi guardò con li occhi pieni
di faville d'amor così divini,
    che, vinta, mia virtute diè le reni,
e quasi mi perdei con li occhi chini.   *142*

Beatrice looked on me with eyes so full of the sparkling of love and so divine that my power, vanquished, took flight, and I almost lost myself with eyes downcast.

PARADISO

"S'io ti fiammeggio nel caldo d'amore
di là dal modo che 'n terra si vede,
sì che del viso tuo vinco il valore,   *3*
non ti maravigliar, ché ciò procede
da perfetto veder, che, come apprende,
così nel bene appreso move il piede.   *6*
Io veggio ben sì come già resplende
ne l'intelletto tuo l'etterna luce,
che, vista, sola e sempre amore accende;   *9*
e s'altra cosa vostro amor seduce,
non è se non di quella alcun vestigio,
mal conosciuto, che quivi traluce.   *12*
Tu vuo' saper se con altro servigio,
per manco voto, si può render tanto
che l'anima sicuri di letigio."   *15*
Sì cominciò Beatrice questo canto;
e sì com' uom che suo parlar non spezza,
continüò così 'l processo santo: *18*
"Lo maggior don che Dio per sua larghezza
fesse creando, e a la sua bontate
più conformato, e quel ch'e' più apprezza,   *21*

48

CANTO V

"I F I flame on you in the warmth of love beyond the measure that is seen on earth and so vanquish the power of your eyes, do not marvel, for it comes from perfect vision which, according as it apprehends, so does it move its foot to the apprehended good. Well do I note how in your intellect already is shining the eternal light which, seen, alone and always kindles love; and if aught else seduce your love, it is naught save some vestige of that light, ill recognized, which therein shines through. You wish to know if for an unfulfilled vow so much can be paid with other service as may secure the soul from suit."

So Beatrice began this canto, and as one who does not interrupt his speech, she thus continued her holy discourse, "The greatest gift which God in His bounty bestowed in creating, and the most conformed to His own goodness and that which He most prizes,

fu de la volontà la libertate;
   di che le creature intelligenti,
   e tutte e sole, fuoro e son dotate.   24
Or ti parrà, se tu quinci argomenti,
   l'alto valor del voto, s'è sì fatto
   che Dio consenta quando tu consenti;   27
ché, nel fermar tra Dio e l'omo il patto,
   vittima fassi di questo tesoro,
   tal quale io dico; e fassi col suo atto.   30
Dunque che render puossi per ristoro?
   Se credi bene usar quel c'hai offerto,
   di maltolletto vuo' far buon lavoro.   33
Tu se' omai del maggior punto certo;
   ma perché Santa Chiesa in ciò dispensa,
   che par contra lo ver ch'i' t'ho scoverto,   36
convienti ancor sedere un poco a mensa,
   però che 'l cibo rigido c'hai preso,
   richiede ancora aiuto a tua dispensa.   39
Apri la mente a quel ch'io ti paleso
   e fermalvi entro; ché non fa scïenza,
   sanza lo ritenere, avere inteso.   42
Due cose si convegnono a l'essenza
   di questo sacrificio: l'una è quella
   di che si fa; l'altr' è la convenenza.   45
Quest' ultima già mai non si cancella
   se non servata; e intorno di lei
   sì preciso di sopra si favella: 48
però necessitato fu a li Ebrei
   pur l'offerere, ancor ch'alcuna offerta
   si permutasse, come saver dei.   51

was the freedom of the will, with which the
creatures that have intelligence, they all and
they alone, were and are endowed. Now, if
you argue from this, the high worth of the
vow will appear to you, if it be such that God
consents when you consent; for in establish-
ing the compact between God and man, this
treasure becomes the sacrifice, such as I pro-
nounce it, and that by its own act. What then
can be given in compensation? If you think
to make good use of that which you have of-
fered, you seek to do good with ill-gotten
gains.

"You are now assured as to the greater point;
but since Holy Church gives dispensation in
this matter, which seems contrary to the truth
I have declared to you, it behooves you to sit
a while longer at table, for the tough food
which you have taken requires still some aid
for your digestion. Open your mind to that
which I reveal to you, and fix it therewithin;
for to have heard without retaining makes
not knowledge.

"Two things constitute the essence of this
sacrifice: the first is that in respect to which
it is made, and the other is the covenant it-
self. This last is never canceled save by being
kept, and concerning this was my preceding
speech so precise. Therefore it was imperative
upon the Hebrews to offer sacrifice in any
case, though the thing offered might some-
times be changed, as you should know.

L'altra, che per materia t'è aperta,
  puote ben esser tal, che non si falla
  se con altra materia si converta.   *54*
Ma non trasmuti carco a la sua spalla
  per suo arbitrio alcun, sanza la volta
  e de la chiave bianca e de la gialla;   *57*
e ogne permutanza credi stolta,
  se la cosa dimessa in la sorpresa
  come 'l quattro nel sei non è raccolta.   *60*
Però qualunque cosa tanto pesa
  per suo valor che tragga ogne bilancia,
  sodisfar non si può con altra spesa.   *63*
Non prendan li mortali il voto a ciancia;
  siate fedeli, e a ciò far non bieci,
  come Ieptè a la sua prima mancia;   *66*
cui più si convenia dicer 'Mal feci,'
  che, servando, far peggio; e così stolto
  ritrovar puoi il gran duca de' Greci,   *69*
onde pianse Efigènia il suo bel volto,
  e fé pianger di sé i folli e i savi
  ch'udir parlar di così fatto cólto.   *72*
Siate, Cristiani, a muovervi più gravi:
  non siate come penna ad ogne vento,
  e non crediate ch'ogne acqua vi lavi.   *75*
Avete il novo e 'l vecchio Testamento,
  e 'l pastor de la Chiesa che vi guida;
  questo vi basti a vostro salvamento.   *78*
Se mala cupidigia altro vi grida,
  uomini siate, e non pecore matte,
  sì che 'l Giudeo di voi tra voi non rida!   *81*

The other, which is known to you as the matter, may indeed be such that there is no fault if it be exchanged for other matter. But let no one shift the load upon his shoulder at his own judgment, without the turning of both the white and the yellow key; and let him hold all changing folly unless the thing laid down be not contained in that which is taken up, as four in six. Therefore, whatever thing weighs so much through its own worth as to tip every scale cannot be made good by any other outlay.

"Let mortals never take the vow in sport. Be faithful, and with that be not perverse, as was Jephthah in his first offering, who ought rather to have said 'I did amiss,' than, by keeping his vow, to do worse. And you can find the great leader of the Greeks in like manner foolish, wherefore Iphigenia wept that her face was fair, and made weep for her both the simple and the wise who heard the tale of such a rite. Be graver, you Christians, in moving. Be not like a feather to every wind, and think not that every water may cleanse you. You have the New Testament and the Old, and the Shepherd of the Church, to guide you: let this suffice for your salvation. If evil greed cry aught else to you, be you men, and not silly sheep, so that the Jew among you may not laugh at you.

Non fate com' agnel che lascia il latte
  de la sua madre, e semplice e lascivo
  seco medesmo a suo piacer combatte!"   *84*
Così Beatrice a me com' ïo scrivo;
  poi si rivolse tutta disïante
  a quella parte ove 'l mondo è più vivo.   *87*
Lo suo tacere e 'l trasmutar sembiante
  puoser silenzio al mio cupido ingegno,
  che già nuove questioni avea davante;   *90*
e sì come saetta che nel segno
  percuote pria che sia la corda queta,
  così corremmo nel secondo regno.   *93*
Quivi la donna mia vid' io sì lieta,
  come nel lume di quel ciel si mise,
  che più lucente se ne fé 'l pianeta.   *96*
E se la stella si cambiò e rise,
  qual mi fec' io che pur da mia natura
  trasmutabile son per tutte guise!   *99*
Come 'n peschiera ch'è tranquilla e pura
  traggonsi i pesci a ciò che vien di fori
  per modo che lo stimin lor pastura,   *102*
sì vid' io ben più di mille splendori
  trarsi ver' noi, e in ciascun s'udia:
  "Ecco chi crescerà li nostri amori."   *105*
E sì come ciascuno a noi venìa,
  vedeasi l'ombra piena di letizia
  nel folgór chiaro che di lei uscia.   *108*
Pensa, lettor, se quel che qui s'inizia
  non procedesse, come tu avresti
  di più savere angosciosa carizia;   *111*

Be not like the lamb that leaves its mother's milk and, silly and wanton, fights with itself at its own pleasure."

Thus Beatrice to me, even as I write; then she turned full of longing to that part where the universe is most alive. Her silence and her changed look imposed silence on my eager mind, which already had new questionings before it. And as an arrow that strikes the target before the bowcord is quiet, so we sped into the second realm. Here I beheld my lady so glad, when she passed into that heaven's light, that the planet itself became the brighter for it; and if the star changed and smiled, what did I become, who by my very nature am subject to every kind of change?

As in a fish-pool that is still and clear the fish draw to that which comes in such manner from without that they deem it something they can feed on, so did I see full more than a thousand splendors draw towards us, and in each was heard, "Lo one who shall increase our loves!" And, as each came up to us, the shade was seen full of joy, by the bright effulgence that issued from it.

Think, reader, if this beginning went no further, how you would feel an anguished craving to know more,

e per te vederai come da questi
    m'era in disio d'udir lor condizioni,
    sì come a li occhi mi fur manifesti.   *114*
"O bene nato a cui veder li troni
    del trïunfo etternal concede grazia
    prima che la milizia s'abbandoni,   *117*
del lume che per tutto il ciel si spazia
    noi semo accesi; e però, se disii
    di noi chiarirti, a tuo piacer ti sazia."   *120*
Così da un di quelli spirti pii
    detto mi fu; e da Beatrice: "Dì, dì
    sicuramente, e credi come a dii."   *123*
"Io veggio ben sì come tu t'annidi
    nel proprio lume, e che de li occhi il traggi,
    perch' e' corusca sì come tu ridi;   *126*
ma non so chi tu se', né perché aggi,
    anima degna, il grado de la spera
    che si vela a' mortai con altrui raggi."   *129*
Questo diss' io diritto a la lumera
    che pria m'avea parlato; ond' ella fessi
    lucente più assai di quel ch'ell' era.   *132*
Sì come il sol che si cela elli stessi
    per troppa luce, come 'l caldo ha róse
    le temperanze d'i vapori spessi,   *135*
per più letizia sì mi si nascose
    dentro al suo raggio la figura santa;
    e così chiusa chiusa mi rispuose
nel modo che 'l seguente canto canta.   *139*

and by yourself you will see what my desire
was, to hear of their conditions from them,
as soon as they became manifest to my eyes.

"O happy-born, to whom Grace concedes to
see the thrones of the eternal triumph before
you leave your time of warfare, we are en-
kindled by the light that ranges through all
heaven; therefore, if you desire to draw light
from us, sate yourself at your own pleasure."
Thus was it said to me by one of those devout
spirits; and by Beatrice, "Speak, speak se-
curely, and trust even as to gods."

"I see well how you do nest yourself in your
own light, and that you dart it from your eyes,
because it sparkles when you smile; but I
know not who you are, nor why, O worthy
spirit, you have your rank in the sphere that
is veiled to mortals by another's rays." This I
said, turned toward the light which first had
spoken to me; whereon it glowed far brighter
than before. Even as the sun, which, when the
heat has consumed the tempering of the dense
vapors, conceals itself by excess of light, so, by
reason of more joy, the holy figure hid itself
from me within its own radiance and, thus
close enclosed, it answered me in such fashion
as the next canto sings.

PARADISO

"Poscia che Costantin l'aquila volse
    contr' al corso del ciel, ch'ella seguio
    dietro a l'antico che Lavina tolse,   *3*
cento e cent' anni e più l'uccel di Dio
    ne lo stremo d'Europa si ritenne,
    vicino a' monti de' quai prima uscìo;   *6*
e sotto l'ombra de le sacre penne
    governò 'l mondo lì di mano in mano,
    e, sì cangiando, in su la mia pervenne.   *9*
Cesare fui e son Iustinïano,
    che, per voler del primo amor ch'i' sento,
    d'entro le leggi trassi il troppo e 'l vano.   *12*
E prima ch'io a l'ovra fossi attento,
    una natura in Cristo esser, non piùe,
    credea, e di tal fede era contento;   *15*
ma 'l benedetto Agapito, che fue
    sommo pastore, a la fede sincera
    mi dirizzò con le parole sue.   *18*

CANTO VI

"After Constantine turned back the Eagle counter to the course of the heavens which it had followed behind the ancient who took Lavinia to wife, a hundred and a hundred years and more the bird of God abode on Europe's limit, near to the mountains from which it first had issued; and there it governed the world beneath the shadow of its sacred wings, from hand to hand, until by succeeding change it came into mine. I was Caesar, and am Justinian, who, by will of the Primal Love which I feel, removed from among the laws what was superfluous and vain. And before I had put my mind to this work, one nature and no more I held to be in Christ, and with that faith I was content; but the blessed Agapetus, who was the supreme pastor, directed me to the true faith by his words.

Io li credetti; e ciò che 'n sua fede era,
   vegg' io or chiaro sì, come tu vedi
   ogne contradizione e falsa e vera.   *21*
Tosto che con la Chiesa mossi i piedi,
   a Dio per grazia piacque di spirarmi
   l'alto lavoro, e tutto 'n lui mi diedi;   *24*
e al mio Belisar commendai l'armi,
   cui la destra del ciel fu sì congiunta,
   che segno fu ch'i' dovessi posarmi.   *27*
Or qui a la question prima s'appunta
   la mia risposta; ma sua condizione
   mi stringe a seguitare alcuna giunta,   *30*
perché tu veggi con quanta ragione
   si move contr' al sacrosanto segno
   e chi 'l s'appropria e chi a lui s'oppone.   *33*
Vedi quanta virtù l'ha fatto degno
   di reverenza; e cominciò da l'ora
   che Pallante morì per darli regno.   *36*
Tu sai ch'el fece in Alba sua dimora
   per trecento anni e oltre, infino al fine
   che i tre a' tre pugnar per lui ancora.   *39*
E sai ch'el fé dal mal de le Sabine
   al dolor di Lucrezia in sette regi,
   vincendo intorno le genti vicine.   *42*
Sai quel ch'el fé portato da li egregi
   Romani incontro a Brenno, incontro a Pirro,
   incontro a li altri principi e collegi;   *45*
onde Torquato e Quinzio, che dal cirro
   negletto fu nomato, i Deci e ' Fabi
   ebber la fama che volontier mirro.   *48*

I believed him, and what he held by faith I now see as clearly as you see that every contradiction is both false and true. So soon as with the Church I moved my feet, it pleased God, of His grace, to inspire me with this high task, and I gave myself entirely to it, committing arms to my Belisarius, with whom Heaven's right hand was so joined that it was a sign for me to rest from them.

"Here ends, then, my answer to the first question; but its condition constrains me to add a certain sequel to it, in order that you may see with how much reason they move against the sacred standard, both those that take it for their own and those that oppose it. See what great virtue made it worthy of reverence, beginning from the hour when Pallas died to give it sway. You know that it made its stay in Alba for three hundred years and more, till at the end, when the three fought against the three for it still. And you know what it did, through seven kings, from the wrong of the Sabine women down to the woe of Lucretia, conquering the neighboring peoples round about. You know what it did when borne by the illustrious Romans against Brennus, against Pyrrhus, and against the rest, princes and governments; whence Torquatus and Quinctius, named from his neglected locks, the Decii and the Fabii, acquired the fame which I gladly embalm.

61

Esso atterrò l'orgoglio de li Aràbi
   che di retro ad Anibale passaro
   l'alpestre rocce, Po, di che tu labi.   *51*
Sott' esso giovanetti trïunfaro
   Scipïone e Pompeo; e a quel colle
   sotto 'l qual tu nascesti parve amaro.   *54*
Poi, presso al tempo che tutto 'l ciel volle
   redur lo mondo a suo modo sereno,
   Cesare per voler di Roma il tolle.   *57*
E quel che fé da Varo infino a Reno,
   Isàra vide ed Era e vide Senna
   e ogne valle onde Rodano è pieno.   *60*
Quel che fé poi ch'elli uscì di Ravenna
   e saltò Rubicon, fu di tal volo,
   che nol seguiteria lingua né penna.   *63*
Inver' la Spagna rivolse lo stuolo,
   poi ver' Durazzo, e Farsalia percosse
   sì ch'al Nil caldo si sentì del duolo.   *66*
Antandro e Simeonta, onde si mosse,
   rivide e là dov' Ettore si cuba;
   e mal per Tolomeo poscia si scosse.   *69*
Da indi scese folgorando a Iuba;
   onde si volse nel vostro occidente,
   ove sentia la pompeana tuba.   *72*
Di quel che fé col baiulo seguente,
   Bruto con Cassio ne l'inferno latra,
   e Modena e Perugia fu dolente.   *75*
Piangene ancor la trista Cleopatra,
   che, fuggendoli innanzi, dal colubro
   la morte prese subitana e atra.   *78*

It cast down the pride of the Arabs that fol-
lowed Hannibal across the Alpine rocks
whence, Po, you do fall. Under it, Scipio and
Pompey triumphed, while yet in their youth,
and to that hill beneath which you were born
it showed itself bitter. Afterward, near the
time when all Heaven willed to bring the
world to its own state of peace, Caesar, by the
will of Rome, laid hold of it; and what it did
from the Var even to the Rhine, the Isere be-
held, and the Loire and the Seine beheld, and
every valley whence Rhone is filled. What it
did after it came forth from Ravenna and
leaped the Rubicon was of such flight as no
tongue nor pen might follow. Towards Spain
it wheeled the host, then towards Durazzo,
and did so smite Pharsalia that grief was felt
on the burning Nile. It saw again Antandros
and the Simois, whence it had set forth, and
there where Hector lies; and then it shook
itself again—the worse for Ptolemy. From
there it fell like lightning on Juba, then
turned to your west, where it heard Pompey's
trumpet. Of what it wrought with the succeed-
ing marshal, Brutus and Cassius howl in Hell,
and Modena and Perugia were doleful. Be-
cause of it sad Cleopatra is still weeping who,
fleeing before it, took from the viper sudden
and black death.

Con costui corse infino al lito rubro;
  con costui puose il mondo in tanta pace,
  che fu serrato a Giano il suo delubro.   *81*
Ma ciò che 'l segno che parlar mi face
  fatto avea prima e poi era fatturo
  per lo regno mortal ch'a lui soggiace,   *84*
diventa in apparenza poco e scuro,
  se in mano al terzo Cesare si mira
  con occhio chiaro e con affetto puro;   *87*
ché la viva giustizia che mi spira,
  li concedette, in mano a quel ch'i' dico,
  gloria di far vendetta a la sua ira.   *90*
Or qui t'ammira in ciò ch'io ti replìco:
  poscia con Tito a far vendetta corse
  de la vendetta del peccato antico.   *93*
E quando il dente longobardo morse
  la Santa Chiesa, sotto le sue ali
  Carlo Magno, vincendo, la soccorse.   *96*
Omai puoi giudicar di quei cotali
  ch'io accusai di sopra e di lor falli,
  che son cagion di tutti vostri mali.   *99*
L'uno al pubblico segno i gigli gialli
  oppone, e l'altro appropria quello a parte,
  sì ch'è forte a veder chi più si falli.   *102*
Faccian li Ghibellin, faccian lor arte
  sott' altro segno, ché mal segue quello
  sempre chi la giustizia e lui diparte;   *105*
e non l'abbatta esto Carlo novello
  coi Guelfi suoi, ma tema de li artigli
  ch'a più alto leon trasser lo vello.   *108*

With him it coursed far as the Red Sea Shore; with him it set the world in such peace that Janus's temple was locked.

"But what the standard that makes me speak had done before, and after was to do throughout the mortal realm subject unto it, becomes in appearance little and obscure if it be looked on in the hand of the third Caesar with clear eye and pure affection; because the living Justice which inspires me granted to it, in his hand of whom I speak, the glory of doing vengeance for Its own wrath. Now marvel here at what I unfold to you: afterwards it sped with Titus to do vengeance for the vengeance of the ancient sin. Then, when the Lombard tooth bit Holy Church, under its wings Charlemagne, conquering, succored her.

"Now you may judge of such as I accused but now, and of their offenses, which are the cause of all your ills. The one opposes to the public standard the yellow lilies, and the other claims it for a party, so that it is hard to see which offends the most. Let the Ghibellines, let them practise their art under another ensign, for this one he ever follows ill who cleaves justice from it. And let not this new Charles strike it down with his Guelphs, but let him fear talons which have stripped the hide from a greater lion.

Molte fïate già pianser li figli
  per la colpa del padre, e non si creda
  che Dio trasmuti l'armi per suoi gigli!   *111*
Questa picciola stella si correda
  d'i buoni spirti che son stati attivi
  perché onore e fama li succeda: *114*
e quando li disiri poggian quivi,
  sì disvïando, pur convien che i raggi
  del vero amore in sù poggin men vivi.   *117*
Ma nel commensurar d'i nostri gaggi
  col merto è parte di nostra letizia,
  perché non li vedem minor né maggi.   *120*
Quindi addolcisce la viva giustizia
  in noi l'affetto sì, che non si puote
  torcer già mai ad alcuna nequizia.   *123*
Diverse voci fanno dolci note;
  così diversi scanni in nostra vita
  rendon dolce armonia tra queste rote.   *126*
E dentro a la presente margarita
  luce la luce di Romeo, di cui
  fu l'ovra grande e bella mal gradita.   *129*
Ma i Provenzai che fecer contra lui
  non hanno riso; e però mal cammina
  qual si fa danno del ben fare altrui.   *132*
Quattro figlie ebbe, e ciascuna reina,
  Ramondo Beringhiere, e ciò li fece
  Romeo, persona umìle e peregrina.   *135*
E poi il mosser le parole biece
  a dimandar ragione a questo giusto,
  che li assegnò sette e cinque per diece,   *138*

Many a time ere now the sons have wept for the sin of the father; and let him not believe that God will change arms for his lilies.

"This little star is adorned with good spirits who have been active in order that honor and fame might come to them. And when desires, thus deviating, tend thitherward, the rays of true love must needs mount upwards less living. But in the equal measure of our rewards with our desert is part of our joy, because we see them neither less nor greater. Hereby the living Justice makes our affection so sweet within us that it can never be bent aside to any evil. Diverse voices make sweet music, so diverse ranks in our life render sweet harmony among these wheels

"And within this present pearl shines the light of Romeo, whose noble and beautiful work was ill rewarded; but the Provençals who wrought against him have not the laugh, and indeed he takes an ill path who makes harm for himself of another's good work. Raymond Berenger had four daughters, each of them a queen, and Romeo, a man of lowly birth and a pilgrim, did this for him. And then crooked words moved him to demand a reckoning of this just man, who had rendered him seven and five for ten.

indi partissi povero e vetusto;
   e se 'l mondo sapesse il cor ch'elli ebbe
   mendicando sua vita a frusto a frusto,
assai lo loda, e più lo loderebbe." *142*

Thereon he departed, poor and old, and if the world but knew the heart he had while begging his bread morsel by morsel, much as it praises him it would praise him more."

PARADISO

"Osanna, sanctus Deus sabaòth,
  superillustrans claritate tua
  felices ignes horum malacòth!"   3
Così, volgendosi a la nota sua,
  fu viso a me cantare essa sustanza,
  sopra la qual doppio lume s'addua;   6
ed essa e l'altre mossero a sua danza,
  e quasi velocissime faville
  mi si velar di sùbita distanza.   9
Io dubitava e dicea "Dille, dille!"
  fra me, "dille" dicea, "a la mia donna
  che mi diseta con le dolci stille."   12
Ma quella reverenza che s'indonna
  di tutto me, pur per *Be* e per *ice*,
  mi richinava come l'uom ch'assonna.   15
Poco sofferse me cotal Beatrice
  e cominciò, raggiandomi d'un riso
  tal, che nel foco faria l'uom felice: 18

CANTO VII

"*Hosanna, sanctus Deus sabaòth,*
superillustrans claritate tua
felices ignes horum malacòth!"
—so, revolving to his melody I saw that
substance sing, on whom a double light is
twinned; and he and the others moved in
their dance, and like swiftest sparks veiled
themselves from me by sudden distance. I
was in doubt, and was saying to myself,
"Speak to her, speak to her," I was saying,
"speak to her, to my lady who slakes my thirst
with her sweet distillings!" But that reverence
which is wholly mistress of me, only by *Be*
and by *ice*, bowed me like one who drowses.
Short while did Beatrice suffer me thus, and
she began, irradiating me with a smile such
as would make a man happy in the fire,

"Secondo mio infallibile avviso,
  come giusta vendetta giustamente
  punita fosse, t'ha in pensier miso;   *21*
ma io ti solverò tosto la mente;
  e tu ascolta, ché le mie parole
  di gran sentenza ti faran presente.   *24*
Per non soffrire a la virtù che vole
  freno a suo prode, quell' uom che non nacque,
  dannando sé, dannò tutta sua prole;   *27*
onde l'umana specie inferma giacque
  giù per secoli molti in grande errore,
  fin ch'al Verbo di Dio discender piacque   *30*
u' la natura, che dal suo fattore
  s'era allungata, unì a sé in persona
  con l'atto sol del suo etterno amore.   *33*
Or drizza il viso a quel ch'or si ragiona:
  questa natura al suo fattore unita,
  qual fu creata, fu sincera e buona;   *36*
ma per sé stessa pur fu ella sbandita
  di paradiso, però che si torse
  da via di verità e da sua vita.   *39*
La pena dunque che la croce porse
  s'a la natura assunta si misura,
  nulla già mai sì giustamente morse;   *42*
e così nulla fu di tanta ingiura,
  guardando a la persona che sofferse,
  in che era contratta tal natura.   *45*
Però d'un atto uscir cose diverse:
  ch'a Dio e a' Giudei piacque una morte;
  per lei tremò la terra e 'l ciel s'aperse.   *48*

"By my judgment, which cannot err, how just vengeance could be justly avenged, has set you pondering; but I will quickly free your mind, and do you listen, for my words will make you the gift of a great doctrine.

"By not enduring for his own good a curb upon the power that wills, that man who never was born, in damning himself damned all his progeny; wherefore the human race lay sick down there for many centuries in great error, until it pleased the word of God to descend where He, by the sole act of His eternal love, united with Himself in person the nature which had estranged itself from its Maker.

"Turn your sight now to that which now I say: this nature, which was thus united to its Maker, was, when it was created, pure and good; but by its own self it had been banished from Paradise, because it turned aside from the way of the truth and its proper life. The penalty therefore which the Cross inflicted, if it be measured by the nature assumed—none ever so justly stung; also none was ever of such great wrong, if we regard the Person who suffered it, with whom that nature was bound up. Therefore from one act issued things diverse, for one same death was pleasing to God and to the Jews; thereat the earth trembled and Heaven was opened.

73

Non ti dee oramai parer più forte,
  quando si dice che giusta vendetta
  poscia vengiata fu da giusta corte.   *51*
Ma io veggi' or la tua mente ristretta
  di pensiero in pensier dentro ad un nodo,
  del qual con gran disio solver s'aspetta.   *54*
Tu dici: 'Ben discerno ciò ch'i' odo;
  ma perché Dio volesse, m'è occulto,
  a nostra redenzion pur questo modo.'   *57*
Questo decreto, frate, sta sepulto
  a li occhi di ciascuno il cui ingegno
  ne la fiamma d'amor non è adulto.   *60*
Veramente, però ch'a questo segno
  molto si mira e poco si discerne,
  dirò perché tal modo fu più degno.   *63*
La divina bontà, che da sé sperne
  ogne livore, ardendo in sé, sfavilla
  sì che dispiega le bellezze etterne.   *66*
Ciò che da lei sanza mezzo distilla
  non ha poi fine, perché non si move
  la sua imprenta quand' ella sigilla.   *69*
Ciò che da essa sanza mezzo piove
  libero è tutto, perché non soggiace
  a la virtute de le cose nove.   *72*
Più l'è conforme, e però più le piace;
  ché l'ardor santo ch'ogne cosa raggia,
  ne la più somigliante è più vivace.   *75*
Di tutte queste dote s'avvantaggia
  l'umana creatura, e s'una manca,
  di sua nobilità convien che caggia.   *78*

No longer, now, should it seem hard to you when it is said that just vengeance was afterwards avenged by a just court.

"But now I see your mind from thought to thought entangled in a knot, from which, with great desire, it awaits release. You say, 'I follow clearly what I hear, but why God willed this sole way for our redemption is hidden from me.' This decree, brother, is buried from the eyes of everyone whose understanding is not matured within love's flame. But inasmuch as at this mark there is much aiming and little discernment, I shall tell why that way was the most fitting.

"The Divine Goodness, which spurns all envy from itself, burning within itself so sparkles that It displays the eternal beauties. That which immediately derives from it thereafter has no end, because when It seals, Its imprint may never be removed. That which rains down from it immediately is wholly free, because it is not subject to the power of the new things. It is the most conformed to it and therefore pleases It the most; for the Holy Ardor, which irradiates everything, is most living in what is most like Itself.

"With all these gifts the human creature is advantaged, and if one fails, it needs must fall from its nobility.

Solo il peccato è quel che la disfranca
  e falla dissimìle al sommo bene,
  per che del lume suo poco s'imbianca;   81
e in sua dignità mai non rivene,
  se non rïempie, dove colpa vòta,
  contra mal dilettar con giuste pene.   84
Vostra natura, quando peccò *tota*
  nel seme suo, da queste dignitadi,
  come di paradiso, fu remota;   87
né ricovrar potiensi, se tu badi
  ben sottilmente, per alcuna via,
  sanza passar per un di questi guadi: 90
o che Dio solo per sua cortesia
  dimesso avesse, o che l'uom per sé isso
  avesse sodisfatto a sua follia.   93
Ficca mo l'occhio per entro l'abisso
  de l'etterno consiglio, quanto puoi
  al mio parlar distrettamente fisso.   96
Non potea l'uomo ne' termini suoi
  mai sodisfar, per non potere ir giuso
  con umiltate obedïendo poi,   99
quanto disobediendo intese ir suso;
  e questa è la cagion per che l'uom fue
  da poter sodisfar per sé dischiuso.   102
Dunque a Dio convenia con le vie sue
  riparar l'omo a sua intera vita,
  dico con l'una, o ver con amendue.   105
Ma perché l'ovra tanto è più gradita
  da l'operante, quanto più appresenta
  de la bontà del core ond' ell' è uscita,   108

Sin alone is that which disfranchises it and makes it unlike the Supreme Good, so that it is little illumined by Its light; and to its dignity it never returns unless, where fault has emptied, it fill up with just penalties against evil delight. Your nature, when it sinned totally in its seed, was removed from these dignities, even as from Paradise; nor could it recover them, if you consider carefully, by any way except the passing of one of these fords: either that God alone, solely by His clemency, had pardoned; or that man should of himself have given satisfaction for his folly. Fix your eyes now within the abyss of the Eternal Counsel, as closely fastened on my words as you are able. Man, within his own limits, could never make satisfaction, for not being able to descend in humility, by subsequent obedience, so far as in his disobedience he had intended to ascend; and this is the reason why man was shut off from power to make satisfaction by himself. Therefore it was needful for God, with His own ways, to restore man to his full life—I mean with one way, or else with both. But because the deed is so much the more prized by the doer, the more it displays of the goodness of the heart whence it issued,

la divina bontà che 'l mondo imprenta,
  di proceder per tutte le sue vie,
  a rilevarvi suso, fu contenta.   *111*
Né tra l'ultima notte e 'l primo die
  sì alto o sì magnifico processo,
  o per l'una o per l'altra, fu o fie: *114*
ché più largo fu Dio a dar sé stesso
  per far l'uom sufficiente a rilevarsi,
  che s'elli avesse sol da sé dimesso;   *117*
e tutti li altri modi erano scarsi
  a la giustizia, se 'l Figliuol di Dio
  non fosse umilïato ad incarnarsi.   *120*
Or per empierti bene ogne disio,
  ritorno a dichiararti in alcun loco,
  perché tu veggi lì così com' io.   *123*
Tu dici: 'Io veggio l'acqua, io veggio il foco,
  l'aere e la terra e tutte lor misture
  venire a corruzione, e durar poco;   *126*
e queste cose pur furon creature;
  per che, se ciò ch'è detto è stato vero,
  esser dovrien da corruzion sicure.'   *129*
Li angeli, frate, e 'l paese sincero
  nel qual tu se', dir si posson creati,
  sì come sono, in loro essere intero;   *132*
ma li alimenti che tu hai nomati
  e quelle cose che di lor si fanno
  da creata virtù sono informati.   *135*
Creata fu la materia ch'elli hanno;
  creata fu la virtù informante
  in queste stelle che 'ntorno a lor vanno.   *138*

the divine Goodness which puts its imprint
on the world, was pleased to proceed by all
Its ways to raise you up again; nor between
the last night and the first day has there been
or will there be so exalted and so magnificent
a procedure, either by one or by the other; for
God was more bounteous in giving Himself
to make man sufficient to uplift himself again,
than if He solely of Himself had remitted;
and all other modes were scanty in respect to
justice, if the Son of God had not humbled
himself to become incarnate.

"Now, to give full satisfaction to your every
wish, I go back to explain to you a certain
place, that you may see it as clearly as I do.
You say, 'I see water, I see fire and air and
earth, and all their mixtures come to corrup-
tion and endure but little, and yet these things
were created things; so that, if what I have
said to you be true, they ought to be secure
against corruption.'

"The angels, brother, and the pure country
in which you are, may be said to be created
even as they are, in their entire being; but
the elements which you have named, and all
things that are compounded of them, are in-
formed by created power. Created was the
matter that is in them, created was the in-
forming virtue in these stars that wheel about
them.

L'anima d'ogne bruto e de le piante
di complession potenzïata tira
lo raggio e 'l moto de le luci sante;   *141*
ma vostra vita sanza mezzo spira
la somma beninanza, e la innamora
di sé sì che poi sempre la disira.   *144*
E quinci puoi argomentare ancora
vostra resurrezion, se tu ripensi
come l'umana carne fessi allora
che li primi parenti intrambo fensi."   *148*

The soul of every beast and of the plants is drawn from a potentiate compound by the shining and the motion of the holy lights; but your life the Supreme Beneficence breathes forth without intermediary, and so enamors it of Itself that it desires It ever after. And hence you further can infer your resurrection, if you reflect how was the making of human flesh then when the first parents were both formed."

PARADISO

Solea creder lo mondo in suo periclo
   che la bella Ciprigna il folle amore
   raggiasse, volta nel terzo epiciclo;   *3*
per che non pur a lei faceano onore
   di sacrificio e di votivo grido
   le genti antiche ne l'antico errore;   *6*
ma Dïone onoravano e Cupido,
   quella per madre sua, questo per figlio,
   e dicean ch'el sedette in grembo a Dido;   *9*
e da costei ond' io principio piglio
   pigliavano il vocabol de la stella
   che 'l sol vagheggia or da coppa or da ciglio.   *12*
Io non m'accorsi del salire in ella;
   ma d'esservi entro mi fé assai fede
   la donna mia ch'i' vidi far più bella.   *15*
E come in fiamma favilla si vede,
   e come in voce voce si discerne,
   quand' una è ferma e altra va e riede,   *18*

CANTO VIII

THE WORLD was wont to believe, to its peril, that the fair Cyprian, wheeling in the third epicycle, rayed down mad love; wherefore the ancient people in their ancient error not only to her did honor with sacrifice and votive cry, but they honored Dione and Cupid, the one as her mother, the other as her son, and they told that he had sat in Dido's lap; and from her with whom I take my start they took the name of the star which the sun woos, now behind her, now before. I was not aware of rising into it, but of being within it my lady gave me full assurance when I saw her become more beautiful.

And as we see a spark within a flame, and as a voice within a voice is distinguished when one holds the note and another comes and goes,

vid' io in essa luce altre lucerne
  muoversi in giro più e men correnti,
  al modo, credo, di lor viste interne.   *21*
Di fredda nube non disceser venti,
  o visibili o no, tanto festini,
  che non paressero impediti e lenti   *24*
a chi avesse quei lumi divini
  veduti a noi venir, lasciando il giro
  pria cominciato in li alti Serafini;   *27*
e dentro a quei che più innanzi appariro
  sonava "*Osanna*" sì, che unque poi
  di rïudir non fui sanza disiro.   *30*
Indi si fece l'un più presso a noi
  e solo incominciò: "Tutti sem presti
  al tuo piacer, perché di noi ti gioi.   *33*
Noi ci volgiam coi principi celesti
  d'un giro e d'un girare e d'una sete,
  ai quali tu del mondo già dicesti: *36*
'*Voi che 'ntendendo il terzo ciel movete*';
  e sem sì pien d'amor, che, per piacerti,
  non fia men dolce un poco di quïete."   *39*
Poscia che li occhi miei si fuoro offerti
  a la mia donna reverenti, ed essa
  fatti li avea di sé contenti e certi,   *42*
rivolsersi a la luce che promessa
  tanto s'avea, e "Deh, chi siete?" fue
  la voce mia di grande affetto impressa.   *45*
E quanta e quale vid' io lei far piùe
  per allegrezza nova che s'accrebbe,
  quando parlai, a l'allegrezze sue!   *48*

I saw within that light other lamps moving in a circle more and less swift according to the measure, I believe, of their internal sight. From a cold cloud winds, whether visible or not, never descended so swiftly that they would not seem impeded and slow to one who had seen those divine lights come to us, leaving the circling first begun among the high Seraphim; and within those that appeared most in front *Hosanna* sounded in such wise that never since have I been without the desire to hear it again.

Then one drew nearer to us, and alone began, "We are all ready at your pleasure, that you may have joy of us. With one circle, with one circling and with one thirst we revolve with the celestial Princes to whom you in the world did once say, '*You who move the third heaven by intellection*'; and we are so full of love that, in order to please you, a little quiet will not be less sweet to us."

After my eyes had been raised with reverence to my lady, and she had satisfied them with assurance of her consent, they turned back to the light which had promised so much; and "Say who you are" was my utterance, stamped with great affection; and, how much I saw it increase in size and brightness, through the new joy which was added to its joys when I spoke!

Così fatta, mi disse: "Il mondo m'ebbe
   giù poco tempo; e se più fosse stato,
   molto sarà di mal, che non sarebbe.   *51*
La mia letizia mi ti tien celato
   che mi raggia dintorno e mi nasconde
   quasi animal di sua seta fasciato.   *54*
Assai m'amasti, e avesti ben onde;
   che s'io fossi giù stato, io ti mostrava
   di mio amor più oltre che le fronde.   *57*
Quella sinistra riva che si lava
   di Rodano poi ch'è misto con Sorga,
   per suo segnore a tempo m'aspettava,   *60*
e quel corno d'Ausonia che s'imborga
   di Bari e di Gaeta e di Catona,
   da ove Tronto e Verde in mare sgorga.   *63*
Fulgeami già in fronte la corona
   di quella terra che 'l Danubio riga
   poi che le ripe tedesche abbandona.   *66*
E la bella Trinacria, che caliga
   tra Pachino e Peloro, sopra 'l golfo
   che riceve da Euro maggior briga,   *69*
non per Tifeo ma per nascente solfo,
   attesi avrebbe li suoi regi ancora,
   nati per me di Carlo e di Ridolfo,   *72*
se mala segnoria, che sempre accora
   li popoli suggetti, non avesse
   mosso Palermo a gridar: 'Mora, mora!'   *75*
E se mio frate questo antivedesse,
   l'avara povertà di Catalogna
   già fuggeria, perché non li offendesse;   *78*

Thus changed, it said to me, "The world held me below but little time; and had it been more, much ill shall be that would not have been. My joy, which rays around me, holds me concealed from you and hides me like a creature swathed in its own silk. Much did you love me, and had good cause; for had I remained below, I would have shown you of my love more than the leaves. That left bank which is bathed by the Rhone, after it has mingled with the Sorgue, awaited me in due time for its lord; so did that corner of Ausonia, down from where Tronto and Verde discharge into the sea, which is skirted by Bari and Gaeta and Catona. Already was shining on my brow the crown of that land which the Danube waters after it has left its German banks. And the fair Trinacria (which between Pachynus and Pelorus, on the gulf most vexed by Eurus, is darkened not by Typhoeus, but by nascent sulphur) would yet have looked to have its kings born through me from Charles and Rudolph, if ill lordship, which ever embitters the subject people, had not moved Palermo to shout, 'Die! Die!' And if my brother foresaw this, he would already shun the rapacious poverty of Catalonia, lest it make trouble for him;

87

ché veramente proveder bisogna
 per lui, o per altrui, sì ch'a sua barca
 carcata più d'incarco non si pogna.   *81*
La sua natura, che di larga parca
 discese, avria mestier di tal milizia
 che non curasse di mettere in arca."   *84*
"Però ch'i' credo che l'alta letizia
 che 'l tuo parlar m'infonde, segnor mio,
 là 've ogne ben si termina e s'inizia,   *87*
per te si veggia come la vegg' io,
 grata m'è più; e anco quest' ho caro
 perché 'l discerni rimirando in Dio.   *90*
Fatto m'hai lieto, e così mi fa chiaro,
 poi che, parlando, a dubitar m'hai mosso
 com' esser può, di dolce seme, amaro."   *93*
Questo io a lui; ed elli a me: "S'io posso
 mostrarti un vero, a quel che tu dimandi
 terrai lo viso come tien lo dosso.   *96*
Lo ben che tutto il regno che tu scandi
 volge e contenta, fa esser virtute
 sua provedenza in questi corpi grandi.   *99*
E non pur le nature provedute
 sono in la mente ch'è da sé perfetta,
 ma esse insieme con la lor salute: *102*
per che quantunque quest' arco saetta
 disposto cade a proveduto fine,
 sì come cosa in suo segno diretta.   *105*
Se ciò non fosse, il ciel che tu cammine
 producerebbe sì li suoi effetti,
 che non sarebbero arti, ma ruine;   *108*

for truly it is needful for him or for some other to look to it, lest upon his laden bark a heavier load be laid. His nature—mean descendant from a generous forebear—would need a knighthood that gave not its care to the filling of coffers."

"Because I believe that the deep joy which your words infuse in me is, even as I see it, seen by you, my lord, there where every good has its end and its beginning, it is the more welcome to me; and this also I hold dear, that you discern it gazing upon God. You have made me glad; and so now do you make clear to me (since in speaking you have raised the question in my mind) how from sweet seed may come forth bitter."

Thus I to him; and he to me, "If I can make one truth plain to you, you will hold your face toward that which you ask, as you now hold your back. The Good which revolves and contents all the realm that you are climbing makes its providence become a power in these great bodies; and not only is the nature of things provided for in the Mind which by itself is perfect, but, along with that nature, their well-being; so that whatever this bow shoots falls disposed to a foreseen end, even as a shaft directed to its mark. Were this not so, the heavens which you are traversing would produce their effects in such wise that they would be not works of art but ruins—

e ciò esser non può, se li 'ntelletti
   che muovon queste stelle non son manchi,
   e manco il primo, che non li ha perfetti.   *111*
Vuo' tu che questo ver più ti s'imbianchi?"
   E io "Non già; ché impossibil veggio
   che la natura, in quel ch'è uopo, stanchi."   *114*
Ond' elli ancora: "Or dì: sarebbe il peggio
   per l'omo in terra, se non fosse cive?"
   "Sì," rispuos' io; "e qui ragion non cheggio."   *117*
"E puot' elli esser, se giù non si vive
   diversamente per diversi offici?
   Non, se 'l maestro vostro ben vi scrive."   *120*
Sì venne deducendo infino a quici;
   poscia conchiuse: "Dunque esser diverse
   convien di vostri effetti le radici: *123*
per ch'un nasce Solone e altro Serse,
   altro Melchisedèch e altro quello
   che, volando per l'aere, il figlio perse.   *126*
La circular natura, ch'è suggello
   a la cera mortal fa ben sua arte,
   ma non distingue l'un da l'altro ostello.   *129*
Quinci addivien ch'Esaù si diparte
   per seme da Iacòb; e vien Quirino
   da sì vil padre, che si rende a Marte.   *132*
Natura generata il suo cammino
   simil farebbe sempre a' generanti,
   se non vincesse il proveder divino.   *135*
Or quel che t'era dietro t'è davanti:
   ma perché sappi che di te mi giova,
   un corollario voglio che t'ammanti.   *138*

and that cannot be, unless the Intelligences
that move these stars be defective, and de-
fective also the Primal Intelligence in that it
did not make them perfect. Do you wish this
truth to be made still clearer to you?"

And I, "No, truly; for I see it to be impos-
sible that Nature should weary in that which
is needful."

Whereupon he again, "Now say, would it
be worse for man on earth if he were not a
citizen?"

"Yes," I replied, "and here I ask for no
proof."

"And can that be, unless men below live in
diverse ways for diverse duties? Not if your
master writes well of this for you." Thus he
came deducing far as here, then he concluded,
"Therefore the roots of your works must
needs be diverse, so that one is born Solon
and another Xerxes, one Melchizedek and an-
other he who flew through the air and lost
his son. Circling nature, which is a seal on
the mortal wax, performs its art well, but does
not distinguish one house from another.
Whence it happens that Esau differs in the
seed from Jacob, and Quirinus comes from so
base a father that he is ascribed to Mars. The
begotten nature would always make its course
like its begetters, did not Divine provision
overrule.

Now that which was behind you is before
you; but, that you may know that I delight in
you, I will have a corollary cloak you round.

Sempre natura, se fortuna trova
   discorde a sé, com' ogne altra semente
   fuor di sua regïon, fa mala prova.   *141*
E se 'l mondo là giù ponesse mente
   al fondamento che natura pone,
   seguendo lui, avria buona la gente.   *144*
Ma voi torcete a la religïone
   tal che fia nato a cignersi la spada,
   e fate re di tal ch'è da sermone;
onde la traccia vostra è fuor di strada."   *148*

Ever does Nature, if she find fortune dis-
cordant with herself, like any kind of seed
out of its proper region, come to ill result.
And if the world there below would give
heed to the foundation which Nature lays,
and followed it, it would have its people good.
But you wrest to religion one born to gird on
the sword, and you make a king of one that
is fit for sermons; so that your track is off
the road."

PARADISO

Da poi che Carlo tuo, bella Clemenza,
    m'ebbe chiarito, mi narrò li 'nganni
    che ricever dovea la sua semenza;   *3*
ma disse: "Taci e lascia muover li anni";
    sì ch'io non posso dir se non che pianto
    giusto verrà di retro ai vostri danni.   *6*
E già la vita di quel lume santo
    rivolta s'era al Sol che la rïempie
    come quel ben ch'a ogne cosa è tanto.   *9*
Ahi anime ingannate e fatture empie,
    che da sì fatto ben torcete i cuori,
    drizzando in vanità le vostre tempie!   *12*
Ed ecco un altro di quelli splendori
    ver' me si fece, e 'l suo voler piacermi
    significava nel chiarir di fori.   *15*
Li occhi di Bëatrice, ch'eran fermi
    sovra me, come pria, di caro assenso
    al mio disio certificato fermi.   *18*

CANTO IX

A<small>FTER YOUR</small> Charles, fair Clemence, had en-
lightened me, he told me of the frauds that
his seed was destined to suffer, but he added,
"Keep silence, and let the years revolve"; so
that I can say nothing except that well-de-
served lamentation shall follow on the wrongs
done you.

And now the life of that holy light had
turned again to the Sun which fills it, as to
that Good which is sufficient to all things.
Ah, souls deceived and creatures impious, who
from such Good turn away your hearts, di-
recting your brows to vanity!

And lo! another of those splendors made
toward me and by brightening outwardly was
signifying its wish to please me. Beatrice's
eyes, fixed on me as before, made me assured
of dear assent to my desire.

"Deh, metti al mio voler tosto compenso,
   beato spirto," dissi, "e fammi prova
   ch'i' possa in te refletter quel ch'io penso!"   *21*
Onde la luce che m'era ancor nova,
   del suo profondo, ond' ella pria cantava,
   seguette come a cui di ben far giova: *24*
"In quella parte de la terra prava
   italica che siede tra Rïalto
   e le fontane di Brenta e di Piava,   *27*
si leva un colle, e non surge molt' alto,
   là onde scese già una facella
   che fece a la contrada un grande assalto.   *30*
D'una radice nacqui e io ed ella:
   Cunizza fui chiamata, e qui refulgo
   perché mi vinse il lume d'esta stella;   *33*
ma lietamente a me medesma indulgo
   la cagion di mia sorte, e non mi noia;
   che parria forse forte al vostro vulgo.   *36*
Di questa luculenta e cara gioia
   del nostro cielo che più m'è propinqua,
   grande fama rimase; e pria che moia,   *39*
questo centesimo anno ancor s'incinqua:
   vedi se far si dee l'omo eccellente,
   sì ch'altra vita la prima relinqua.   *42*
E ciò non pensa la turba presente
   che Tagliamento e Adice richiude,
   né per esser battuta ancor si pente;   *45*
ma tosto fia che Padova al palude
   cangerà l'acqua che Vincenza bagna,
   per essere al dover le genti crude;   *48*

"Pray, blessed spirit," I said, "afford speedy fulfillment to my wish, and give me proof that what I think I can reflect on you." Whereon the light which was still new to me, from out of its depth where it first was singing, continued, as one rejoicing to do a kindness: "In that region of the depraved land of Italy that lies between the Rialto and the springs of the Brenta and the Piave there rises a hill of no great height, whence once descended a firebrand that made a great assault on the country round. I and he sprang from the same root. I was called Cunizza, and I am refulgent here because the light of this star overcame me. But I gladly pardon in myself the reason of my lot, and it does not grieve me—which might perhaps seem strange to your vulgar herd. Of this resplendent and precious jewel of our heaven which is nearest to me great fame has remained, and before it dies away this centennial year shall yet be fived. See if man should make himself excel, so that the first life may leave another after it! And this the present crowd which the Tagliamento and the Adige shut in considers not; nor yet, though it be scourged, does it repent. But soon it shall come to pass that, because her people are stubborn against duty, Padua at the marsh will stain the waters that bathe Vicenza.

97

e dove Sile e Cagnan s'accompagna,
   tal signoreggia e va con la testa alta,
   che già per lui carpir si fa la ragna.   *51*
Piangerà Feltro ancora la difalta
   de l'empio suo pastor, che sarà sconcia
   sì, che per simil non s'entrò in Malta.   *54*
Troppo sarebbe larga la bigoncia
   che ricevesse il sangue ferrarese,
   e stanco chi 'l pesasse a oncia a oncia,   *57*
che donerà questo prete cortese
   per mostrarsi di parte; e cotai doni
   conformi fieno al viver del paese.   *60*
Sù sono specchi, voi dicete Troni,
   onde refulge a noi Dio giudicante;
   sì che questi parlar ne paion buoni."   *63*
Qui si tacette; e fecemi sembiante
   che fosse ad altro volta, per la rota
   in che si mise com' era davante.   *66*
L'altra letizia, che m'era già nota
   per cara cosa, mi si fece in vista
   qual fin balasso in che lo sol percuota.   *69*
Per letiziar là sù fulgor s'acquista,
   sì come riso qui; ma giù s'abbuia
   l'ombra di fuor, come la mente è trista.   *72*
"Dio vede tutto, e tuo veder s'inluia,"
   diss' io, "beato spirto, sì che nulla
   voglia di sé a te puot' esser fuia.   *75*
Dunque la voce tua, che 'l ciel trastulla
   sempre col canto di quei fuochi pii
   che di sei ali facen la coculla,   *78*

And where Sile joins Cagnano, one lords it and
goes with his head high, for catching whom
the web is already being made. Feltre shall
yet bewail the crime of its impious shepherd,
which will be so foul that for the like nobody
ever entered Malta. Great indeed would be
the vat that should receive the blood of the
Ferrarese and weary him that should weigh
it ounce by ounce, which this courteous priest
will offer to show himself a member of his
party—and such gifts will suit the country's
way of life. Aloft are mirrors—you name
them Thrones—whence God in judgment
shines upon us, so that these words approve
themselves to us." Here she was silent, and
had to me the semblance of being turned to
other heeding, by the wheel in which she set
herself as she was before.

The other joy, which was already known
to me as precious, became to my sight like
a fine ruby on which the sun is striking.
Through rejoicing, effulgence is gained there
on high, even as a smile here; but below, the
shade darkens outwardly as the mind is sad.

"God sees all, and into Him your vision
sinks, blessed spirit," I said, "so that no wish
may steal itself from you. Why then does
your voice, which ever gladdens Heaven—
together with the singing of those devout fires
that make themselves a cowl with the six
wings—

perché non satisface a' miei disii?
  Già non attendere' io tua dimanda,
  s'io m'intuassi, come tu t'inmii."   *81*
"La maggior valle in che l'acqua si spanda,"
  incominciaro allor le sue parole,
  "fuor di quel mar che la terra inghirlanda,   *84*
tra ' discordanti liti contra 'l sole
  tanto sen va, che fa meridïano
  là dove l'orizzonte pria far suole.   *87*
Di quella valle fu' io litorano
  tra Ebro e Macra, che per cammin corto
  parte lo Genovese dal Toscano.   *90*
Ad un occaso quasi e ad un orto
  Buggea siede e la terra ond' io fui,
  che fé del sangue suo già caldo il porto.   *93*
Folco mi disse quella gente a cui
  fu noto il nome mio; e questo cielo
  di me s'imprenta, com' io fe' di lui;   *96*
ché più non arse la figlia di Belo,
  noiando e a Sicheo e a Creusa,
  di me infin che si convenne al pelo;   *99*
né quella Rodopëa che delusa
  fu da Demofoonte, né Alcide
  quando Iole nel core ebbe rinchiusa.   *102*
Non però qui si pente, ma si ride,
  non de la colpa, ch'a mente non torna,
  ma del valor ch'ordinò e provide.   *105*
Qui si rimira ne l'arte ch'addorna
  cotanto affetto, e discernesi 'l bene
  per che 'l mondo di sù quel di giù torna.   *108*

not satisfy my longings? Surely I should not wait for your request, were I in you, even as you are in me."

"The greatest valley in which the water spreads from the sea that encircles the world," he then began, "extends its discordant shores so far counter to the sun that it makes meridian of the place where before it made horizon. I was a dweller on that valley's shore, between the Ebro and the Magra, which with short course divides the Genoese from the Tuscan; and with almost the same sunset and sunrise lie Bougie and the city whence I came, which with its own blood once made its harbor warm. Folco the people called me to whom my name was known, and this heaven is imprinted by me, as I was by it: for the daughter of Belus, wronging both Sichaeus and Creusa, burned not more than I, as long as it befitted my locks; nor yet the Rhodopean maid who was deluded by Demophoön, nor Alcides when he had enclosed Iole in his heart. Yet here we repent not, but we smile, not for the fault, which returns not to mind, but for the Power that ordained and foresaw. Here we contemplate the art which so much love adorns, and we discern the good by reason of which the world below again becomes the world above.

Ma perché tutte le tue voglie piene
　　ten porti che son nate in questa spera,
　　procedere ancor oltre mi convene.　　　　　　*111*
Tu vuo' saper chi è in questa lumera
　　che qui appresso me così scintilla
　　come raggio di sole in acqua mera.　　　　　　*114*
Or sappi che là entro si tranquilla
　　Raab; e a nostr' ordine congiunta,
　　di lei nel sommo grado si sigilla.　　　　　　*117*
Da questo cielo, in cui l'ombra s'appunta
　　che 'l vostro mondo face, pria ch'altr' alma
　　del trïunfo di Cristo fu assunta.　　　　　　*120*
Ben si convenne lei lasciar per palma
　　in alcun cielo de l'alta vittoria
　　che s'acquistò con l'una e l'altra palma,　　　　*123*
perch' ella favorò la prima gloria
　　di Iosüè in su la Terra Santa,
　　che poco tocca al papa la memoria.　　　　　　*126*
La tua città, che di colui è pianta
　　che pria volse le spalle al suo fattore
　　e di cui è la 'nvidia tanto pianta,　　　　　　*129*
produce e spande il maladetto fiore
　　c'ha disvïate le pecore e li agni,
　　però che fatto ha lupo del pastore.　　　　　　*132*
Per questo l'Evangelio e i dottor magni
　　son derelitti, e solo ai Decretali
　　si studia, sì che pare a' lor vivagni.　　　　　*135*
A questo intende il papa e ' cardinali;
　　non vanno i lor pensieri a Nazarette,
　　là dove Gabrïello aperse l'ali.　　　　　　　*138*

"But in order that you may bear away with you all your desires fulfilled which have been born in this sphere, I must proceed yet further. You wish to know who is within this light which so sparkles here beside me as a sunbeam on clear water. Now know that therewithin Rahab is at rest, and being joined with our order, it is sealed by her in the highest degree. By this heaven—in which the shadow that your earth casts comes to a point—she was taken up before any other soul of Christ's triumph. And it was well-befitting to leave her in some heaven as a trophy of the lofty victory which was achieved by the one and the other palm, because she favored Joshua's first glory in the Holy Land—which little touches the memory of the Pope.

"Your city—which was planted by him who first turned his back on his Maker, and whose envy has been so bewept—produces and scatters the accursed flower that has caused the sheep and the lambs to stray, because it has made a wolf of the shepherd. For this the Gospel and the great Doctors are deserted, and only the Decretals are studied, as may be seen by their margins. Thereon the Pope and Cardinals are intent. Their thoughts go not to Nazareth whither Gabriel spread his wings.

Ma Vaticano e l'altre parti elette
di Roma che son state cimitero
a la milizia che Pietro seguette,
tosto libere fien de l'avoltero."   *142*

But the Vatican and the other chosen parts
of Rome which have been the burial place for
the soldiery that followed Peter shall soon be
free from this adultery."

PARADISO

GUARDANDO NEL suo Figlio con l'Amore
   che l'uno e l'altro etternalmente spira,
   lo primo e ineffabile Valore   *3*
quanto per mente e per loco si gira
   con tant' ordine fé ch'esser non puote
   sanza gustar di lui chi ciò rimira.   *6*
Leva dunque, lettore, a l'alte rote
   meco la vista, dritto a quella parte
   dove l'un moto e l'altro si percuote;   *9*
e lì comincia a vagheggiar ne l'arte
   di quel maestro che dentro a sé l'ama,
   tanto che mai da lei l'occhio non parte.   *12*
Vedi come da indi si dirama
   l'oblico cerchio che i pianeti porta,
   per sodisfare al mondo che li chiama.   *15*
Che se la strada lor non fosse torta,
   molta virtù nel ciel sarebbe in vano,
   e quasi ogne potenza qua giù morta;   *18*

CANTO X

Looking upon His Son with the love which the One and the Other eternally breathe forth, the primal and ineffable Power made everything that revolves through the mind or through space with such order that he who contemplates it cannot but taste of Him. Lift then your sight with me, reader, to the lofty wheels, straight to that part where the one motion strikes the other; and amorously there begin to gaze upon that Master's art who within Himself so loves it that His eye never turns from it. See how from there the oblique circle which bears the planets branches off, to satisfy the world which calls on them: and were their pathway not aslant, much virtue in the heavens would be vain, and well-nigh every potency dead here below;

e se dal dritto più o men lontano
  fosse 'l partire, assai sarebbe manco
  e giù e sù de l'ordine mondano.   *21*
Or ti riman, lettor, sovra 'l tuo banco,
  dietro pensando a ciò che si preliba,
  s'esser vuoi lieto assai prima che stanco.   *24*
Messo t'ho innanzi; omai per te ti ciba;
  ché a sé torce tutta la mia cura
  quella materia ond' io son fatto scriba.   *27*
Lo ministro maggior de la natura,
  che del valor del ciel lo mondo imprenta
  e col suo lume il tempo ne misura,   *30*
con quella parte che sù si rammenta
  congiunto, si girava per le spire
  in che più tosto ognora s'appresenta;   *33*
e io era con lui; ma del salire
  non m'accors' io, se non com' uom s'accorge,
  anzi 'l primo pensier, del suo venire.   *36*
È Bëatrice quella che sì scorge
  di bene in meglio, sì subitamente
  che l'atto suo per tempo non si sporge.   *39*
Quant' esser convenia da sé lucente
  quel ch'era dentro al sol dov' io entra'mi,
  non per color, ma per lume parvente!   *42*
Perch' io lo 'ngegno e l'arte e l'uso chiami,
  sì nol direi che mai s'imaginasse;
  ma creder puossi e di veder si brami.   *45*
E se le fantasie nostre son basse
  a tanta altezza, non è maraviglia;
  ché sopra 'l sol non fu occhio ch'andasse.   *48*

and if it parted farther or less far from the
straight course, much of the order of the
world, both above and below, would be de-
fective.

Now remain, reader, upon your bench, re-
flecting on this of which you have a foretaste,
if you would be glad far sooner than weary.
I have set before you; now feed yourself,
because that matter of which I am made the
scribe wrests to itself all my care.

The greatest minister of nature, which im-
prints the world with heavenly worth and
with its light measures time for us, being in
conjunction with the part I have noted, was
wheeling through the spirals in which it pre-
sents itself earlier every day. And I was with
him, but of my ascent I was no more aware
than is a man, before his first thought, aware
of its coming. It is Beatrice who thus conducts
from good to better, so swiftly that her act
does not extend through time.

How shining in itself must have been that
which was within the sun where I entered it,
showing not by color but by light! Though I
should call on genius, art, and practice, I
could not tell it so that it could ever be
imagined; but one may believe it—and let
him long to see it. And if our fantasies are
low for such a loftiness, it is no marvel, for our
eyes never knew a light brighter than the sun.

Tal era quivi la quarta famiglia
   de l'alto Padre, che sempre la sazia,
   mostrando come spira e come figlia.   *51*
E Bëatrice cominciò: "Ringrazia,
   ringrazia il Sol de li angeli, ch'a questo
   sensibil t'ha levato per sua grazia."   *54*
Cor di mortal non fu mai sì digesto
   a divozione e a rendersi a Dio
   con tutto 'l suo gradir cotanto presto,   *57*
come a quelle parole mi fec' io;
   e sì tutto 'l mio amore in lui si mise,
   che Bëatrice eclissò ne l'oblio.   *60*
Non le dispiacque, ma sì se ne rise,
   che lo splendor de li occhi suoi ridenti
   mia mente unita in più cose divise.   *63*
Io vidi più folgór vivi e vincenti
   far di noi centro e di sé far corona,
   più dolci in voce che in vista lucenti: *66*
così cinger la figlia di Latona
   vedem talvolta, quando l'aere è pregno,
   sì che ritenga il fil che fa la zona.   *69*
Ne la corte del cielo, ond' io rivegno,
   si trovan molte gioie care e belle
   tanto che non si posson trar del regno;   *72*
e 'l canto di quei lumi era di quelle;
   chi non s'impenna sì che là sù voli,
   dal muto aspetti quindi le novelle.   *75*
Poi, sì cantando, quelli ardenti soli
   si fuor girati intorno a noi tre volte,
   come stelle vicine a' fermi poli,   *78*

Such was here the fourth family of the ex-
alted Father who ever satisfies it, showing
how He breathes forth, and how He begets.
And Beatrice began, "Give thanks, give
thanks to the Sun of the Angels who of His
grace has raised you to this visible one."

Never was heart of mortal so disposed unto
devotion and so ready, with all its gratitude,
to give itself to God, as I became at those
words. And all my love was so set on Him
that it eclipsed Beatrice in oblivion; nor did
this displease her, but she so smiled thereat
that the splendor of her smiling eyes divided
upon many things my mind intent on one.

I saw many flashing lights of surpassing
brightness make of us a center and of them-
selves a crown, more sweet in voice than shin-
ing in aspect. Thus girt we sometimes see
Latona's daughter when the air is so im-
pregnate that it holds the thread which makes
her zone. In the court of Heaven, whence I
have returned, are many gems so precious and
beautiful that they may not be taken out of
the kingdom, and of these was the song of
those lights. Let him who does not wing him-
self so that he may fly up thither await tidings
thence from the dumb.

When, so singing, those blazing suns had
circled three times round about us, like stars
neighboring the fixed poles,

donne mi parver, non da ballo sciolte,
    ma che s'arrestin tacite, ascoltando
    fin che le nove note hanno ricolte.   *81*
E dentro a l'un senti' cominciar: "Quando
    lo raggio de la grazia, onde s'accende
    verace amore e che poi cresce amando,   *84*
multiplicato in te tanto resplende,
    che ti conduce su per quella scala
    u' sanza risalir nessun discende;   *87*
qual ti negasse il vin de la sua fiala
    per la tua sete, in libertà non fora
    se non com' acqua ch'al mar non si cala.   *90*
Tu vuo' saper di quai piante s'infiora
    questa ghirlanda che 'ntorno vagheggia
    la bella donna ch'al ciel t'avvalora.   *93*
Io fui de li agni de la santa greggia
    che Domenico mena per cammino
    u' ben s'impingua se non si vaneggia.   *96*
Questi che m'è a destra più vicino,
    frate e maestro fummi, ed esso Alberto
    è di Cologna, e io Thomas d'Aquino.   *99*
Se sì di tutti li altri esser vuo' certo,
    di retro al mio parlar ten vien col viso
    girando su per lo beato serto.   *102*
Quell' altro fiammeggiare esce del riso
    di Grazïan, che l'uno e l'altro foro
    aiutò sì che piace in paradiso.   *105*
L'altro ch'appresso addorna il nostro coro,
    quel Pietro fu che con la poverella
    offerse a Santa Chiesa suo tesoro.   *108*

they seemed as ladies not released from the dance, but who stop silent, listening till they have caught the new notes. And within one I heard begin, "Since the ray of grace, by which true love is kindled and which then grows by loving, shines so multiplied in you that it brings you up that stair which none descends but to mount again, he who should deny to you the wine of his flask for your thirst would no more be at liberty than water that flows not down to the sea. You wish to know what plants these are that enflower this garland, which amorously circles round the fair lady who strengthens you for heaven. I was of the lambs of the holy flock which Dominic leads on the path where there is good fattening if they do not stray. He that is next beside me on the right was my brother and my master, and he is Albert of Cologne, and I Thomas of Aquino. If thus of all the rest you would be informed, come, following my speech with your sight, going round the blessed wreath. That next flaming comes from the smile of Gratian who served the one and the other court so well that it pleases in Paradise. The other who next adorns our choir was that Peter who, like the poor widow, offered his treasure to Holy Church.

La quinta luce, ch'è tra noi più bella,
   spira di tale amor, che tutto 'l mondo
   là giù ne gola di saper novella: *111*
entro v'è l'alta mente u' sì profondo
   saver fu messo, che, se 'l vero è vero,
   a veder tanto non surse il secondo.   *114*
Appresso vedi il lume di quel cero
   che giù in carne più a dentro vide
   l'angelica natura e 'l ministero.   *117*
Ne l'altra piccioletta luce ride
   quello avvocato de' tempi cristiani
   del cui latino Augustin si provide.   *120*
Or se tu l'occhio de la mente trani
   di luce in luce dietro a le mie lode,
   già de l'ottava con sete rimani.   *123*
Per vedere ogne ben dentro vi gode
   l'anima santa che 'l mondo fallace
   fa manifesto a chi di lei ben ode.   *126*
Lo corpo ond' ella fu cacciata giace
   giuso in Cieldauro; ed essa da martiro
   e da essilio venne a questa pace.   *129*
Vedi oltre fiammeggiar l'ardente spiro
   d'Isidoro, di Beda e di Riccardo,
   che a considerar fu più che viro.   *132*
Questi onde a me ritorna il tuo riguardo,
   è 'l lume d'uno spirto che 'n pensieri
   gravi a morir li parve venir tardo: *135*
essa è la luce etterna di Sigieri,
   che, leggendo nel Vico de li Strami,
   silogizzò invidïosi veri."   *138*

The fifth light, which is the most beautiful among us, breathes with such love that all the world there below thirsts to know tidings of it. Within it is the lofty mind to which was given wisdom so deep that, if the truth be true, there never rose a second of such full vision. At its side behold the light of that candle which, below in the flesh, saw deepest into the angelic nature and its ministry. In the next little light smiles that defender of the Christian times, of whose discourse Augustine made use. If now you are bringing your mind's eye from light to light after my praises, you are already thirsting for the eighth. Therewithin, through seeing every good, the sainted soul rejoices who makes the fallacious world manifest to any who listen well to him. The body from which it was driven lies down below in Cieldauro, and he came from martyrdom and exile to this peace. See, flaming beyond, the glowing breath of Isidore, of Bede, and of Richard who in contemplation was more than man. This one from whom your look returns to me is the light of a spirit to whom, in his grave thoughts, it seemed that death came slow. It is the eternal light of Siger who, lecturing in Straw Street, demonstrated invidious truths."

Indi, come orologio che ne chiami
  ne l'ora che la sposa di Dio surge
  a mattinar lo sposo perché l'ami,   *141*
che l'una parte e l'altra tira e urge,
  tin tin sonando con sì dolce nota,
  che 'l ben disposto spirto d'amor turge;   *144*
così vid' ïo la gloriosa rota
  muoversi e render voce a voce in tempra
  e in dolcezza ch'esser non pò nota
se non colà dove gioir s'insempra.   *148*

Then, like a clock which calls us at the hour when the Bride of God rises to sing her matins to her Bridegroom, that he may love her, in which the one part draws or drives the other, sounding *ting! ting!* with notes so sweet that the well-disposed spirit swells with love, so did I see the glorious wheel move and render voice to voice with harmony and sweetness that cannot be known except there where joy is everlasting.

PARADISO

O INSENSATA CURA de' mortali,
quanto son difettivi silogismi
quei che ti fanno in basso batter l'ali!   *3*

Chi dietro a *iura* e chi ad amforismi
sen giva, e chi seguendo sacerdozio,
e chi regnar per forza o per sofismi,   *6*

e chi rubare e chi civil negozio,
chi nel diletto de la carne involto
s'affaticava e chi si dava a l'ozio,   *9*

quando, da tutte queste cose sciolto,
con Bëatrice m'era suso in cielo
cotanto glorïosamente accolto.   *12*

Poi che ciascuno fu tornato ne lo
punto del cerchio in che avanti s'era,
fermossi, come a candellier candelo.   *15*

E io senti' dentro a quella lumera
che pria m'avea parlato, sorridendo
incominciar, faccendosi più mera: *18*

"Così com' io del suo raggio resplendo,
sì, riguardando ne la luce etterna,
li tuoi pensieri onde cagioni apprendo.   *21*

CANTO XI

O INSENSATE care of mortals! how false are the reasonings that make you beat your wings in downward flight. One was following after the laws, another after the *Aphorisms*, one was pursuing priesthood, and one dominion by force or craft, and another plunder, and another civil business, one was moiling, caught in the pleasures of the flesh, and another was giving himself to idleness, the while, free from all these things, I was high in heaven with Beatrice, thus gloriously received.

After each had come to the point of the circle where it was before, it stayed itself, as the taper in its stand. And within that light which first had spoken to me I heard begin, while it smiled and grew brighter, "Even as I glow with its beams, so, gazing into the Eternal Light, I perceive your thoughts and the cause of them.

Tu dubbi, e hai voler che si ricerna
  in sì aperta e 'n sì distesa lingua
  lo dicer mio, ch'al tuo sentir si sterna,   24
ŏve dinanzi dissi: 'U' ben s'impingua,'
  e là u' dissi: 'Non nacque il secondo';
  e qui è uopo che ben si distingua.   27
La provedenza, che governa il mondo
  con quel consiglio nel quale ogne aspetto
  creato è vinto pria che vada al fondo,   30
però che andasse ver' lo suo diletto
  la sposa di colui ch'ad alte grida
  disposò lei col sangue benedetto,   33
in sé sicura e anche a lui più fida,
  due principi ordinò in suo favore,
  che quinci e quindi le fosser per guida.   36
L'un fu tutto serafico in ardore;
  l'altro per sapïenza in terra fue
  di cherubica luce uno splendore.   39
De l'un dirò, però che d'amendue
  si dice l'un pregiando, qual ch'om prende,
  perch' ad un fine fur l'opere sue.   42
Intra Tupino e l'acqua che discende
  del colle eletto dal beato Ubaldo,
  fertile costa d'alto monte pende,   45
onde Perugia sente freddo e caldo
  da Porta Sole; e di rietro le piange
  per grave giogo Nocera con Gualdo.   48
Di questa costa, là dov' ella frange
  più sua rattezza, nacque al mondo un sole,
  come fa questo talvolta di Gange.   51

You are perplexed and would fain have my words made clearer, in plain and explicit language leveled to your understanding, where I said just now 'where there is good fattening,' and again where I said, 'there never rose a second'; and here is need that one distinguish well.

"The Providence that governs the world with that counsel in which every created vision is vanquished before it reaches the bottom, in order that the Bride of Him who, with loud cries, espoused her with the blessed blood, might go to her Delight, secure within herself and also more faithful to Him, ordained on her behalf two princes, who on this side and that might be her guides. The one was all seraphic in ardor, the other, for wisdom, was on earth a splendor of cherubic light. I will speak of one, because in praising one, whichever be taken, both are spoken of, for their labors were to one same end.

"Between the Topino and the stream that drops from the hill chosen by the blessed Ubaldo, a fertile slope hangs from a lofty mountain wherefrom Perugia feels cold and heat through Porta Sole, while behind it Nocera and Gualdo grieve under a heavy yoke. From this slope, where most it breaks its steepness a sun rose on the world, even as this is wont to rise from Ganges.

Però chi d'esso loco fa parole,
   non dica Ascesi, ché direbbe corto,
   ma Orïente, se proprio dir vuole.   *54*
Non era ancor molto lontan da l'orto,
   ch'el cominciò a far sentir la terra
   de la sua gran virtute alcun conforto;   *57*
ché per tal donna, giovinetto, in guerra
   del padre corse, a cui, come a la morte,
   la porta del piacer nessun diserra;   *60*
e dinanzi a la sua spirital corte
   et coram patre le si fece unito;
   poscia di dì in dì l'amò più forte.   *63*
Questa, privata del primo marito,
   millecent' anni e più dispetta e scura
   fino a costui si stette sanza invito;   *66*
né valse udir che la trovò sicura
   con Amiclate, al suon de la sua voce,
   colui ch'a tutto 'l mondo fé paura;   *69*
né valse esser costante né feroce,
   sì che, dove Maria rimase giuso,
   ella con Cristo pianse in su la croce.   *72*
Ma perch' io non proceda troppo chiuso,
   Francesco e Povertà per questi amanti
   prendi oramai nel mio parlar diffuso.   *75*
La lor concordia e i lor lieti sembianti,
   amore e maraviglia e dolce sguardo
   facieno esser cagion di pensier santi;   *78*
tanto che 'l venerabile Bernardo
   si scalzò prima, e dietro a tanta pace
   corse e, correndo, li parve esser tardo.   *81*

Therefore let him who talks of this place not say *Ascesi*, which would be to speak short, but *Orient*, if he would name it rightly. He was not yet very far from his rising when he began to make the earth feel, from his great virtue, a certain strengthening; for, while still a youth, he rushed into strife against his father for such a lady, to whom, as to death, none willingly unlocks the door; and before his spiritual court *et coram patre* he was joined to her, and thereafter, from day to day, he loved her ever more ardently. She, bereft of her first husband, for eleven hundred years and more, despised and obscure, remained unwooed till he came; nor had it availed to hear that he who caused fear to all the world found her undisturbed with Amyclas at the sound of his voice; nor had it availed to have been constant and undaunted so that, where Mary remained below, she wept with Christ upon the Cross.

"But, lest I should proceed too darkly, take now Francis and Poverty for these lovers in all that I have said. Their harmony and joyous semblance made love and wonder and tender looks the cause of holy thoughts; so that the venerable Bernard first bared his feet, following such great peace, and running, it seemed to him that he was slow.

Oh ignota ricchezza! oh ben ferace!
  Scalzasi Egidio, scalzasi Silvestro
  dietro a lo sposo, sì la sposa piace.   *84*
Indi sen va quel padre e quel maestro
  con la sua donna e con quella famiglia
  che già legava l'umile capestro.   *87*
Né li gravò viltà di cuor le ciglia
  per esser fi' di Pietro Bernardone,
  né per parer dispetto a maraviglia;   *90*
ma regalmente sua dura intenzione
  ad Innocenzio aperse, e da lui ebbe
  primo sigillo a sua relïgïone.   *93*
Poi che la gente poverella crebbe
  dietro a costui, la cui mirabil vita
  meglio in gloria del ciel si canterebbe,   *96*
di seconda corona redimita
  fu per Onorio da l'Etterno Spiro
  la santa voglia d'esto archimandrita.   *99*
E poi che, per la sete del martiro,
  ne la presenza del Soldan superba
  predicò Cristo e li altri che 'l seguiro,   *102*
e per trovare a conversione acerba
  troppo la gente e per non stare indarno,
  redissi al frutto de l'italica erba,   *105*
nel crudo sasso intra Tevero e Arno
  da Cristo prese l'ultimo sigillo,
  che le sue membra due anni portarno.   *108*
Quando a colui ch'a tanto ben sortillo
  piacque di trarlo suso a la mercede
  ch'el meritò nel suo farsi pusillo,   *111*

Oh wealth unknown, oh fertile good! Egidius bares his feet, Silvester bares his feet, following the spouse, so does the bride delight them. Then that father and master goes his way, with his lady and with that family which was already girt with the lowly cord. Nor did abjectness of heart weigh down his brow that he was Pietro Bernardone's son, nor for appearing marvelously despised; but royally he opened his stern resolve to Innocent, and had from him the first seal upon his Order.

"After the poor folk had increased behind him, whose wondrous life were better sung in Heaven's glory, then was the holy will of this chief shepherd circled with a second crown by the Eternal Spirit through Honorius. And when, in thirst for martyrdom, he, in the proud presence of the Sultan, had preached Christ and them that followed him, and, finding the people too unripe for conversion and in order not to stay in vain, had returned to the harvest of the Italian fields, then on the harsh rock between Tiber and Arno he received from Christ the last seal, which his limbs bore for two years. When it pleased Him, who had allotted him to such great good, to draw him up to the reward that he had gained in making himself lowly,

a' frati suoi, sì com' a giuste rede,
   raccomandò la donna sua più cara,
   e comandò che l'amassero a fede;   *114*
e del suo grembo l'anima preclara
   mover si volle, tornando al suo regno,
   e al suo corpo non volle altra bara.   *117*
Pensa oramai qual fu colui che degno
   collega fu a mantener la barca
   di Pietro in alto mar per dritto segno;   *120*
e questo fu il nostro patrïarca;
   per che qual segue lui, com' el comanda,
   discerner puoi che buone merce carca.   *123*
Ma 'l suo peculio di nova vivanda
   è fatto ghiotto, sì ch'esser non puote
   che per diversi salti non si spanda;   *126*
e quanto le sue pecore remote
   e vagabunde più da esso vanno,
   più tornano a l'ovil di latte vòte.   *129*
Ben son di quelle che temono 'l danno
   e stringonsi al pastor; ma son sì poche,
   che le cappe fornisce poco panno.   *132*
Or, se le mie parole non son fioche,
   se la tua audïenza è stata attenta,
   se ciò ch'è detto a la mente revoche,   *135*
in parte fia la tua voglia contenta,
   perché vedrai la pianta onde si scheggia,
   e vedra' il corrègger che argomenta
'U' ben s'impingua, se non si vaneggia.' "   *139*

to his brethren as to rightful heirs he com-
mended his most dear lady and bade them
love her faithfully; and from her bosom the
glorious soul chose to set forth, returning to
its own realm, and for its body would have
no other bier.

"Think now what he was that was a worthy
colleague to keep Peter's bark on the right
course in the high sea; and such was our
Patriarch; wherefore you can see that whoever
follows him as he commands freights good
merchandise. But his flock has grown so
greedy of new fare that it cannot but be scat-
tered through wild pastures; and the farther
his sheep, remote and vagabond, go from him,
the more empty of milk do they return to the
fold. Some of them indeed there are who fear
the harm, and keep close to the shepherd, but
they are so few that little cloth suffices for
their cowls.

"Now if my words have not been faint, if
your listening has been intent, if you recall to
mind what I have said, your wish will be con-
tent in part, for you will see the plant which
is whittled away, and you will see what is in-
tended by the correction 'where there is good
fattening if they do not stray.'"

PARADISO

Sì tosto come l'ultima parola
   la benedetta fiamma per dir tolse,
   a rotar cominciò la santa mola;   *3*
e nel suo giro tutta non si volse
   prima ch'un'altra di cerchio la chiuse,
   e moto a moto e canto a canto colse;   *6*
canto che tanto vince nostre muse,
   nostre serene in quelle dolci tube,
   quanto primo splendor quel ch'e' refuse. *9*
Come si volgon per tenera nube
   due archi paralelli e concolori,
   quando Iunone a sua ancella iube,   *12*
nascendo di quel d'entro quel di fori,
   a guisa del parlar di quella vaga
   ch'amor consunse come sol vapori,   *15*
e fanno qui la gente esser presaga,
   per lo patto che Dio con Noè puose,
   del mondo che già mai più non s'allaga: *18*

CANTO XII

As soon as the blessed flame took to speak-
ing its last word the holy millstone began to
turn, and it had not yet made a full circle
when a second enclosed it round and matched
motion with motion and song with song:
song which, in those sweet pipes, as much
surpasses our Muses, our Sirens, as a first
splendor that which it throws back. As two
bows, parallel and like in color, bend across a
thin cloud when Juno gives the order to her
handmaid—the one without born of the one
within, like the voice of that wandering
nymph whom love consumed as the sun does
vapors—and make the people here presage,
by reason of the covenant that God made
with Noah, that the world shall never again
be flooded;

così di quelle sempiterne rose
   volgiensi circa noi le due ghirlande,
   e sì l'estrema a l'intima rispuose.   *21*
Poi che 'l tripudio e l'altra festa grande,
   sì del cantare e sì del fiammeggiarsi
   luce con luce gaudïose e blande,   *24*
insieme a punto e a voler quetarsi,
   pur come li occhi ch'al piacer che i move
   conviene insieme chiudere e levarsi;   *27*
del cor de l'una de le luci nove
   si mosse voce, che l'ago a la stella
   parer mi fece in volgermi al suo dove;   *30*
e cominciò: "L'amor che mi fa bella
   mi tragge a ragionar de l'altro duca
   per cui del mio sì ben ci si favella.   *33*
Degno è che, dov' è l'un, l'altro s'induca:
   sì che, com' elli ad una militaro,
   così la gloria loro insieme luca.   *36*
L'essercito di Cristo, che sì caro
   costò a rïarmar, dietro a la 'nsegna
   si movea tardo, sospeccioso e raro,   *39*
quando lo 'mperador che sempre regna
   provide a la milizia, ch'era in forse,
   per sola grazia, non per esser degna;   *42*
e, come è detto, a sua sposa soccorse
   con due campioni, al cui fare, al cui dire
   lo popol disvïato si raccorse.   *45*
In quella parte ove surge ad aprire
   Zefiro dolce le novelle fronde
   di che si vede Europa rivestire,   *48*

so the two garlands of those sempiternal roses circled round us, and so did the outer correspond to the inner.

When the dance and all the great festival of both song and flames, light with light, gladsome and benign, stopped together at one instant and with one consent (even as the eyes which, at the pleasure that moves them, must needs be closed and lifted in accord), from the heart of one of the new lights there came a voice which made me seem as the needle to the star in turning me to where it was; and it began, "The love that makes me beautiful draws me to speak of the other leader on whose account such fair utterance is made here concerning mine. It is fit that where one is, the other be brought in, so that, as they warred for one same end, so together may their glory shine.

"Christ's army, which cost so dear to rearm, was moving behind the standard, slow, mistrustful and scanty, when the Emperor who reigns eternally took thought for His soldiery that was in peril, of His grace only, not that it was worthy, and, as has been said, succored His bride with two champions by whose deeds, by whose words, the scattered people were rallied.

"In that region where sweet Zephyr rises to open the new leaves wherewith Europe sees herself reclad,

non molto lungi al percuoter de l'onde
 dietro a le quali, per la lunga foga,
 lo sol talvolta ad ogne uom si nasconde,   *51*
siede la fortunata Calaroga
 sotto la protezion del grande scudo
 in che soggiace il leone e soggioga: *54*
dentro vi nacque l'amoroso drudo
 de la fede cristiana, il santo atleta
 benigno a' suoi e a' nemici crudo;   *57*
e come fu creata, fu repleta
 sì la sua mente di viva vertute
 che, ne la madre, lei fece profeta.   *60*
Poi che le sponsalizie fuor compiute
 al sacro fonte intra lui e la Fede,
 u' si dotar di mutüa salute,   *63*
la donna che per lui l'assenso diede,
 vide nel sonno il mirabile frutto
 ch'uscir dovea di lui e de le rede;   *66*
e perché fosse qual era in costrutto,
 quinci si mosse spirito a nomarlo
 del possessivo di cui era tutto.   *69*
Domenico fu detto; e io ne parlo
 sì come de l'agricola che Cristo
 elesse a l'orto suo per aiutarlo.   *72*
Ben parve messo e famigliar di Cristo:
 ché 'l primo amor che 'n lui fu manifesto,
 fu al primo consiglio che diè Cristo.   *75*
Spesse fïate fu tacito e desto
 trovato in terra da la sua nutrice,
 come dicesse: 'Io son venuto a questo.'   *78*

not far from the smiting of the waves, behind
which the sun, after his long course, some-
times hides himself from every man, sits for-
tunate Calaroga under the protection of the
mighty shield whereon the lion is subject and
sovereign. Therein was born the ardent lover
of the Christian faith, the holy athlete, be-
nignant to his own and harsh to his foes.
And his mind, as soon as it was created, was
so full of living virtue that in his mother's
womb he made her a prophetess. When the
espousals were completed at the sacred font
between him and the faith, where they
dowered each other with mutual salvation,
the lady who gave the assent for him saw in
a dream the marvelous fruit destined to issue
from him and from his heirs, and, that he
might in very construing be what he was, a
spirit from up here went forth to name him
by the possessive of Him whose he wholly
was. Dominic he was named, and I speak of
him as of the husbandman whom Christ
chose to help Him in His garden. Well did
he show himself a messenger and familiar of
Christ; for the first love manifested in him
was for the first counsel that Christ gave.
Oftentimes his nurse found him silent and
awake upon the ground, as though he would
say, 'I am come for this.'

Oh padre suo veramente Felice!
    oh madre sua veramente Giovanna,
    se, interpretata, val come si dice!   81
Non per lo mondo, per cui mo s'affanna
    di retro ad Ostïense e a Taddeo,
    ma per amor de la verace manna   84
in picciol tempo gran dottor si feo;
    tal che si mise a circüir la vigna
    che tosto imbianca, se 'l vignaio è reo.   87
E a la sedia che fu già benigna
    più a' poveri giusti, non per lei,
    ma per colui che siede, che traligna,   90
non dispensare o due o tre per sei,
    non la fortuna di prima vacante,
    non *decimas, quae sunt pauperum Dei,*   93
addimandò, ma contro al mondo errante
    licenza di combatter per lo seme
    del qual ti fascian ventiquattro piante.   96
Poi, con dottrina e con volere insieme,
    con l'officio appostolico si mosse
    quasi torrente ch'alta vena preme;   99
e ne li sterpi eretici percosse
    l'impeto suo, più vivamente quivi
    dove le resistenze eran più grosse.   102
Di lui si fecer poi diversi rivi
    onde l'orto catolico si riga,
    sì che i suoi arbuscelli stan più vivi.   105
Se tal fu l'una rota de la biga
    in che la Santa Chiesa si difese
    e vinse in campo la sua civil briga,   108

Oh father of him, Felice indeed! Oh mother of him, Giovanna indeed, if this, being interpreted, means as is said!

"Not for the world for whose sake men now toil after him of Ostia and after Thaddeus, but for love of the true manna, in short time he became a mighty teacher, such that he set himself to go round the vineyard, which soon turns gray if the vine-dresser is negligent. And of the seat which once was more benign to the righteous poor—not in itself, but in him who sits on it and degenerates—he asked, not to dispense two or three for six, not for the fortune of the first vacancy, not for *decimas quae sunt pauperum Dei*, but for leave to fight against the erring world for that seed of which four and twenty plants surround you. Then both with doctrine and with will, together with the apostolic office, he went forth like a torrent which a lofty vein presses out, and on the heretical stocks his force struck with most vigor where the resistances were most obstinate. From him there sprang then various streamlets whereby the catholic garden is watered, so that its bushes are more living.

"If such was the one wheel of the chariot in which Holy Church defended herself and won in the field her civil strife,

ben ti dovrebbe assai esser palese
  l'eccellenza de l'altra, di cui Tomma
  dinanzi al mio venir fu sì cortese.   *111*
Ma l'orbita che fé la parte somma
  di sua circunferenza, è derelitta,
  sì ch'è la muffa dov' era la gromma.   *114*
La sua famiglia, che si mosse dritta
  coi piedi a le sue orme, è tanto volta,
  che quel dinanzi a quel di retro gitta;   *117*
e tosto si vedrà de la ricolta
  de la mala coltura, quando il loglio
  si lagnerà che l'arca li sia tolta.   *120*
Ben dico, chi cercasse a foglio a foglio
  nostro volume, ancor troveria carta
  u' leggerebbe 'I' mi son quel ch'i' soglio';   *123*
ma non fia da Casal né d'Acquasparta,
  là onde vegnon tali a la scrittura,
  ch'uno la fugge e altro la coarta.   *126*
Io son la vita di Bonaventura
  da Bagnoregio, che ne' grandi offici
  sempre pospuosi la sinistra cura.   *129*
Illuminato e Augustin son quici,
  che fuor de' primi scalzi poverelli
  che nel capestro a Dio si fero amici.   *132*
Ugo da San Vittore è qui con elli,
  e Pietro Mangiadore e Pietro Spano,
  lo qual giù luce in dodici libelli;   *135*
Natàn profeta e 'l metropolitano
  Crisostomo e Anselmo e quel Donato
  ch'a la prim' arte degnò porre mano.   *138*

surely the excellence of the other must be very plain to you, concerning whom, before I came, Thomas was so courteous. But the track made by the topmost part of its rim is derelict; so that there is mould where the crust was. His household, which set out aright with their feet upon his footprints, is so turned about that the forward foot moves to that behind; and soon shall be seen some harvest of the bad tillage, when the tare will complain that the bin is taken from it. Nevertheless, I say, he who should search our volume leaf by leaf might still find a page where he would read, 'I am as I always was'; but it will not be from Casale or from Acquasparta, whence come such to the writing that one shuns it and the other contracts it.

"I am the living soul of Bonaventura of Bagnorea, who in the great offices always put the left-hand care behind. Illuminato and Augustine are here, who were of the first unshod poor brethren that with the cord made themselves God's friends. Hugh of St. Victor is here with them, and Peter Comestor, and Peter of Spain, who down below shines in twelve books; Nathan the prophet, and the Metropolitan Chrysostom, and Anselm, and that Donatus who deigned to set his hand to the first art;

Rabano è qui, e lucemi dallato
  il calavrese abate Giovacchino
  di spirito profetico dotato.   *141*
Ad inveggiar cotanto paladino
  mi mosse l'infiammata cortesia
  di fra Tommaso e 'l discreto latino;
e mosse meco questa compagnia."   *145*

Rabanus is here, and beside me shines the Calabrian abbot Joachim, who was endowed with prophetic spirit.

"The glowing courtesy and the well-judged discourse of Brother Thomas has moved me to celebrate so great a paladin, and with me has moved this company."

PARADISO

IMAGINI, CHI bene intender cupe
   quel ch'i' or vidi — e ritegna l'image,
   mentre ch'io dico, come ferma rupe —,   *3*
quindici stelle che 'n diverse plage
   lo cielo avvivan di tanto sereno
   che soperchia de l'aere ogne compage;   *6*
imagini quel carro a cu' il seno
   basta del nostro cielo e notte e giorno,
   sì ch'al volger del temo non vien meno;   *9*
imagini la bocca di quel corno
   che si comincia in punta de lo stelo
   a cui la prima rota va dintorno,   *12*
aver fatto di sé due segni in cielo,
   qual fece la figliuola di Minoi
   allora che sentì di morte il gelo;   *15*
e l'un ne l'altro aver li raggi suoi,
   e amendue girarsi per maniera
   che l'uno andasse al primo e l'altro al poi;   *18*

CANTO XIII

L ET HIM imagine, who would rightly grasp
what I now beheld (and, while I speak, let
him hold the image firm as a rock), fifteen
stars which in different regions vivify the
heaven with such great brightness that it over-
comes every thickness of the air; let him
imagine that Wain for which the bosom of
our heaven suffices night and day so that with
the turning of the pole it does not disappear;
let him imagine the mouth of that Horn
which begins at the end of the axle on which
the first wheel revolves—all to have made of
themselves two signs in the heavens like that
which the daughter of Minos made when she
felt the chill of death; and one to have its
rays within the other, and both to revolve in
such manner that one should go first and the
other after;

e avrà quasi l'ombra de la vera
   costellazione e de la doppia danza
   che circulava il punto dov' io era: *21*
poi ch'è tanto di là da nostra usanza,
   quanto di là dal mover de la Chiana
   si move il ciel che tutti li altri avanza.   *24*
Lì si cantò non Bacco, non Peana,
   ma tre persone in divina natura,
   e in una persona essa e l'umana.   *27*
Compié 'l cantare e 'l volger sua misura;
   e attersersi a noi quei santi lumi,
   felicitando sé di cura in cura.   *30*
Ruppe il silenzio ne' concordi numi
   poscia la luce in che mirabil vita
   del poverel di Dio narrata fumi,   *33*
e disse: "Quando l'una paglia è trita,
   quando la sua semenza è già riposta,
   a batter l'altra dolce amor m'invita.   *36*
Tu credi che nel petto onde la costa
   si trasse per formar la bella guancia
   il cui palato a tutto 'l mondo costa,   *39*
e in quel che, forato da la lancia,
   e prima e poscia tanto sodisfece,
   che d'ogne colpa vince la bilancia,   *42*
quantunque a la natura umana lece
   aver di lume, tutto fosse infuso
   da quel valor che l'uno e l'altro fece;   *45*
e però miri a ciò ch'io dissi suso,
   quando narrai che non ebbe 'l secondo
   lo ben che ne la quinta luce è chiuso.   *48*

and he will have as it were a shadow of the
true constellation, and of the double dance,
which was circling round the point where I
was; for it is as far beyond our experience as
the motion of the heaven that outspeeds all
the rest is beyond the motion of the Chiana.
There they sang not Bacchus, and not Paean,
but Three Persons in the divine nature, and
it and the human nature in one Person. The
singing and the circling completed each its
measure, and those holy lights gave heed to us,
rejoicing as they passed from care to care.

Then the light within which the wondrous
life of the poor man of God had been nar-
rated to me broke the silence among the con-
cordant souls, and said, "Since one straw is
threshed, since its grain is now garnered,
sweet charity bids me beat out the other. You
believe that into the breast from which the
rib was drawn to form her beautiful cheek
whose palate costs dear to all the world, and
into that which, pierced by the lance, made
such satisfaction, both after and before, that it
turns the scale against all fault, whatever of
light it is allowed human nature to have was
all infused by that Power which made the one
and the other; and therefore you wonder at
what I said above, when I declared that the
excellence which is enclosed in the fifth light
never had a second.

Or apri li occhi a quel ch'io ti rispondo,
    e vedräi il tuo credere e 'l mio dire
    nel vero farsi come centro in tondo.   *51*
Ciò che non more e ciò che può morire
    non è se non splendor di quella idea
    che partorisce, amando, il nostro Sire;   *54*
ché quella viva luce che sì mea
    dal suo lucente, che non si disuna
    da lui né da l'amor ch'a lor s'intrea,   *57*
per sua bontate il suo raggiare aduna,
    quasi specchiato, in nove sussistenze,
    etternalmente rimanendosi una.   *60*
Quindi discende a l'ultime potenze
    giù d'atto in atto, tanto divenendo,
    che più non fa che brevi contingenze;   *63*
e queste contingenze essere intendo
    le cose generate, che produce
    con seme e sanza seme il ciel movendo.   *66*
La cera di costoro e chi la duce
    non sta d'un modo; e però sotto 'l segno
    idëale poi più e men traluce.   *69*
Ond' elli avvien ch'un medesimo legno,
    secondo specie, meglio e peggio frutta;
    e voi nascete con diverso ingegno.   *72*
Se fosse a punto la cera dedutta
    e fosse il cielo in sua virtù suprema,
    la luce del suggel parrebbe tutta;   *75*
ma la natura la dà sempre scema,
    similemente operando a l'artista
    ch'a l'abito de l'arte ha man che trema.   *78*

Now open your eyes to that which I answer
you, and you will see your belief and what I
say become in the truth as the center in a
circle.

"That which dies not and that which can
die are naught but the splendor of that Idea
which in His love our Sire begets; for that liv-
ing light which so streams from its Lucent
Source that It is not disunited from It, nor
from the Love which is intrined with them,
does of Its own goodness collect Its rays, as
though reflected, in nine subsistences, Itself
eternally remaining One. Thence It descends
to the ultimate potentialities, downward from
act to act becoming such that finally it makes
but brief contingencies; and these contingen-
cies I understand to be the generated things
which the moving heavens produce with seed
and without it. The wax of these and that
which molds it are not always in the same
condition, and therefore under the ideal stamp
it then shines now more, now less; hence it
comes that one same plant, in respect to spe-
cies, fruits better or worse, and that you are
born with diverse dispositions. If the wax
were exactly worked, and the heavens were at
the height of their power, the light of the
whole seal would be apparent. But nature al-
ways gives it defectively, working like the art-
ist who in the practice of his art has a hand
that trembles.

Però se 'l caldo amor la chiara vista
  de la prima virtù dispone e segna,
  tutta la perfezion quivi s'acquista.   *81*
Così fu fatta già la terra degna
  di tutta l'animal perfezïone;
  così fu fatta la Vergine pregna;   *84*
sì ch'io commendo tua oppinïone,
  che l'umana natura mai non fue
  né fia qual fu in quelle due persone.   *87*
Or s'i' non procedesse avanti piùe,
  'Dunque, come costui fu sanza pare?'
  comincerebber le parole tue.   *90*
Ma perché paia ben ciò che non pare,
  pensa chi era, e la cagion che 'l mosse,
  quando fu detto 'Chiedi,' a dimandare.   *93*
Non ho parlato sì, che tu non posse
  ben veder ch'el fu re, che chiese senno
  acciò che re sufficïente fosse;   *96*
non per sapere il numero in che enno
  li motor di qua sù, o se *necesse*
  con contingente mai *necesse* fenno;   *99*
non *si est dare primum motum esse*,
  o se del mezzo cerchio far si puote
  trïangol sì ch'un retto non avesse.   *102*
Onde, se ciò ch'io dissi e questo note,
  regal prudenza è quel vedere impari
  in che lo stral di mia intenzion percuote;   *105*
e se al "surse" drizzi li occhi chiari,
  vedrai aver solamente respetto
  ai regi, che son molti, e ' buon son rari.   *108*

Yet, if the fervent Love disposes and imprints the clear Vision of the primal Power, complete perfection is there acquired. Thus was the dust once made fit for the full perfection of a living creature, thus was the Virgin made to be with child; so that I approve your opinion that human nature never was, nor shall be, what it was in those two persons.

"Now, if I went no further, 'How, then, was that other without an equal?' would your words begin. But in order that that which is not apparent may clearly appear, consider who he was and the cause which moved him to make request when it was said to him, 'Ask.' I have not so spoken that you cannot plainly see that he was a king, who asked for wisdom, in order that he might be a worthy king; not to know the number of the mover spirits here above, nor if *necesse* with a contingent ever made *necesse*; nor *si est dare primum motum esse*; nor if in a semicircle a triangle can be so constructed that it shall have no right angle. Wherefore, if you note this along with what I said, kingly prudence is that peerless vision on which the arrow of my intention strikes. And if to 'rose' you turn your discerning eyes, you will see it has respect only to kings—who are many and the good are rare.

Con questa distinzion prendi 'l mio detto;
 e così puote star con quel che credi
 del primo padre e del nostro Diletto.   *111*
E questo ti sia sempre piombo a' piedi,
 per farti mover lento com' uom lasso
 e al sì e al no che tu non vedi: *114*
ché quelli è tra li stolti bene a basso,
 che sanza distinzione afferma e nega
 ne l'un così come ne l'altro passo;   *117*
perch' elli 'ncontra che più volte piega
 l'oppinïon corrente in falsa parte,
 e poi l'affetto l'intelletto lega.   *120*
Vie più che 'ndarno da riva si parte,
 perché non torna tal qual e' si move,
 chi pesca per lo vero e non ha l'arte.   *123*
E di ciò sono al mondo aperte prove
 Parmenide, Melisso e Brisso e molti,
 li quali andaro e non sapëan dove;   *126*
sì fé Sabellio e Arrio e quelli stolti
 che furon come spade a le Scritture
 in render torti li diritti volti.   *129*
Non sien le genti, ancor, troppo sicure
 a giudicar, sì come quei che stima
 le biade in campo pria che sien mature;   *132*
ch'i' ho veduto tutto 'l verno prima
 lo prun mostrarsi rigido e feroce,
 poscia portar la rosa in su la cima;   *135*
e legno vidi già dritto e veloce
 correr lo mar per tutto suo cammino,
 perire al fine a l'intrar de la foce.   *138*

Take my words with this distinction, and
they can stand thus with what you believe of
the first father and of our Beloved.

"And let this ever be as lead to your feet,
to make you slow, like a weary man, in mov-
ing either to the *yes* or the *no* which you see
not; for he is right low down among the fools,
alike in the one and in the other case, who
affirms or denies without distinguishing; be-
cause it happens that oftentimes hasty opinion
inclines to the wrong side, and then fondness
for it binds the intellect. Far worse than in
vain does he leave the shore (since he returns
not as he puts forth) who fishes for the truth
and has not the art. And of this Parmenides,
Melissus, Bryson, are open proofs to the world,
as are the many others who went on but knew
not whither. Thus did Sabellius, and Arius,
and those fools who were to the Scriptures
like swords, in rendering straight counte-
nances distorted.

Moreover, let folk not be too secure in judg-
ment, like one who should count the ears in
the field before they are ripe; for I have seen
first, all winter through, the thorn display it-
self hard and stiff, and then upon its summit
bear the rose. And I have seen ere now a ship
fare straight and swift over the sea through
all her course, and perish at the last as she
entered the harbor.

149

Non creda donna Berta e ser Martino,
   per vedere un furare, altro offerere,
   vederli dentro al consiglio divino;
ché quel può surgere, e quel può cadere."   *142*

Let not dame Bertha and squire Martin, if
they see one steal and one make offering, be-
lieve to see them within the Divine Counsel:
for the one may rise and the other may fall."

PARADISO

Dal centro al cerchio, e sì dal cerchio al centro
movesi l'acqua in un ritondo vaso,
secondo ch'è percosso fuori o dentro: *3*
ne la mia mente fé sùbito caso
questo ch'io dico, sì come si tacque
la glorïosa vita di Tommaso,   *6*
per la similitudine che nacque
del suo parlare e di quel di Beatrice,
a cui sì cominciar, dopo lui, piacque: *9*
"A costui fa mestieri, e nol vi dice
né con la voce né pensando ancora,
d'un altro vero andare a la radice.   *12*
Diteli se la luce onde s'infiora
vostra sustanza, rimarrà con voi
etternalmente sì com' ell' è ora;   *15*
e se rimane, dite come, poi
che sarete visibili rifatti,
esser porà ch'al veder non vi nòi."   *18*
Come, da più letizia pinti e tratti,
a la fïata quei che vanno a rota
levan la voce e rallegrano li atti,   *21*

CANTO XIV

From the center to the rim, and so from the rim to the center, the water in a round vessel moves, according as it is struck from without or within. This which I say fell suddenly into my mind as the glorious life of Thomas became silent, because of the likeness which was born of his speech and that of Beatrice, who was pleased to begin thus after him, "This man has need, and does not tell you of it, either by word or as yet in thought, to go to the root of another truth. Tell him if the light wherewith your substance blooms will remain with you eternally even as it is now; and, if it does remain, tell how, after you are made visible again, it can be that it will not hurt your sight."

As when urged and drawn on by increasing delight, those who are dancing in a ring from time to time raise their voices and gladden their motions,

così, a l'orazion pronta e divota,
  li santi cerchi mostrar nova gioia
  nel torneare e ne la mira nota.   24
Qual si lamenta perché qui si moia
  per viver colà sù, non vide quive
  lo refrigerio de l'etterna ploia.   27
Quell' uno e due e tre che sempre vive
  e regna sempre in tre e 'n due e 'n uno,
  non circunscritto, e tutto circunscrive,   30
tre volte era cantato da ciascuno
  di quelli spiriti con tal melodia,
  ch'ad ogne merto saria giusto muno.   33
E io udi' ne la luce più dia
  del minor cerchio una voce modesta,
  forse qual fu da l'angelo a Maria,   36
risponder: "Quanto fia lunga la festa
  di paradiso, tanto il nostro amore
  si raggerà dintorno cotal vesta.   39
La sua chiarezza séguita l'ardore;
  l'ardor la visïone, e quella è tanta,
  quant' ha di grazia sovra suo valore.   42
Come la carne glorïosa e santa
  fia rivestita, la nostra persona
  più grata fia per esser tutta quanta;   45
per che s'accrescerà ciò che ne dona
  di gratüito lume il sommo bene,
  lume ch'a lui veder ne condiziona;   48
onde la visïon crescer convene,
  crescer l'ardor che di quella s'accende,
  crescer lo raggio che da esso vene.   51

so at that prompt and devout petition the holy circles showed new joy in their revolving and in their marvelous melody. Whoso laments because we die here to live there on high has not seen there the refreshment of the eternal rain.

That One and Two and Three which ever lives, and ever reigns in Three and Two and One, uncircumscribed, and circumscribing all things, was thrice sung by each of those spirits with such a melody as would be adequate reward for every merit. And I heard in the divinest light of the lesser circle a modest voice, perhaps such as was that of the Angel to Mary, make answer, "As long as the feast of Paradise shall be, so long shall our love radiate around us such a garment. Its brightness follows our ardor, the ardor our vision, and that is in the measure which each has of grace beyond his merit. When the flesh, glorious and sanctified, shall be clothed on us again, our persons will be more acceptable for being all complete; wherefore whatever of gratuitous light the Supreme Good gives us will be increased, light which fits us to see Him; so that our vision needs must increase, our ardor increase which by that is kindled, our radiance increase which comes from this.

Ma sì come carbon che fiamma rende,
  e per vivo candor quella soverchia,
  sì che la sua parvenza si difende;   *54*
così questo folgór che già ne cerchia
  fia vinto in apparenza da la carne
  che tutto dì la terra ricoperchia;   *57*
né potrà tanta luce affaticarne:
  ché li organi del corpo saran forti
  a tutto ciò che potrà dilettarne."   *60*
Tanto mi parver sùbiti e accorti
  e l'uno e l'altro coro a dicer "Amme!"
  che ben mostrar disio d'i corpi morti: *63*
forse non pur per lor, ma per le mamme,
  per li padri e per li altri che fuor cari
  anzi che fosser sempiterne fiamme.   *66*
Ed ecco intorno, di chiarezza pari,
  nascere un lustro sopra quel che v'era,
  per guisa d'orizzonte che rischiari.   *69*
E sì come al salir di prima sera
  comincian per lo ciel nove parvenze,
  sì che la vista pare e non par vera,   *72*
parvemi lì novelle sussistenze
  cominciare a vedere, e fare un giro
  di fuor da l'altre due circunferenze.   *75*
Oh vero sfavillar del Santo Spiro!
  come si fece sùbito e candente
  a li occhi miei che, vinti, nol soffriro!   *78*
Ma Bëatrice sì bella e ridente
  mi si mostrò, che tra quelle vedute
  si vuol lasciar che non seguir la mente.   *81*

But even as a coal which gives forth flame, and with its white glow outshines it, so that its visibility is maintained, so shall this effulgence which already surrounds us be surpassed in brightness by the flesh which the earth still covers; nor will such light have power to fatigue us, for the organs of the body will be strong for everything that can delight us."

So sudden and eager both the one and the other chorus seemed to me in saying "Amen," that truly they showed desire for their dead bodies—perhaps not only for themselves, but also for their mothers, for their fathers, and for the others who were dear before they became eternal flames.

And lo! round about and of equal brightness rose a lustre beyond that which was there, like a brightening horizon. And as, at rise of early evening, new lights begin to show in heaven, so that the sight does, and yet does not, seem real, it seemed to me that there I began to perceive new subsistences making a ring beyond the other two circumferences. Oh true sparkling of the Holy Spirit! how suddenly glowing it became to my eyes, which, vanquished, endured it not. But Beatrice showed herself to me so beautiful and smiling that it must be left among those sights which followed not my memory.

Quindi ripreser li occhi miei virtute
  a rilevarsi; e vidimi translato
  sol con mia donna in più alta salute.   *84*
Ben m'accors' io ch'io era più levato,
  per l'affocato riso de la stella,
  che mi parea più roggio che l'usato.   *87*
Con tutto 'l core e con quella favella
  ch'è una in tutti, a Dio feci olocausto,
  qual conveniesi a la grazia novella.   *90*
E non er' anco del mio petto essausto
  l'ardor del sacrificio, ch'io conobbi
  esso litare stato accetto e fausto;   *93*
ché con tanto lucore e tanto robbi
  m'apparvero splendor dentro a due raggi,
  ch'io dissi: "O Eliòs che sì li addobbi!"   *96*
Come distinta da minori e maggi
  lumi biancheggia tra ' poli del mondo
  Galassia sì, che fa dubbiar ben saggi;   *99*
sì costellati facean nel profondo
  Marte quei raggi il venerabil segno
  che fan giunture di quadranti in tondo.   *102*
Qui vince la memoria mia lo 'ngegno;
  ché quella croce lampeggiava Cristo,
  sì ch'io non so trovare essempro degno;   *105*
ma chi prende sua croce e segue Cristo,
  ancor mi scuserà di quel ch'io lasso,
  vedendo in quell' albor balenar Cristo.   *108*
Di corno in corno e tra la cima e 'l basso
  si movien lumi, scintillando forte
  nel congiugnersi insieme e nel trapasso: *111*

Therefrom my eyes regained power to raise
themselves again, and I saw myself, alone
with my lady, translated to a more exalted
blessedness. That I was more uplifted I per-
ceived clearly by the fiery smile of the star
which seemed to me ruddier than its wont.
With all my heart, and with that speech
which is one in all men, I made a holocaust
to God such as befitted the new grace; and
the burning of the sacrifice was not yet com-
pleted in my breast when I knew the of-
fering to be accepted and propitious, for
with such a glow and such a ruddiness splen-
dors appeared to me within two rays that I
said, "O Helios, who dost so adorn them!"

As, pricked out with greater and lesser
lights, between the poles of the Universe, the
Milky Way so gleams as to cause even the
wise to question, so did those beams, thus
constellated, make in the depth of Mars the
venerable sign which joinings of quadrants
make in a circle. Here my memory outstrips
my wit, for that Cross so flashed forth Christ
that I can find for it no fit comparison; but
he that takes up his cross and follows Christ
shall yet forgive me for what I leave untold
when he sees Christ flash in that dawn.

From horn to horn and between the top and
the base, lights were moving that sparkled
brightly as they met and passed;

così si veggion qui diritte e torte,
  veloci e tarde, rinovando vista,
  le minuzie d'i corpi, lunghe e corte,   *114*
moversi per lo raggio onde si lista
  talvolta l'ombra che, per sua difesa,
  la gente con ingegno e arte acquista.   *117*
E come giga e arpa, in tempra tesa
  di molte corde, fa dolce tintinno
  a tal da cui la nota non è intesa,   *120*
così da' lumi che lì m'apparinno
  s'accogliea per la croce una melode
  che mi rapiva, sanza intender l'inno.   *123*
Ben m'accors' io ch'elli era d'alte lode,
  però ch'a me venìa "Resurgi" e "Vinci"
  come a colui che non intende e ode.   *126*
Ïo m'innamorava tanto quinci,
  che 'nfino a lì non fu alcuna cosa
  che mi legasse con sì dolci vinci.   *129*
Forse la mia parola par troppo osa,
  posponendo il piacer de li occhi belli,
  ne' quai mirando mio disio ha posa;   *132*
ma chi s'avvede che i vivi suggelli
  d'ogne bellezza più fanno più suso,
  e ch'io non m'era lì rivolto a quelli,   *135*
escusar puommi di quel ch'io m'accuso
  per escusarmi, e vedermi dir vero:
  ché 'l piacer santo non è qui dischiuso,
perché si fa, montando, più sincero.   *139*

so we see here, straight and athwart, swift and slow, changing appearance, the motes of bodies, long and short, moving through the ray that sometimes streaks the shade which men with skill and art contrive for their defense. And as viol and harp, strung with many cords in harmony, chime sweetly for one who does not catch the tune, so from the lights that appeared to me there a melody gathered through the cross which held me rapt, though I followed not the hymn. Well I discerned it to be of lofty praise, for there came to me: "Rise" and "Conquer," as to one who understands not, but hears; by which I was so moved to love that till then nothing had bound me with such sweet bonds. Perhaps my word appears too daring, as though slighting the pleasure of the beautiful eyes, gazing into which my longing has repose. But he who considers that the living seals of every beauty have more effect the higher they are, and that I there had not yet turned to them, may excuse me for that whereof I accuse myself in order to excuse myself, and may see that I speak truth; for the holy pleasure is not excluded here, because it becomes the purer as one mounts.

PARADISO

Benigna volontade in che si liqua
sempre l'amor che drittamente spira,
come cupidità fa ne la iniqua,   *3*
silenzio puose a quella dolce lira,
e fece quïetar le sante corde
che la destra del cielo allenta e tira.   *6*
Come saranno a' giusti preghi sorde
quelle sustanze che, per darmi voglia
ch'io le pregassi, a tacer fur concorde?   *9*
Bene è che sanza termine si doglia
chi, per amor di cosa che non duri
etternalmente, quello amor si spoglia.   *12*
Quale per li seren tranquilli e puri
discorre ad ora ad or sùbito foco,
movendo li occhi che stavan sicuri,   *15*
e pare stella che tramuti loco,
se non che da la parte ond' e' s'accende
nulla sen perde, ed esso dura poco: *18*

CANTO XV

GRACIOUS WILL, wherein right-breathing love always resolves itself, as cupidity does into grudging will, imposed silence on that sweet lyre and quieted the holy strings which the right hand of Heaven slackens and draws tight. How shall those beings be deaf to righteous prayers, who, in order to prompt me to beg of them, became silent with one consent? Right it is that he should grieve without end who, for the love of what does not endure forever, robs himself of that love.

As, through the still and cloudless evening sky a sudden fire shoots from time to time, moving the eyes that were at rest, and seeming a star that changes place, save that from where it kindles no star is lost, and it lasts but short while;

tale dal corno che 'n destro si stende
   a piè di quella croce corse un astro
   de la costellazion che lì resplende;   *21*
né si partì la gemma dal suo nastro,
   ma per la lista radïal trascorse,
   che parve foco dietro ad alabastro.   *24*
Sì pïa l'ombra d'Anchise si porse,
   se fede merta nostra maggior musa,
   quando in Eliso del figlio s'accorse.   *27*
"O sanguis meus, o superinfusa
   gratïa Deï, sicut tibi cui
   bis unquam celi ianüa reclusa?"   *30*
Così quel lume: ond' io m'attesi a lui;
   poscia rivolsi a la mia donna il viso,
   e quinci e quindi stupefatto fui;   *33*
ché dentro a li occhi suoi ardeva un riso
   tal, ch'io pensai co' miei toccar lo fondo
   de la mia gloria e del mio paradiso.   *36*
Indi, a udire e a veder giocondo,
   giunse lo spirto al suo principio cose,
   ch'io non lo 'ntesi, sì parlò profondo;   *39*
né per elezïon mi si nascose,
   ma per necessità, ché 'l suo concetto
   al segno d'i mortal si soprapuose.   *42*
E quando l'arco de l'ardente affetto
   fu sì sfogato, che 'l parlar discese
   inver' lo segno del nostro intelletto,   *45*
la prima cosa che per me s'intese,
   "Benedetto sia tu," fu, "trino e uno,
   che nel mio seme se' tanto cortese!"   *48*

so, from the horn that extends on the right, there darted a star of the resplendent constellation that is there, down to the foot of that cross; nor did the gem depart from its ribbon, but coursed along the radial strip, and seemed like fire behind alabaster. With like affection did the shade of Anchises stretch forward (if our greatest Muse merits belief), when in Elysium he perceived his son.

"*O sanguis meus, O superinfusa gratia Dei, sicut tibi cui bis unquam celi ianua reclusa?*" Thus that light; wherefore I gave my heed to it, then I turned back my sight to my lady, and on this side and that I was amazed, for in her eyes was blazing such a smile that I thought with mine I had touched the limit both of my beatitude and of my paradise.

Then, a joy to hearing and to sight, the spirit added to his first words things I did not comprehend, so deep was his speech; nor did he conceal himself from me by choice, but of necessity, for his conception was set above the mark of mortals. And when the bow of his ardent affection was so relaxed that his speech descended toward the mark of our intellect, the first thing I understood was, "Blessed be Thou, Three and One, who show such favor to my seed."

E seguì: "Grato e lontano digiuno,
  tratto leggendo del magno volume
  du' non si muta mai bianco né bruno,   *51*
solvuto hai, figlio, dentro a questo lume
  in ch'io ti parlo, mercé di colei
  ch'a l'alto volo ti vestì le piume.   *54*
Tu credi che a me tuo pensier mei
  da quel ch'è primo, così come raia
  da l'un, se si conosce, il cinque e 'l sei;   *57*
e però ch'io mi sia e perch' io paia
  più gaudïoso a te, non mi domandi,
  che alcun altro in questa turba gaia.   *60*
Tu credi 'l vero; ché i minori e ' grandi
  di questa vita miran ne lo speglio
  in che, prima che pensi, il pensier pandi;   *63*
ma perché 'l sacro amore in che io veglio
  con perpetüa vista e che m'asseta
  di dolce disïar, s'adempia meglio,   *66*
la voce tua sicura, balda e lieta
  suoni la volontà, suoni 'l disio,
  a che la mia risposta è già decreta!"   *69*
Io mi volsi a Beatrice, e quella udio
  pria ch'io parlassi, e arrisemi un cenno
  che fece crescer l'ali al voler mio.   *72*
Poi cominciai così: "L'affetto e 'l senno,
  come la prima equalità v'apparse,
  d'un peso per ciascun di voi si fenno,   *75*
però che 'l sol che v'allumò e arse,
  col caldo e con la luce è sì iguali,
  che tutte simiglianze sono scarse.   *78*

And he continued, "Happy and long-felt hunger, derived from reading in the great volume where white or dark is never changed, you have relieved, my son, within this light in which I speak to you, thanks to her who clothed you with plumes for the lofty flight. You believe that your thought flows to me from Him who is First, even as from the unit, if that be known, ray out the five and the six; and therefore who I am, and why I seem to you more joyous than another in this festive throng, you do not ask me. You believe the truth, for the lesser and the great of this life gaze into that mirror in which, before you think, you display your thought. But in order that holy love, in which I watch with perpetual vision, and which makes me thirst with sweet longing, may be the better fulfilled, let your voice, confident and bold and glad, sound forth the will, sound forth the desire, whereto my answer is already decreed."

I turned to Beatrice, and she heard before I spoke, and smiled to me a sign that made the wings of my desire increase. And I began thus, "Love and intelligence, as soon as the first Equality became visible to you, became of one weight for each of you, because the Sun which illumined you and warmed you is of such equality in its heat and light that all comparisons fall short.

Ma voglia e argomento ne' mortali,
   per la cagion ch'a voi è manifesta,
   diversamente son pennuti in ali;   *81*
ond' io, che son mortal, mi sento in questa
   disagguaglianza, e però non ringrazio
   se non col core a la paterna festa.   *84*
Ben supplico io a te, vivo topazio
   che questa gioia prezïosa ingemmi,
   perché mi facci del tuo nome sazio."   *87*
"O fronda mia in che io compiacemmi
   pur aspettando, io fui la tua radice":
   cotal principio, rispondendo, femmi.   *90*
Poscia mi disse: "Quel da cui si dice
   tua cognazione e che cent' anni e piùe
   girato ha 'l monte in la prima cornice,   *93*
mio figlio fu e tuo bisavol fue:
   ben si convien che la lunga fatica
   tu li raccorci con l'opere tue.   *96*
Fiorenza dentro da la cerchia antica,
   ond' ella toglie ancora e terza e nona,
   si stava in pace, sobria e pudica.   *99*
Non avea catenella, non corona,
   non gonne contigiate, non cintura
   che fosse a veder più che la persona.   *102*
Non faceva, nascèndo, ancor paura
   la figlia al padre, ché 'l tempo e la dote
   non fuggien quinci e quindi la misura.   *105*
Non avea case di famiglia vòte;
   non v'era giunto ancor Sardanapalo
   a mostrar ciò che 'n camera si puote.   *108*

But will and faculty in mortals, for the reason that is plain to you, are not equally feathered in their wings, so that I, who am mortal, feel myself in this inequality, and therefore can only give thanks with the heart for your paternal welcome. But I beseech you, living topaz who are a gem in this precious jewel, that you satisfy me with your name."

"O my branch, in whom I took delight only expecting you, I was your root." Thus he began his answer to me, then said, "He from whom your family has its name and who a hundred years and more has circled the mountain on the first ledge, was my son and was your grandfather's father. Truly it is fitting that you should shorten his long toil with your good offices.

"Florence, within her ancient circle from which she still takes tierce and nones, abode in peace, sober and chaste. There was no necklace, no coronal, no embroidered gowns, no girdle that was more to be looked at than the person. Not yet did the daughter at her birth cause fear to the father, for the time and the dowry did not outrun due measure on this side and that. Houses empty of family there were none, nor had Sardanapalus arrived yet to show what could be done in the chamber.

Non era vinto ancora Montemalo
    dal vostro Uccellatoio, che, com' è vinto
    nel montar sù, così sarà nel calo.   *111*
Bellincion Berti vid' io andar cinto
    di cuoio e d'osso, e venir da lo specchio
    la donna sua sanza 'l viso dipinto;   *114*
e vidi quel d'i Nerli e quel del Vecchio
    esser contenti a la pelle scoperta,
    e le sue donne al fuso e al pennecchio.   *117*
Oh fortunate! ciascuna era certa
    de la sua sepultura, e ancor nulla
    era per Francia nel letto diserta.   *120*
L'una vegghiava a studio de la culla,
    e, consolando, usava l'idïoma
    che prima i padri e le madri trastulla;   *123*
l'altra, traendo a la rocca la chioma,
    favoleggiava con la sua famiglia
    d'i Troiani, di Fiesole e di Roma.   *126*
Saria tenuta allor tal maraviglia
    una Cianghella, un Lapo Salterello,
    qual or saria Cincinnato e Corniglia.   *129*
A così riposato, a così bello
    viver di cittadini, a così fida
    cittadinanza, a così dolce ostello,   *132*
Maria mi diè, chiamata in alte grida;
    e ne l'antico vostro Batisteo
    insieme fui cristiano e Cacciaguida.   *135*
Moronto fu mio frate ed Eliseo;
    mia donna venne a me di val di Pado,
    e quindi il sopranome tuo si feo.   *138*

Not yet was Montemalo surpassed by your Uccellatoio, which, as it has been passed in the uprising, so shall it be in the fall. Bellincion Berti have I seen go girt with leather and bone, and his wife come from her mirror with unpainted face. I have seen de' Nerli and del Vecchio content in unlined skin, and their wives at the spindle and the distaff. O happy they! each one of them sure of her burial place, and none as yet deserted in her bed because of France. The one kept watch in minding the cradle, and, soothing, spoke that speech which first delights fathers and mothers. Another, as she drew the threads from the distaff, would tell her household about the Trojans, and Fiesole, and Rome. Then a Cianghella or a Lapo Salterello would have been as great a marvel as Cincinnatus and Cornelia would be now.

"To so reposeful, to so fair a life of citizens, to such a trusty community, to so sweet an abode, Mary, called on with loud cries, gave me, and in your ancient Baptistery I became at once a Christian and Cacciaguida. Moronto was my brother, and Eliseo. My wife came to me from the valley of the Po, and thence was derived your surname.

Poi seguitai lo 'mperador Currado;
   ed el mi cinse de la sua milizia,
   tanto per bene ovrar li venni in grado.   *141*
Dietro li andai incontro a la nequizia
   di quella legge il cui popolo usurpa,
   per colpa d'i pastor, vostra giustizia.   *144*
Quivi fu' io da quella gente turpa
   disviluppato dal mondo fallace,
   lo cui amor molt'anime deturpa;
e venni dal martiro a questa pace."   *148*

Afterward I followed the Emperor Conrad, who girt me with his knighthood, so much did I win his favor by good work. I went, in his train, against the iniquity of that law whose people, through fault of the Pastors, usurp your right. There by that foul folk was I released from the deceitful world, the love of which debases many souls, and I came from martyrdom to this peace."

PARADISO

O POCA NOSTRA nobiltà di sangue,
se gloriar di te la gente fai
qua giù dove l'affetto nostro langue,   *3*
mirabil cosa non mi sarà mai:
ché là dove appetito non si torce,
dico nel cielo, io me ne gloriai.   *6*
Ben se' tu manto che tosto raccorce:
sì che, se non s'appon di dì in die,
lo tempo va dintorno con le force.   *9*
Dal "voi" che prima a Roma s'offerie,
in che la sua famiglia men persevra,
ricominciaron le parole mie;   *12*
onde Beatrice, ch'era un poco scevra,
ridendo, parve quella che tossio
al primo fallo scritto di Ginevra.   *15*
Io cominciai: "Voi siete il padre mio;
voi mi date a parlar tutta baldezza;
voi mi levate sì, ch'i' son più ch'io.   *18*

CANTO XVI

O our petty nobility of blood! if you make folk glory in you here below where our affections languish, it will nevermore be a marvel to me, since there where appetite is not warped, I mean in Heaven, I myself gloried in you. Truly you are a mantle that soon shrinks, so that if naught be added from day to day, time goes round about you with its shears.

With that *You* which was first used in Rome and in which her family least perseveres, my words began again; at which Beatrice, who was a little withdrawn, smiled and seemed to me like her who coughed at the first fault that is written of Guinevere. I began, "You are my father, you give me full boldness to speak, you so uplift me that I am more than I.

Per tanti rivi s'empie d'allegrezza
  la mente mia, che di sé fa letizia
  perché può sostener che non si spezza.   *21*
Ditemi dunque, cara mia primizia,
  quai fuor li vostri antichi e quai fuor li anni
  che si segnaro in vostra püerizia;   *24*
ditemi de l'ovil di San Giovanni
  quanto era allora, e chi eran le genti
  tra esso degne di più alti scanni."   *27*
Come s'avviva a lo spirar d'i venti
  carbone in fiamma, così vid' io quella
  luce risplendere a' miei blandimenti;   *30*
e come a li occhi miei si fé più bella,
  così con voce più dolce e soave,
  ma non con questa moderna favella,   *33*
dissemi: "Da quel dì che fu detto *'Ave'*
  al parto in che mia madre, ch'è or santa,
  s'alleviò di me ond' era grave,   *36*
al suo Leon cinquecento cinquanta
  e trenta fiate venne questo foco
  a rinfiammarsi sotto la sua pianta.   *39*
Li antichi miei e io nacqui nel loco
  dove si truova pria l'ultimo sesto
  da quei che corre il vostro annüal gioco.   *42*
Basti d'i miei maggiori udirne questo:
  chi ei si fosser e onde venner quivi,
  più è tacer che ragionare onesto.   *45*
Tutti color ch'a quel tempo eran ivi
  da poter arme tra Marte e 'l Batista,
  erano il quinto di quei ch'or son vivi.   *48*

By so many streams my mind is filled with gladness that it rejoices in itself that it can bear this and not burst. Tell me then, dear stock from which I spring, what was your ancestry and what were the years that were reckoned in your boyhood. Tell me of the sheepfold of St. John, how large it was then, and who were the folk within it worthy of the highest seats."

As a coal quickens into flame at the breathing of the winds, so did I see that light glow at my blandishments; and as it became more beautiful to my eyes, so with a voice more sweet and gentle, but not in this our modern speech, he said to me, "From that day on which *Ave* was uttered, to the birth in which my mother, who now is sainted, was lightened of me with whom she had been burdened, this fire had come to its Lion five hundred, fifty, and thirty times to rekindle itself beneath his paw. My ancestors and I were born at the place where the furthest ward is first reached by the runner in your annual game. Let it suffice to hear thus much of my forebears; as to who they were and whence they came hither, silence is more becoming than speech.

"All those able to bear arms who at that time were there, between Mars and the Baptist, were the fifth of the number now living;

Ma la cittadinanza, ch'è or mista
   di Campi, di Certaldo e di Fegghine,
   pura vediesi ne l'ultimo artista.   *51*
Oh quanto fora meglio esser vicine
   quelle genti ch'io dico, e al Galluzzo
   e a Trespiano aver vostro confine,   *54*
che averle dentro e sostener lo puzzo
   del villan d'Aguglion, di quel da Signa,
   che già per barattare ha l'occhio aguzzo!   *57*
Se la gente ch'al mondo più traligna
   non fosse stata a Cesare noverca,
   ma come madre a suo figlio benigna,   *60*
tal fatto è fiorentino e cambia e merca,
   che si sarebbe vòlto a Simifonti,
   là dove andava l'avolo a la cerca;   *63*
sariesi Montemurlo ancor de' Conti;
   sarieno i Cerchi nel piovier d'Acone,
   e forse in Valdigrieve i Buondelmonti.   *66*
Sempre la confusion de le persone
   principio fu del mal de la cittade,
   come del vostro il cibo che s'appone;   *69*
e cieco toro più avaccio cade
   che cieco agnello; e molte volte taglia
   più e meglio una che le cinque spade.   *72*
Se tu riguardi Luni e Orbisaglia
   come sono ite, e come se ne vanno
   di retro ad esse Chiusi e Sinigaglia,   *75*
udir come le schiatte si disfanno
   non ti parrà nòva cosa né forte,
   poscia che le cittadi termine hanno.   *78*

but the citizenship, which is now mixed with
Campi, with Certaldo, and with Figline, saw
itself pure down to the humblest artisan. Oh,
how much better it would be that those folk
of whom I speak were neighbors, and to have
your boundary at Galluzzo and at Trespiano,
than to have them within and to endure the
stench of the churl of Aguglione, and of him
of Signa, who already has his eye sharp for
jobbery.

"If the folk who are the most degenerate in
the world had not been a stepmother to
Caesar, but, like a mother, benignant to her
son, there is one who has become a Florentine
and is a money-changer and trader, who
would have lived on at Simifonti where his
own grandfather went a-begging. Monte-
murlo would still belong to its Counts, the
Cerchi would be in the parish of Acone, and
perhaps the Buondelmonti in Valdigreve. The
intermingling of people was ever the begin-
ning of harm to the city, as to you the food
which is loaded on is to the body. And a blind
bull falls more headlong than the blind lamb,
and oftentimes one sword cuts better and
more than five.

"If you regard Luni and Urbisaglia, how
they have perished, and how are following
after them Chiusi and Senigallia, it will not
appear to you a strange thing or a hard, to
hear how families are undone, since cities
have their term.

Le vostre cose tutte hanno lor morte,
  sì come voi; ma celasi in alcuna
  che dura molto, e le vite son corte.   *81*
E come 'l volger del ciel de la luna
  cuopre e discuopre i liti sanza posa,
  così fa di Fiorenza la Fortuna: *84*
per che non dee parer mirabil cosa
  ciò ch'io dirò de li alti Fiorentini
  onde è la fama nel tempo nascosa.   *87*
Io vidi li Ughi e vidi i Catellini,
  Filippi, Greci, Ormanni e Alberichi,
  già nel calare, illustri cittadini;   *90*
e vidi così grandi come antichi,
  con quel de la Sannella, quel de l'Arca,
  e Soldanieri e Ardinghi e Bostichi.   *93*
Sovra la porta ch'al presente è carca
  di nova fellonia di tanto peso
  che tosto fia iattura de la barca,   *96*
erano i Ravignani, ond' è disceso
  il conte Guido e qualunque del nome
  de l'alto Bellincione ha poscia preso.   *99*
Quel de la Pressa sapeva già come
  regger si vuole, e avea Galigaio
  dorata in casa sua già l'elsa e 'l pome.   *102*
Grand' era già la colonna del Vaio,
  Sacchetti, Giuochi, Fifanti e Barucci
  e Galli e quei ch'arrossan per lo staio.   *105*
Lo ceppo di che nacquero i Calfucci
  era già grande, e già eran tratti
  a le curule Sizii e Arrigucci.   *108*

Your affairs all have their death, even as have
you; but it is concealed in some things that
last long, whereas lives are short. And as the
revolution of the heaven of the moon covers
and uncovers the shores without pause, so
Fortune does with Florence; wherefore it
should appear no wondrous thing which I
shall tell of the great Florentines whose fame
is hidden by time. I saw the Ughi and I saw
the Catellini, Filippi, Greci, Ormanni, and
Alberichi, illustrious citizens, already in de-
cline; and I saw, great as they were ancient,
dell'Arca with della Sannella, and Soldanieri
and Ardinghi and Bostichi. Over the gate
which at present is laden with new felony of
such great weight that there will soon be
jettison from the bark, were the Ravignani of
whose line the Count Guido is descended and
whosoever has since taken the name of the
high Bellincione. Della Pressa knew already
how to rule, and Galligaio had already in his
house the hilt and the pommel gilded. Great
already were the Vair column, the Sacchetti,
Giuochi, Fifanti, Barucci, and Galli, and those
that blush for the bushel. The stock from
which the Calfucci sprang was already great,
and already the Sizii and Arrigucci had been
raised to the highest seats.

Oh quali io vidi quei che son disfatti
  per lor superbia! e le palle de l'oro
  fiorian Fiorenza in tutt' i suoi gran fatti.   *111*
Così facieno i padri di coloro
  che, sempre che la vostra chiesa vaca,
  si fanno grassi stando a consistoro.   *114*
L'oltracotata schiatta che s'indraca
  dietro a chi fugge, e a chi mostra 'l dente
  o ver la borsa, com' agnel si placa,   *117*
già venìa sù, ma di picciola gente;
  sì che non piacque ad Ubertin Donato
  che poï il suocero il fé lor parente.   *120*
Già era 'l Caponsacco nel mercato
  disceso giù da Fiesole, e già era
  buon cittadino Giuda e Infangato.   *123*
Io dirò cosa incredibile e vera:
  nel picciol cerchio s'entrava per porta
  che si nomava da quei de la Pera.   *126*
Ciascun che de la bella insegna porta
  del gran barone il cui nome e 'l cui pregio
  la festa di Tommaso riconforta,   *129*
da esso ebbe milizia e privilegio;
  avvegna che con popol si rauni
  oggi colui che la fascia col fregio.   *132*
Già eran Gualterotti e Importuni;
  e ancor saria Borgo più quïeto,
  se di novi vicin fosser digiuni.   *135*
La casa di che nacque il vostro fleto,
  per lo giusto disdegno che v'ha morti
  e puose fine al vostro viver lieto,   *138*

Oh, how great have I seen those now undone
by their pride! and the balls of gold adorned
Florence in all her great doings. So did the
fathers of those who, whenever your church
is vacant, fatten themselves by staying in con-
sistory. The insolent breed that plays the
dragon behind him that flees, and to whoever
shows his teeth—or else his purse—becomes
mild as a lamb, was already on the rise, but of
humble stock, so that it did not please Ubertin
Donato that his father-in-law afterward
should make him their kinsman. Already had
Caponsacco descended into the market-place
down from Fiesole, and already was Giuda a
good citizen, and Infangato. One thing I will
tell, incredible and true: the little circuit was
entered by a gate named after the Della Pera.
Everyone who bears the fair ensign of the
great Baron whose name and whose worth
the feast of Thomas keeps fresh, from him
had knighthood and privilege, although he
who fringes it round is siding now with the
people. Already there were Gualterotti and
Importuni; and the Borgo would still be
quiet if they had gone fasting of new neigh-
bors. The house of which was born your
weeping, by reason of its just resentment
which has slain you and put an end to your
glad living,

era onorata, essa e suoi consorti:
  o Buondelmonte, quanto mal fuggisti
  le nozze süe per li altrui conforti! 141
Molti sarebber lieti, che son tristi,
  se Dio t'avesse conceduto ad Ema
  la prima volta ch'a città venisti. 144
Ma conveniesi, a quella pietra scema
  che guarda 'l ponte, che Fiorenza fesse
  vittima ne la sua pace postrema. 147
Con queste genti, e con altre con esse,
  vid' io Fiorenza in sì fatto riposo,
  che non avea cagione onde piangesse. 150
Con queste genti vid' io glorïoso
  e giusto il popol suo, tanto che 'l giglio
  non era ad asta mai posto a ritroso,
né per divisïon fatto vermiglio." 154

was honored, both itself and its consorts. O
Buondelmonte, how ill for you that you did
fly from its nuptials at the promptings of an-
other. Many would be happy who now are sad
if God had committed you to the Ema the first
time you came to the city! but it was fitting
that Florence, in her last peace, should offer
a victim to that mutilated stone which guards
the bridge.

"With these families, and with others with
them, I saw Florence in such repose that she
had no cause for wailing. With these families
I saw her people so glorious and so just, that
the lily was never set reversed upon the staff,
nor made vermilion by division."

PARADISO

Qual venne a Climenè, per accertarsi
   di ciò ch'avëa incontro a sé udito,
   quei ch'ancor fa li padri ai figli scarsi;   *3*
tal era io, e tal era sentito
   e da Beatrice e da la santa lampa
   che pria per me avea mutato sito.   *6*
Per che mia donna "Manda fuor la vampa
   del tuo disio," mi disse, "sì ch'ella esca
   segnata bene de la interna stampa: *9*
non perché nostra conoscenza cresca
   per tuo parlare, ma perché t'ausi
   a dir la sete, sì che l'uom ti mesca."   *12*
"O cara piota mia che sì t'insusi,
   che, come veggion le terrene menti
   non capere in trïangol due ottusi,   *15*
così vedi le cose contingenti
   anzi che sieno in sé, mirando il punto
   a cui tutti li tempi son presenti;   *18*

CANTO XVII

As HE who still makes fathers chary toward their sons came to Clymene to be reassured about that which he had heard against himself, such was I, and such was I perceived to be both by Beatrice and by the holy lamp which already, for my sake, had changed its place. Wherefore my lady said to me, "Put forth the flame of your desire, so that it may issue imprinted well by the internal stamp; not in order that our knowledge may increase through your speech, but that you may learn to tell your thirst, so that one may pour out drink for you."

"O dear root of me, who are so uplifted that, even as earthly minds see that two obtuse angles can not be contained in a triangle, so you, gazing upon the Point to which all times are present, do see contingent things before they exist in themselves;

mentre ch'io era a Virgilio congiunto
  su per lo monte che l'anime cura
  e discendendo nel mondo defunto,   *21*
dette mi fuor di mia vita futura
  parole gravi, avvegna ch'io mi senta
  ben tetragono ai colpi di ventura;   *24*
per che la voglia mia saria contenta
  d'intender qual fortuna mi s'appressa:
  ché saetta prevista vien più lenta."   *27*
Così diss' io a quella luce stessa
  che pria m'avea parlato; e come volle
  Beatrice, fu la mia voglia confessa.   *30*
Né per ambage, in che la gente folle
  già s'inviscava pria che fosse anciso
  l'Agnel di Dio che le peccata tolle,   *33*
ma per chiare parole e con preciso
  latin rispuose quello amor paterno,
  chiuso e parvente del suo proprio riso: *36*
"La contingenza, che fuor del quaderno
  de la vostra matera non si stende,
  tutta è dipinta nel cospetto etterno;   *39*
necessità però quindi non prende
  se non come dal viso in che si specchia
  nave che per torrente giù discende.   *42*
Da indi, sì come viene ad orecchia
  dolce armonia da organo, mi viene
  a vista il tempo che ti s'apparecchia.   *45*
Qual si partio Ipolito d'Atene
  per la spietata e perfida noverca,
  tal di Fiorenza partir ti convene.   *48*

while I was in Virgil's company, up the mountain that heals the souls, and while descending through the dead world, heavy words were said to me about my future life, though I feel myself truly foursquare against the blows of chance; so that my will would be well content to hear what fortune is drawing near me, because an arrow foreseen comes slower." Thus said I to that same light which had spoken to me before, and, as Beatrice willed, my wish was confessed.

In no dark sayings, such as those in which the foolish folk of old once ensnared themselves, before the Lamb of God who takes away sins was slain, but in clear words and with precise discourse that paternal love replied, hidden and revealed by his own smile, "Contingency, which does not extend beyond the volume of your material world, is all depicted in the Eternal Vision. Yet thence it takes not necessity, any more than from the eyes in which it is mirrored does a ship which is going down the stream. Therefrom, even as sweet harmony comes from an organ to the ear, comes to my sight the time that is in store for you. As Hippolytus departed from Athens, by reason of his pitiless and perfidious stepmother, so from Florence must you depart.

Questo si vuole e questo già si cerca,
  e tosto verrà fatto a chi ciò pensa
  là dove Cristo tutto dì si merca.   *51*

La colpa seguirà la parte offensa
  in grido, come suol; ma la vendetta
  fia testimonio al ver che la dispensa.   *54*

Tu lascerai ogne cosa diletta
  più caramente; e questo è quello strale
  che l'arco de lo essilio pria saetta.   *57*

Tu proverai sì come sa di sale
  lo pane altrui, e come è duro calle
  lo scendere e 'l salir per l'altrui scale.   *60*

E quel che più ti graverà le spalle,
  sarà la compagnia malvagia e scempia
  con la qual tu cadrai in questa valle;   *63*

che tutta ingrata, tutta matta ed empia
  si farà contr' a te; ma, poco appresso,
  ella, non tu, n'avrà rossa la tempia.   *66*

Di sua bestialitate il suo processo
  farà la prova; sì ch'a te fia bello
  averti fatta parte per te stesso.   *69*

Lo primo tuo refugio e 'l primo ostello
  sarà la cortesia del gran Lombardo
  che 'n su la scala porta il santo uccello;   *72*

ch'in te avrà sì benigno riguardo,
  che del fare e del chieder, tra voi due,
  fia primo quel che tra li altri è più tardo.   *75*

Con lui vedrai colui che 'mpresso fue,
  nascendo, sì da questa stella forte,
  che notabili fier l'opere sue.   *78*

So is it willed, so already plotted, and so shall
be accomplished soon by him who ponders
upon it in the place where every day Christ
is bought and sold. The blame, as always, will
follow the injured party, in outcry; but venge-
ance shall bear witness to the truth which
dispenses it. You shall leave everything be-
loved most dearly; and this is the arrow
which the bow of exile shoots first. You shall
come to know how salt is the taste of an-
other's bread, and how hard the path to de-
scend and mount by another man's stairs.
And that which shall most weigh your
shoulders down will be the evil and senseless
company with which you shall fall into this
vale; which shall then become all ungrateful,
all mad and malevolent against you, but, soon
after, their brows, not yours, shall redden for it.
Of their brutish folly their own conduct shall
afford the proof, so that it will be for your fair
fame to have made you a party by yourself.

"Your first refuge and first inn shall be
the courtesy of the great Lombard who bears
the holy bird upon the ladder, and he will
have for you such benign regard that, in do-
ing and in asking, between you two, that will
be first which between others is the slowest.
With him you shall see one who, at his birth,
was so stamped by this strong star, that nota-
ble shall be his deeds.

Non se ne son le genti ancora accorte
  per la novella età, ché pur nove anni
  son queste rote intorno di lui torte;   *81*
ma pria che 'l Guasco l'alto Arrigo inganni,
  parran faville de la sua virtute
  in non curar d'argento né d'affanni.   *84*
Le sue magnificenze conosciute
  saranno ancora, sì che ' suoi nemici
  non ne potran tener le lingue mute.   *87*
A lui t'aspetta e a' suoi benefici;
  per lui fia trasmutata molta gente,
  cambiando condizion ricchi e mendici;   *90*
e portera'ne scritto ne la mente
  di lui, e nol dirai"; e disse cose
  incredibili a quei che fier presente.   *93*
Poi giunse: "Figlio, queste son le chiose
  di quel che ti fu detto; ecco le 'nsidie
  che dietro a pochi giri son nascose.   *96*
Non vo' però ch'a' tuoi vicini invidie,
  poscia che s'infutura la tua vita
  via più là che 'l punir di lor perfidie."   *99*
Poi che, tacendo, si mostrò spedita
  l'anima santa di metter la trama
  in quella tela ch'io le porsi ordita,   *102*
io cominciai, come colui che brama,
  dubitando, consiglio da persona
  che vede e vuol dirittamente e ama: *105*
"Ben veggio, padre mio, sì come sprona
  lo tempo verso me, per colpo darmi
  tal, ch'è più grave a chi più s'abbandona;   *108*

Not yet have folk taken due note of him,
because of his young age, for these wheels
have revolved around him only nine years;
but before the Gascon deceives the lofty
Henry, some sparks of his virtue shall appear,
in his caring naught for money or for toils.
His magnificence shall hereafter be so known,
that his very foes will not be able to keep
silent tongues about him. Look you to him
and to his benefits. By him shall many folk
be changed, the rich and the beggarly altering
their condition. And you shall bear hence
written of him in your mind, but you shall
not tell it";—and he told things past the belief
even of those who shall see them. Then he
added, "Son, these are the glosses on what
was said to you; behold the snares which are
hidden behind but a few circlings. Yet I
would not have you envious of your neigh-
bors, since your life shall be prolonged far be-
yond the punishment of their perfidies."

When by his silence the holy soul showed
he had finished setting the woof across the
warp I had held out in readiness to him, I
began, as he who, in doubt, craves counsel of
one who sees and rightly wills and loves, "I
see well, my father, how time spurs toward me
to give me such a blow as is heaviest to who-
soever is most heedless;

per che di provedenza è buon ch'io m'armi,
   sì che, se loco m'è tolto più caro,
   io non perdessi li altri per miei carmi.   *111*
Giù per lo mondo sanza fine amaro,
   e per lo monte del cui bel cacume
   li occhi de la mia donna mi levaro,   *114*
e poscia per lo ciel, di lume in lume,
   ho io appreso quel che s'io ridico,
   a molti fia sapor di forte agrume;   *117*
e s'io al vero son timido amico,
   temo di perder viver tra coloro
   che questo tempo chiameranno antico."   *120*
La luce in che rideva il mio tesoro
   ch'io trovai lì, si fé prima corusca,
   quale a raggio di sole specchio d'oro;   *123*
indi rispuose: "Coscïenza fusca
   o de la propria o de l'altrui vergogna
   pur sentirà la tua parola brusca.   *126*
Ma nondimen, rimossa ogne menzogna,
   tutta tua visïon fa manifesta;
   e lascia pur grattar dov' è la rogna.   *129*
Ché se la voce tua sarà molesta
   nel primo gusto, vital nodrimento
   lascerà poi, quando sarà digesta.   *132*
Questo tuo grido farà come vento,
   che le più alte cime più percuote;
   e ciò non fa d'onor poco argomento.   *135*
Però ti son mostrate in queste rote,
   nel monte e ne la valle dolorosa
   pur l'anime che son di fama note,   *138*

wherefore it is good that I arm myself with foresight, so that if the dearest place be taken from me, I lose not all the rest by reason of my songs. Down in the world endlessly bitter, and upon the mountain from whose fair summit my lady's eyes uplifted me, and after, through the heavens from light to light, I have learned that which, if I tell again, will have for many a savor of great bitterness; and if I am a timid friend to the truth, I fear to lose life among those who shall call this time ancient."

The light wherein was smiling the treasure I had found there first became flashing as a golden mirror in the sun, then it replied, "A conscience dark, either with its own or with another's shame, will indeed feel your speech to be harsh. But none the less, all falsehood set aside, make manifest all that you have seen; and then let them scratch where the itch is. For if at first taste your voice be grievous, yet shall it leave thereafter vital nourishment when digested. This cry of yours shall do as does the wind, which smites most upon the loftiest summits; and this shall be no little cause of honor. Therefore only the souls known of fame have been shown to you within these wheels, upon the mountain, and in the woeful valley;

che l'animo di quel ch'ode, non posa
   né ferma fede per essempro ch'aia
   la sua radice incognita e ascosa,
né per altro argomento che non paia."   *142*

for the mind of him who hears rests not nor confirms its faith by an example that has its roots unknown or hidden, nor for other proof that is not manifest."

PARADISO

Già si godeva solo del suo verbo
quello specchio beato, e io gustava
lo mio, temprando col dolce l'acerbo;   *3*
e quella donna ch'a Dio mi menava
disse: "Muta pensier; pensa ch'i' sono
presso a colui ch'ogne torto disgrava."   *6*
Io mi rivolsi a l'amoroso suono
del mio conforto; e qual io allor vidi
ne li occhi santi amor, qui l'abbandono: *9*
non perch' io pur del mio parlar diffidi,
ma per la mente che non può redire
sovra sé tanto, s'altri non la guidi.   *12*
Tanto poss' io di quel punto ridire,
che, rimirando lei, lo mio affetto
libero fu da ogne altro disire,   *15*
fin che 'l piacere etterno, che diretto
raggiava in Bëatrice, dal bel viso
mi contentava col secondo aspetto.   *18*

CANTO XVIII

Already that blessed mirror was enjoying only its own thoughts, and I was tasting mine, tempering the bitter with the sweet, when the lady who was leading me to God said, "Change your thought: consider that I am in His presence who lightens the burden of every wrong."

I turned round at the loving sound of my Comfort, and what love I then saw in the holy eyes I leave here untold; not only because I distrust my own speech, but because of memory, which cannot return on itself so far unless Another guide it. This much of that moment can I retell, that as I gazed upon her my affection was freed from every other desire so long as the Eternal Joy that shone direct on Beatrice satisfied me from the fair eyes with its reflected aspect.

Vincendo me col lume d'un sorriso,
  ella mi disse: "Volgiti e ascolta;
  ché non pur ne' miei occhi è paradiso."   *21*
Come si vede qui alcuna volta
  l'affetto ne la vista, s'elli è tanto,
  che da lui sia tutta l'anima tolta,   *24*
così nel fiammeggiar del folgór santo,
  a ch'io mi volsi, conobbi la voglia
  in lui di ragionarmi ancora alquanto.   *27*
El cominciò: "In questa quinta soglia
  de l'albero che vive de la cima
  e frutta sempre e mai non perde foglia,   *30*
spiriti son beati, che giù, prima
  che venissero al ciel, fuor di gran voce,
  sì ch'ogne musa ne sarebbe opima.   *33*
Però mira ne' corni de la croce:
  quello ch'io nomerò, lì farà l'atto
  che fa in nube il suo foco veloce."   *36*
Io vidi per la croce un lume tratto
  dal nomar Iosuè, com' el si feo;
  né mi fu noto il dir prima che 'l fatto.   *39*
E al nome de l'alto Macabeo
  vidi moversi un altro roteando,
  e letizia era ferza del paleo.   *42*
Così per Carlo Magno e per Orlando
  due ne seguì lo mio attento sguardo,
  com' occhio segue suo falcon volando.   *45*
Poscia trasse Guiglielmo e Rinoardo
  e 'l duca Gottifredi la mia vista
  per quella croce, e Ruberto Guiscardo.   *48*

Overcoming me with the light of a smile, she said to me, "Turn and listen, for not only in my eyes is Paradise."

As sometimes here the affection is seen in the countenance if it be such that all the mind is taken up by it, so in the flaming of the holy glow to which I turned I recognized his wish to have some further speech with me; and he began, "In this fifth tier of the tree, which has life from its top and is always in fruit and never sheds its leaves, are blessed spirits which below, before they came to heaven, were of such great renown that every Muse would be rich with them. Look, therefore, upon the horns of the cross: he whom I shall name there will do as in a cloud its swift fire does."

At the naming of Joshua, even as it was done, I saw a light drawn along the cross, nor was the word noted by me before the fact; and at the name of the great Maccabeus I saw another move, wheeling, and gladness was the whip of the top. So for Charlemagne and Roland my intent gaze followed two of them, as the eye follows its falcon as he flies; next William, and Renouard and Duke Godfrey drew my sight along that cross, and Robert Guiscard too.

Indi, tra l'altre luci mota e mista,
   mostrommi l'alma che m'avea parlato
   qual era tra i cantor del cielo artista.   *51*
Io mi rivolsi dal mio destro lato
   per vedere in Beatrice il mio dovere,
   o per parlare o per atto, segnato;   *54*
e vidi le sue luci tanto mere,
   tanto gioconde, che la sua sembianza
   vinceva li altri e l'ultimo solere.   *57*
E come, per sentir più dilettanza
   bene operando, l'uom di giorno in giorno
   s'accorge che la sua virtute avanza,   *60*
sì m'accors' io che 'l mio girare intorno
   col cielo insieme avea cresciuto l'arco,
   veggendo quel miracol più addorno.   *63*
E qual è 'l trasmutare in picciol varco
   di tempo in bianca donna, quando 'l volto
   suo si discarchi di vergogna il carco,   *66*
tal fu ne li occhi miei, quando fui vòlto,
   per lo candor de la temprata stella
   sesta, che dentro a sé m'avea ricolto.   *69*
Io vidi in quella giovïal facella
   lo sfavillar de l'amor che lì era
   segnare a li occhi miei nostra favella.   *72*
E come augelli surti di rivera,
   quasi congratulando a lor pasture,
   fanno di sé or tonda or altra schiera,   *75*
sì dentro ai lumi sante creature
   volitando cantavano, e faciensi
   or *D*, or *I*, or *L* in sue figure.   *78*

Then, moving and mingling among the other lights, the soul which had spoken with me showed me how great an artist it was among the singers of that heaven.

I turned to my right side, to see in Beatrice my duty, signified either by speech or by gesture, and I saw her eyes so clear, so joyful, that her aspect surpassed all it had been at other times, even the last. And as from feeling more delight in doing well, a man from day to day becomes aware that his virtue makes advance, so did I perceive that my circling round with the heaven had increased its arc, when I saw that miracle even more adorned. And such change as comes in a moment over the face of a pale lady, when her countenance frees itself from a burden of modest shame, was presented to my eyes when I turned, because of the whiteness of the temperate sixth star which had received me within itself.

I saw in that torch of Jove the sparkling of the love that was there, trace out our speech to my eyes; and as birds, risen from the shore, as if rejoicing together at their pasture, make of themselves now a round flock, now some other shape, so within the lights holy creatures were singing as they flew, and in their figures made of themselves now *D*, now *I*, now *L*.

Prima, cantando, a sua nota moviensi;
  poi, diventando l'un di questi segni,
  un poco s'arrestavano e taciensi.   *81*
O diva Pegasëa che li 'ngegni
  fai glorïosi e rendili longevi,
  ed essi teco le cittadi e ' regni,   *84*
illustrami di te, sì ch'io rilevi
  le lor figure com' io l'ho concette:
  paia tua possa in questi versi brevi!   *87*
Mostrarsi dunque in cinque volte sette
  vocali e consonanti; e io notai
  le parti sì, come mi parver dette.   *90*
"*DILIGITE IUSTITIAM*," primai
  fur verbo e nome di tutto 'l dipinto;
  "*QUI IUDICATIS TERRAM*," fur sezzai.   *93*
Poscia ne l'emme del vocabol quinto
  rimasero ordinate; sì che Giove
  pareva argento lì d'oro distinto.   *96*
E vidi scendere altre luci dove
  era il colmo de l'emme, e lì quetarsi
  cantando, credo, il ben ch'a sé le move.   *99*
Poi, come nel percuoter d'i ciocchi arsi
  surgono innumerabili faville,
  onde li stolti sogliono agurarsi,   *102*
resurger parver quindi più di mille
  luci e salir, qual assai e qual poco,
  sì come 'l sol che l'accende sortille;   *105*
e quïetata ciascuna in suo loco,
  la testa e 'l collo d'un'aguglia vidi
  rappresentare a quel distinto foco.   *108*

At first, as they sang, they moved to their own notes; then, as they became one of these characters, they stopped a little and were silent.

O divine Pegasea, who give glory unto men of genius and render them long-lived, as they, through you, the cities and the kingdoms, illumine me with yourself that I may set forth their shapes, as I have them in conception; let your power appear in these brief lines.

They displayed themselves then, in five times seven vowels and consonants; and I took note of the parts as they appeared in utterance to me. *DILIGITE IUSTITIAM* were the first verb and substantive of all the design, *QUI IUDICATIS TERRAM* were the last. Then, ordered in the *M* of the fifth word they stayed, so that Jove seemed silver in that place, pricked out with gold; and I saw other lights descending where the top of the *M* was, and become quiet there, singing, I believe, the Good that draws them to Itself. Then, as on the striking of burning logs there rise innumerable sparks, wherefrom the foolish are wont to draw auguries, so thence there seemed to rise again more than a thousand lights, and mount, some much, some little, even as the Sun which kindles them allotted them; and when each had rested in its place, I saw the head and the neck of an eagle represented by that patterned fire.

Quei che dipinge lì, non ha chi 'l guidi;
 ma esso guida, e da lui si rammenta
 quella virtù ch'è forma per li nidi. *111*
L'altra bëatitudo, che contenta
 pareva prima d'ingigliarsi a l'emme,
 con poco moto seguitò la 'mprenta. *114*
O dolce stella, quali e quante gemme
 mi dimostraro che nostra giustizia
 effetto sia del ciel che tu ingemme! *117*
Per ch'io prego la mente in che s'inizia
 tuo moto e tua virtute, che rimiri
 ond' esce il fummo che 'l tuo raggio vizia; *120*
sì ch'un'altra fïata omai s'adiri
 del comperare e vender dentro al templo
 che si murò di segni e di martìri. *123*
O milizia del ciel cu' io contemplo,
 adora per color che sono in terra
 tutti svïati dietro al malo essemplo! *126*
Già si solea con le spade far guerra;
 ma or si fa togliendo or qui or quivi
 lo pan che 'l pïo Padre a nessun serra. *129*
Ma tu che sol per cancellare scrivi,
 pensa che Pietro e Paulo, che moriro
 per la vigna che guasti, ancor son vivi. *132*
Ben puoi tu dire: "I' ho fermo 'l disiro
 sì a colui che volle viver solo
 e che per salti fu tratto al martiro,
ch'io non conosco il pescator né Polo." *136*

He who there paints has none to guide Him,
but He Himself does guide, and from Him
is recognized that virtue which shapes nests.
The rest of the blessed spirits, which at first
seemed content to form a lily on the *M*, with
a slight motion completed the design.

O sweet star, how many and how bright
were the gems which made it plain to me that
our justice is the effect of the heaven which
you engem! Wherefore I pray the Mind, in
which your motion and your virtue have their
beginning, that It look on the place whence
issues the smoke that dims your radiance, so
that once again It may be wroth at the buying
and the selling in the temple which made its
walls of miracles and martyrdoms. O soldiery
of Heaven whom I look upon, pray for all
those who have gone astray on earth, follow-
ing the ill example. Of old it was the wont to
make war with swords, but now it is made by
taking away, now here now there, the bread
which the tender Father bars from none.

But you that write only to cancel, bethink
you that Peter and Paul, who died for the
vineyard that you are laying waste, are still
alive. Though you indeed may say, "I have
my desire so set on him who willed to live
alone, and who, for a dance, was dragged to
martyrdom, that I know not the Fisherman
nor Paul."

PARADISO

Pᴀʀᴇᴀ ᴅɪɴᴀɴᴢɪ a me con l'ali aperte
   la bella image che nel dolce *frui*
   liete facevan l'anime conserte;   *3*
parea ciascuna rubinetto in cui
   raggio di sole ardesse sì acceso,
   che ne' miei occhi rifrangesse lui.   *6*
E quel che mi convien ritrar testeso,
   non portò voce mai, né scrisse incostro,
   né fu per fantasia già mai compreso;   *9*
ch'io vidi e anche udi' parlar lo rostro,
   e sonar ne la voce e "io" e "mio,"
   quand' era nel concetto e "noi" e "nostro."   *12*
E cominciò: "Per esser giusto e pio
   son io qui essaltato a quella gloria
   che non si lascia vincere a disio;   *15*
e in terra lasciai la mia memoria
   sì fatta, che le genti lì malvage
   commendan lei, ma non seguon la storia." *18*

CANTO XIX

Wᴛ ᴏᴜᴛsᴛʀᴇᴛᴄʜᴇᴅ wings appeared before me the beautiful image which those inter woven souls, joyful in their sweet fruition, were making. Each of them seemed a little ruby on which a ray of sun should glow so enkindled as to reflect it into my eyes. And that which I must now tell, never did voice report nor ink record, nor was it ever comprised by phantasy; for I saw and also heard the beak speaking, and uttering with its voice *I* and *Mine* when in conception it was *We* and *Our*. And it began, "For being just and duteous am I here exalted to that glory which cannot be surpassed by desire; and upon earth have I left such a memory that the wicked people there commend it, but follow not its story."

Così un sol calor di molte brage
  si fa sentir, come di molti amori
  usciva solo un suon di quella image.   *21*
Ond' io appresso: "O perpetüi fiori
  de l'etterna letizia, che pur uno
  parer mi fate tutti vostri odori,   *24*
solvetemi, spirando, il gran digiuno
  che lungamente m'ha tenuto in fame,
  non trovandoli in terra cibo alcuno.   *27*
Ben so io che, se 'n cielo altro reame
  la divina giustizia fa suo specchio,
  che 'l vostro non l'apprende con velame.   *30*
Sapete come attento io m'apparecchio
  ad ascoltar; sapete qual è quello
  dubbio che m'è digiun cotanto vecchio."   *33*
Quasi falcone ch'esce del cappello,
  move la testa e con l'ali si plaude,
  voglia mostrando e faccendosi bello,   *36*
vid' io farsi quel segno, che di laude
  de la divina grazia era contesto,
  con canti quai si sa chi là sù gaude.   *39*
Poi cominciò: "Colui che volse il sesto
  a lo stremo del mondo, e dentro ad esso
  distinse tanto occulto e manifesto,   *42*
non poté suo valor sì fare impresso
  in tutto l'universo, che 'l suo verbo
  non rimanesse in infinito eccesso.   *45*
E ciò fa certo che 'l primo superbo,
  che fu la somma d'ogne creatura,
  per non aspettar lume, cadde acerbo;   *48*

Thus one sole heat makes itself felt from many embers, even as from many loves one sole sound issued from that image.

And I then, "O perpetual flowers of the eternal bliss, who make all your odors seem to me but one, breathe forth and deliver me from the great fast which has long held me hungering, not finding any food for it on earth. Well do I know that if the Divine Justice makes another realm in heaven Its mirror, yours does not apprehend It through a veil. You know how eager I prepare myself to listen; you know what is that question which is so old a fast to me."

As the falcon which, issuing from the hood, moves his head and flaps his wings, showing his will and making himself fine, such did I see that ensign which was woven of praises of the Divine Grace become, with songs such as he knows who thereabove rejoices. Then it began, "He that turned His compass round the limit of the world, and within it marked out so much both hidden and revealed, could not so imprint His power on all the universe that His word should not remain in infinite excess; and this is certified by that first proud one, who was the highest of all creatures and who, through not awaiting light, fell unripe;

e quinci appar ch'ogne minor natura
è corto recettacolo a quel bene
che non ha fine e sé con sé misura.   *51*

Dunque vostra veduta, che convene
essere alcun de' raggi de la mente
di che tutte le cose son ripiene,   *54*

non pò da sua natura esser possente
tanto, che suo principio non discerna
molto di là da quel che l'è parvente.   *57*

Però ne la giustizia sempiterna
la vista che riceve il vostro mondo,
com' occhio per lo mare, entro s'interna;   *60*

che, ben che da la proda veggia il fondo,
in pelago nol vede; e nondimeno
èli, ma cela lui l'esser profondo.   *63*

Lume non è, se non vien dal sereno
che non si turba mai; anzi è tenèbra
od ombra de la carne o suo veleno.   *66*

Assai t'è mo aperta la latebra
che t'ascondeva la giustizia viva,
di che facei question cotanto crebra;   *69*

ché tu dicevi: 'Un uom nasce a la riva
de l'Indo, e quivi non è chi ragioni
di Cristo né chi legga né chi scriva;   *72*

e tutti suoi voleri e atti buoni
sono, quanto ragione umana vede,
sanza peccato in vita o in sermoni.   *75*

Muore non battezzato e sanza fede:
ov' è questa giustizia che 'l condanna?
ov' è la colpa sua, se ei non crede?'   *78*

from which it is plain that every lesser nature
is too scant a vessel for that Good which has
no limit and measures Itself by Itself. Thus
your vision, which must needs be one of the
rays of the Mind with which all things are
replete, cannot of its own nature be of such
power that it should not perceive its origin to
be far beyond all that is apparent to it. There-
fore the sight that is granted to your world
penetrates within the Eternal Justice as the
eye into the sea; which, though from the
shore it can see the bottom, in the open sea
it sees it not, and none the less it is there, but
the depth conceals it. There is no light unless
it comes from that serene which is never
clouded, else is it darkness, either shadow of
the flesh or its poison.

"Now is laid well open to you the hiding-
place which concealed from you the living
Justice concerning which you have made
question so incessantly. For you said, 'A man
is born on the bank of the Indus, and none is
there to speak, or read, or write, of Christ, and
all his wishes and acts are good, so far as hu-
man reason sees, without sin in life or in
speech. He dies unbaptized, and without
faith. Where is this justice which condemns
him? Where is his sin if he does not believe?'

Or tu chi se', che vuo' sedere a scranna,
  per giudicar di lungi mille miglia
  con la veduta corta d'una spanna?   *81*
Certo a colui che meco s'assottiglia,
  se la Scrittura sovra voi non fosse,
  da dubitar sarebbe a maraviglia.   *84*
Oh terreni animali! oh menti grosse!
  La prima volontà, ch'è da sé buona,
  da sé, ch'è sommo ben, mai non si mosse.   *87*
Cotanto è giusto quanto a lei consuona:
  nullo creato bene a sé la tira,
  ma essa, radïando, lui cagiona."   *90*
Quale sovresso il nido si rigira
  poi c'ha pasciuti la cicogna i figli,
  e come quel ch'è pasto la rimira;   *93*
cotal si fece, e sì levài i cigli,
  la benedetta imagine, che l'ali
  movea sospinte da tanti consigli.   *96*
Roteando cantava, e dicea: "Quali
  son le mie note a te, che non le 'ntendi,
  tal è il giudicio etterno a voi mortali."   *99*
Poi si quetaro quei lucenti incendi
  de lo Spirito Santo ancor nel segno
  che fé i Romani al mondo reverendi,   *102*
esso ricominciò: "A questo regno
  non salì mai chi non credette 'n Cristo,
  né pria né poi ch'el si chiavasse al legno.   *105*
Ma vedi: molti gridan 'Cristo, Cristo!'
  che saranno in giudicio assai men *prope*
  a lui, che tal che non conosce Cristo;   *108*

Now who are you who would sit upon the
seat to judge at a thousand miles away with
the short sight that carries but a span? As-
suredly, for him who subtilizes with me, if
the Scriptures were not set over you, there
would be marvelous occasion for questioning.
O earthly animals! O gross minds! The
primal Will, which of Itself is good, has never
moved from Itself, which is the supreme
Good. All is just that accords with It; no
created good draws It to itself, but It, raying
forth, is the cause of it."

As the stork circles over her nest, when
she has fed her young, and as the one which
she has fed looks up to her, such became (and
I so raised my brows) the blessed image
which, impelled by so many counsels, moved
its wings. Wheeling it sang and said, "As are
my notes to you who understand them not,
such is the Eternal Judgment to you mortals."

After those glowing flames of the Holy
Spirit became quiet, still in the sign which
made the Romans reverend to the world, it
began again, "To this realm none ever rose
who believed not in Christ, either before or
after he was nailed to the tree. But behold,
many cry Christ, Christ, who, at the Judg-
ment, shall be far less near to Him than he
who knows not Christ;

e tai Cristian dannerà l'Etïòpe,
   quando si partiranno i due collegi,
   l'uno in etterno ricco e l'altro inòpe.   *111*
Che poran dir li Perse a' vostri regi,
   come vedranno quel volume aperto
   nel qual si scrivon tutti suoi dispregi?   *114*
Lì si vedrà, tra l'opere d'Alberto,
   quella che tosto moverà la penna,
   per che 'l regno di Praga fia diserto.   *117*
Lì si vedrà il duol che sovra Senna
   induce, falseggiando la moneta,
   quel che morrà di colpo di cotenna.   *120*
Lì si vedrà la superbia ch'asseta,
   che fa lo Scotto e l'Inghilese folle,
   sì che non può soffrir dentro a sua meta.   *123*
Vedrassi la lussuria e 'l viver molle
   di quel di Spagna e di quel di Boemme,
   che mai valor non conobbe né volle.   *126*
Vedrassi al Ciotto di Ierusalemme
   segnata con un i la sua bontate,
   quando 'l contrario segnerà un emme.   *129*
Vedrassi l'avarizia e la viltate
   di quei che guarda l'isola del foco,
   ove Anchise finì la lunga etate;   *132*
e a dare ad intender quanto è poco,
   la sua scrittura fian lettere mozze,
   che noteranno molto in parvo loco.   *135*
E parranno a ciascun l'opere sozze
   del barba e del fratel, che tanto egregia
   nazione e due corone han fatte bozze.   *138*

and the Ethiop will condemn such Christians when the two companies shall be separated, the one forever rich, and the other poor. What may the Persians say to your kings, when they shall see that volume open in which are recorded all their dispraises? There shall be seen, among the deeds of Albert, that which will soon set the pen in motion, by which the Kingdom of Prague shall be made a desert. There shall be seen the woe which he who shall die by a boarskin blow is bringing upon the Seine by falsifying the coin. There shall be seen the pride that quickens thirst, which makes the Scot and the Englishman mad, so that neither can keep within his own bounds. It will show the lechery and effeminate life of him of Spain, and him of Bohemia, who never knew valor nor wished it. It will show the Cripple of Jerusalem, his goodness marked with an *I*, while an *M* will mark the opposite. It will show the avarice and cowardice of him who has in ward the Isle of Fire where Anchises ended his long life; and to give to understand how paltry he is, the writing for him shall be in contractions that will note much in little space. And plain to all shall be revealed the foul deeds of his uncle and his brother, which have dishonored so eminent a lineage and two crowns.

E quel di Portogallo e di Norvegia
   lì si conosceranno, e quel di Rascia
   che male ha visto il conio di Vinegia.   *141*
O beata Ungheria, se non si lascia
   più malmenare! e beata Navarra,
   se s'armasse del monte che la fascia!   *144*
E creder de' ciascun che già, per arra
   di questo, Niccosïa e Famagosta
   per la lor bestia si lamenti e garra,
che dal fianco de l'altre non si scosta."   *148*

And he of Portugal and he of Norway shall be known there, and he of Rascia, who, to his harm, has seen the coin of Venice.

"Oh happy Hungary, if she no longer allow herself to be maltreated! and happy Navarre, if she arm herself with the mountains which bind her round! And all should believe that, for earnest of this, Nicosia and Famagosta are now lamenting and complaining because of their beast who departs not from the side of the others."

PARADISO

Quando colui che tutto 'l mondo alluma
  de l'emisperio nostro sì discende,
  che 'l giorno d'ogne parte si consuma,   *3*
lo ciel, che sol di lui prima s'accende,
  subitamente si rifà parvente
  per molte luci, in che una risplende;   *6*
e questo atto del ciel mi venne a mente,
  come 'l segno del mondo e de' suoi duci
  nel benedetto rostro fu tacente;   *9*
però che tutte quelle vive luci,
  vie più lucendo, cominciaron canti
  da mia memoria labili e caduci.   *12*
O dolce amor che di riso t'ammanti,
  quanto parevi ardente in que' flailli,
  ch'avieno spirto sol di pensier santi!   *15*
Poscia che i cari e lucidi lapilli
  ond' io vidi ingemmato il sesto lume
  puoser silenzio a li angelici squilli,   *18*

CANTO XX

W HEN HE who illumines all the world descends from our hemisphere so that day on every side is spent, the heaven, which before is kindled by him alone, suddenly shows itself again with many lights wherein one alone is shining; and this change in the sky came to my mind when the ensign of the world and of its leaders became silent in the blessed beak; because all those living lights, shining far more brightly, began songs that have lapsed and fallen from my memory.

O sweet Love, that mantlest thyself in a smile, how glowing didst thou appear in those pipes that were filled only with the breath of holy thoughts!

When the bright and precious jewels wherewith I saw the sixth luminary engemmed had imposed silence on these angelic chimes,

udir mi parve un mormorar di fiume
  che scende chiaro giù di pietra in pietra,
  mostrando l'ubertà del suo cacume.   *21*
E come suono al collo de la cetra
  prende sua forma, e sì com' al pertugio
  de la sampogna vento che penètra,   *24*
così, rimosso d'aspettare indugio,
  quel mormorar de l'aguglia salissi
  su per lo collo, come fosse bugio.   *27*
Fecesi voce quivi, e quindi uscissi
  per lo suo becco in forma di parole,
  quali aspettava il core ov' io le scrissi.   *30*
"La parte in me che vede e pate il sole
  ne l'aguglie mortali," incominciommi,
  "or fisamente riguardar si vole,   *33*
perché d'i fuochi ond' io figura fommi,
  quelli onde l'occhio in testa mi scintilla,
  e' di tutti lor gradi son li sommi.   *36*
Colui che luce in mezzo per pupilla,
  fu il cantor de lo Spirito Santo,
  che l'arca traslatò di villa in villa: *39*
ora conosce il merto del suo canto,
  in quanto effetto fu del suo consiglio,
  per lo remunerar ch'è altrettanto.   *42*
Dei cinque che mi fan cerchio per ciglio,
  colui che più al becco mi s'accosta,
  la vedovella consolò del figlio: *45*
ora conosce quanto caro costa
  non seguir Cristo, per l'esperïenza
  di questa dolce vita e de l'opposta.   *48*

I seemed to hear the murmuring of a river
which falls down clear from rock to rock,
showing the abundance of its high source.
And as the sound takes its form at the neck
of the lute, and the wind at the vent of the
pipe it fills, so, without keeping me waiting
longer, that murmuring of the Eagle rose up
through the neck, as if it were hollow. There
it became voice, and thence it issued through
the beak in the form of words such as the
heart whereon I wrote them was awaiting.

"That part in me which in mortal eagles
sees and endures the sun you must now gaze
on intently," it began to me, "because, of the
fires whereof I make my shape, those with
which the eye in my head is sparkling are of
all their ranks the chiefs. He that shines mid-
most, as the pupil, was the singer of the Holy
Ghost, who bore the ark about from town to
town. Now he knows the merit of his song,
so far as it was the effect of his own counsel,
by the reward which is proportioned to it. Of
the five which make an arch for my brow, he
who is nearest to my beak consoled the poor
widow for her son. Now he knows, by ex-
perience of this sweet life and of the opposite,
how dear it costs not to follow Christ.

E quel che segue in la circunferenza
 di che ragiono, per l'arco superno,
 morte indugiò per vera penitenza: *51*
ora conosce che 'l giudicio etterno
 non si trasmuta, quando degno preco
 fa crastino là giù de l'odïerno.   *54*
L'altro che segue, con le leggi e meco,
 sotto buona intenzion che fé mal frutto,
 per cedere al pastor si fece greco: *57*
ora conosce come il mal dedutto
 dal suo bene operar non li è nocivo,
 avvegna che sia 'l mondo indi distrutto.   *60*
E quel che vedi ne l'arco declivo,
 Guiglielmo fu, cui quella terra plora
 che piagne Carlo e Federigo vivo: *63*
ora conosce come s'innamora
 lo ciel del giusto rege, e al sembiante
 del suo fulgore il fa vedere ancora.   *66*
Chi crederebbe giù nel mondo errante
 che Rifëo Troiano in questo tondo
 fosse la quinta de le luci sante?   *69*
Ora conosce assai di quel che 'l mondo
 veder non può de la divina grazia,
 ben che sua vista non discerna il fondo." *72*
Quale allodetta che 'n aere si spazia
 prima cantando, e poi tace contenta
 de l'ultima dolcezza che la sazia,   *75*
tal mi sembiò l'imago de la 'mprenta
 de l'etterno piacere, al cui disio
 ciascuna cosa qual ell' è diventa.   *78*

And he who follows on the circumference whereof I speak, upon the upward arc, by true penitence delayed death. Now he knows that the eternal judgment is not changed when worthy prayer there below makes tomorrow's that which was today's. The next who follows, with a good intention which bore bad fruit, made himself Greek, together with the laws and me, in order to give place to the Pastor. Now he knows how the evil derived from his good action does not harm him, even though the world should be destroyed thereby. And him you see in the downward arc was William, for whom that land mourns that weeps on account of the living Charles and Frederick. Now he knows how Heaven is enamored of the righteous king, as by the effulgence of his aspect he yet makes this evident. Who would believe, down in the erring world, that Ripheus the Trojan was the fifth of the holy lights in this circle? Now he knows much of the divine grace that the world cannot see, even though his sight discerns not the bottom."

Like the lark that soars in the air, first singing, then silent, content with the last sweetness that satiates it, so seemed to me the image of the imprint of the Eternal Pleasure, by whose will everything becomes that which it is.

E avvegna ch'io fossi al dubbiar mio
 lì quasi vetro a lo color ch'el veste,
 tempo aspettar tacendo non patio,   *81*
ma de la bocca, "Che cose son queste?"
 mi pinse con la forza del suo peso:
 per ch'io di coruscar vidi gran feste.   *84*
Poi appresso, con l'occhio più acceso,
 lo benedetto segno mi rispuose
 per non tenermi in ammirar sospeso: *87*
"Io veggio che tu credi queste cose
 perch' io le dico, ma non vedi come;
 sì che, se son credute, sono ascose.   *90*
Fai come quei che la cosa per nome
 apprende ben, ma la sua quiditate
 veder non può se altri non la prome.   *93*
Regnum celorum vïolenza pate
 da caldo amore e da viva speranza,
 che vince la divina volontate: *96*
non a guisa che l'omo a l'om sobranza,
 ma vince lei perché vuole esser vinta,
 e, vinta, vince con sua beninanza.   *99*
La prima vita del ciglio e la quinta
 ti fa maravigliar, perché ne vedi
 la regïon de li angeli dipinta.   *102*
D'i corpi suoi non uscir, come credi,
 Gentili, ma Cristiani, in ferma fede
 quel d'i passuri e quel d'i passi piedi.   *105*
Ché l'una de lo 'nferno, u' non si riede
 già mai a buon voler, tornò a l'ossa;
 e ciò di viva spene fu mercede: *108*

And albeit there I was to my questioning like
glass to the color that it clothes, yet would it
not endure to bide its time in silence, but by
its weight and pressure forced from my lips,
"How can these things be?" At which I saw
a great festival of flashing lights. And then,
its eye kindling yet more, the blessed sign,
not to keep me in suspense and amazement,
replied, "I see that you believe these things
because I tell them, but you see not the *how*,
so that, though believed in, they are hidden.
You do as one who well apprehends a thing
by name, but may not see its quiddity unless
another explain it. *Regnum celorum* suffers
violence from fervent love and from living
hope which vanquishes the Divine will: not
as man overcomes man, but vanquishes it
because it wills to be vanquished, and van-
quished, vanquishes with its own benignity.
The first soul of the eyebrow and the fifth
make you marvel, because you see the region of
the Angels decked with them. They came forth
from their bodies not as you think, Gentiles,
but Christians, with firm faith, the one in the
Feet that were to suffer, the other in the Feet
that had suffered. For the one came back to
his bones from Hell, where none ever returns
to right will; and this was the reward of liv-
ing hope,

di viva spene, che mise la possa
　ne' prieghi fatti a Dio per suscitarla,
　sì che potesse sua voglia esser mossa.　　　*111*
L'anima glorïosa onde si parla,
　tornata ne la carne, in che fu poco,
　credette in lui che potëa aiutarla;　　　*114*
e credendo s'accese in tanto foco
　di vero amor, ch'a la morte seconda
　fu degna di venire a questo gioco.　　　*117*
L'altra, per grazia che da sì profonda
　fontana stilla, che mai creatura
　non pinse l'occhio infino a la prima onda,　　　*120*
tutto suo amor là giù pose a drittura:
　per che, di grazia in grazia, Dio li aperse
　l'occhio a la nostra redenzion futura;　　　*123*
ond' ei credette in quella, e non sofferse
　da indi il puzzo più del paganesmo;
　e riprendiene le genti perverse.　　　*126*
Quelle tre donne li fur per battesmo
　che tu vedesti da la destra rota,
　dinanzi al battezzar più d'un millesmo.　　　*129*
O predestinazion, quanto remota
　è la radice tua da quelli aspetti
　che la prima cagion non veggion *tota*!　　　*132*
E voi, mortali, tenetevi stretti
　a giudicar: ché noi, che Dio vedemo,
　non conosciamo ancor tutti li eletti;　　　*135*
ed ènne dolce così fatto scemo,
　perché il ben nostro in questo ben s'affina,
　che quel che vole Iddio, e noi volemo."　　　*138*

of living hope that gave power to the prayers made to God to raise him up, that it might be possible for his will to be moved. The glorious soul I tell of, having returned to the flesh for a short time, believed in Him that was able to help him; and, believing, was kindled to such a fire of true love that on his second death he was worthy to come to this rejoicing. The other, through grace that wells from a fountain so deep that never did creature thrust eye down to its first wave, set all his love below on righteousness; wherefore, from grace to grace, God opened his eye to our future redemption, so that he believed in it, and thenceforth endured not the stench of paganism, and reproved the perverse peoples for it. Those three ladies whom you saw by the right wheel stood for baptism to him more than a thousand years before baptizing.

"O predestination, how remote is thy root from the vision of those who see not the First Cause entire! And you mortals, keep yourselves restrained in judging; for we, who see God, know not yet all the elect. And to us such defect is sweet, because our good in this good is refined, that what God wills we also will."

Così da quella imagine divina,
   per farmi chiara la mia corta vista,
   data mi fu soave medicina.   *141*
E come a buon cantor buon citarista
   fa seguitar lo guizzo de la corda,
   in che più di piacer lo canto acquista,   *144*
sì, mentre ch'e' parlò, sì mi ricorda
   ch'io vidi le due luci benedette,
   pur come batter d'occhi si concorda,
con le parole mover le fiammette.   *148*

Thus, to make my short sight clear, sweet medicine was given to me by that divine image. And as a good lutanist makes the vibration of the string accompany a good singer, by which the song gains more pleasantness, so, I remember that, while it spoke, I saw the two blessed lights, just as the winking of the eyes concords, making their flames quiver to the words.

PARADISO

Già eran li occhi miei rifissi al volto
de la mia donna, e l'animo con essi,
e da ogne altro intento s'era tolto.   *3*
E quella non ridea; ma "S'io ridessi,"
mi cominciò, "tu ti faresti quale
fu Semelè quando di cener fessi: *6*
ché la bellezza mia, che per le scale
de l'etterno palazzo più s'accende,
com' hai veduto, quanto più si sale,   *9*
se non si temperasse, tanto splende,
che 'l tuo mortal podere, al suo fulgore,
sarebbe fronda che trono scoscende.   *12*
Noi sem levati al settimo splendore,
che sotto 'l petto del Leone ardente
raggia mo misto giù del suo valore.   *15*
Ficca di retro a li occhi tuoi la mente,
e fa di quelli specchi a la figura
che 'n questo specchio ti sarà parvente."   *18*

CANTO XXI

ALREADY MY eyes were fixed again on the face of my lady, and with them my mind, and from every other intent it was withdrawn; and she did not smile, but, "Were I to smile," she began to me, "you would become such as was Semele when she turned to ashes; for my beauty which, along the steps of the eternal palace, is kindled the more, as you have seen, the higher the ascent, were it not tempered, is so resplendent that your mortal powers at its flash would be like the bough shattered by a thunderbolt. We have risen to the seventh splendor which beneath the breast of the burning Lion rays down now mingled with its power. Fix your mind after your eyes, and make of them mirrors to the figure which in this mirror shall be shown to you."

Qual savesse qual era la pastura
  del viso mio ne l'aspetto beato
  quand' io mi trasmutai ad altra cura,   *21*
conoscerebbe quanto m'era a grato
  ubidire a la mia celeste scorta,
  contrapesando l'un con l'altro lato.   *24*
Dentro al cristallo che 'l vocabol porta,
  cerchiando il mondo, del suo caro duce
  sotto cui giacque ogne malizia morta,   *27*
di color d'oro in che raggio traluce
  vid' io uno scaleo eretto in suso
  tanto, che nol seguiva la mia luce.   *30*
Vidi anche per li gradi scender giuso
  tanti splendor, ch'io pensai ch'ogne lume
  che par nel ciel, quindi fosse diffuso.   *33*
E come, per lo natural costume,
  le pole insieme, al cominciar del giorno,
  si movono a scaldar le fredde piume;   *36*
poi altre vanno via sanza ritorno,
  altre rivolgon sé onde son mosse,
  e altre roteando fan soggiorno;   *39*
tal modo parve me che quivi fosse
  in quello sfavillar che 'nsieme venne,
  sì come in certo grado si percosse.   *42*
E quel che presso più ci si ritenne,
  si fé sì chiaro, ch'io dicea pensando:
  "Io veggio ben l'amor che tu m'accenne.   *45*
Ma quella ond' io aspetto il come e 'l quando
  del dire e del tacer, si sta; ond' io,
  contra 'l disio, fo ben ch'io non dimando."   *48*

He who should know what was the pasture of my sight in her blessed aspect, when I transferred me to another care, would recognize how much it rejoiced me to be obedient to my heavenly guide, weighing the one with the other side.

Within the crystal which bears the name, circling round the world, of its beloved leader beneath whom every wickedness lay dead, I saw, of the color of gold on which a sunbeam is shining, a ladder rising up so high that my sight might not follow it. I saw, moreover, so many splendors descending along the steps, that I thought every light which appears in heaven had been poured down from it.

And, as by their natural custom, the daws move about together, at the beginning of the day, to warm their cold feathers, then some fly away not to return, some wheel round to whence they had started, while others wheeling make a stay; such movements, it seemed to me, were in that sparkling, which came in a throng, as soon as it smote upon a certain step.

And that one which stopped nearest to us became so bright that in my thought I said, "I clearly perceive the love which you are signaling to me. But she from whom I await the how and the when of speech and of silence pauses, and therefore I, counter to desire, do well not to ask."

235

Per ch'ella, che vedëa il tacer mio
  nel veder di colui che tutto vede,
  mi disse: "Solvi il tuo caldo disio."   *51*
E io incominciai: "La mia mercede
  non mi fa degno de la tua risposta;
  ma per colei che 'l chieder mi concede,   *54*
vita beata che ti stai nascosta
  dentro a la tua letizia, fammi nota
  la cagion che sì presso mi t'ha posta;   *57*
e dì perché si tace in questa rota
  la dolce sinfonia di paradiso,
  che giù per l'altre suona sì divota."   *60*
"Tu hai l'udir mortal sì come il viso,"
  rispuose a me; "onde qui non si canta
  per quel che Bëatrice non ha riso.   *63*
Giù per li gradi de la scala santa
  discesi tanto sol per farti festa
  col dire e con la luce che mi ammanta;   *66*
né più amor mi fece esser più presta,
  ché più e tanto amor quinci sù ferve,
  sì come il fiammeggiar ti manifesta.   *69*
Ma l'alta carità, che ci fa serve
  pronte al consiglio che 'l mondo governa,
  sorteggia qui sì come tu osserve."   *72*
"Io veggio ben," diss' io, "sacra lucerna,
  come libero amore in questa corte
  basta a seguir la provedenza etterna;   *75*
ma questo è quel ch'a cerner mi par forte,
  perché predestinata fosti sola
  a questo officio tra le tue consorte."   *78*

Whereupon she, who saw my silence in His sight who sees all, said to me, "Loose your warm desire." And I began, "My own merit does not make me worthy of your answer, but for her sake who gives me leave to ask, O blessed life that are hidden within your own joy, make known to me the cause that has placed you so near me; and tell why in this wheel the sweet symphony of Paradise is silent, which below through the others so devoutly sounds."

"You have the hearing as the sight of mortals," it replied to me, "wherefore here is no song, for that same reason for which Beatrice has not smiled. Down by the steps of the sacred ladder I descended so far only to give you glad welcome with my speech and with the light that mantles me; nor was it greater love that made me swifter; for love as much and more is burning up there, even as the flaming manifests to you; but the high charity which makes us prompt servants of the counsel which governs the world allots here as you perceive."

"I see well," said I, "O holy lamp, how free love suffices in this Court for following the eternal Providence; but this is what seems to me hard to discern, why you alone among your consorts were predestined to this office."

Né venni prima a l'ultima parola,
  che del suo mezzo fece il lume centro,
  girando sé come veloce mola;   *81*
poi rispuose l'amor che v'era dentro:
  "Luce divina sopra me s'appunta,
  penetrando per questa in ch'io m'inventro,   *84*
la cui virtù, col mio veder congiunta,
  mi leva sopra me tanto, ch'i' veggio
  la somma essenza de la quale è munta.   *87*
Quinci vien l'allegrezza ond' io fiammeggio;
  per ch'a la vista mia, quant' ella è chiara,
  la chiarità de la fiamma pareggio.   *90*
Ma quell' alma nel ciel che più si schiara,
  quel serafin che 'n Dio più l'occhio ha fisso,
  a la dimanda tua non satisfara,   *93*
però che sì s'innoltra ne lo abisso
  de l'etterno statuto quel che chiedi,
  che da ogne creata vista è scisso.   *96*
E al mondo mortal, quando tu riedi,
  questo rapporta, sì che non presumma
  a tanto segno più mover li piedi.   *99*
La mente, che qui luce, in terra fumma;
  onde riguarda come può là giùe
  quel che non pote perché 'l ciel l'assumma." *102*
Sì mi prescrisser le parole sue,
  ch'io lasciai la quistione e mi ritrassi
  a dimandarla umilmente chi fue.   *105*
"Tra ' due liti d'Italia surgon sassi,
  e non molto distanti a la tua patria,
  tanto che ' troni assai suonan più bassi,   *108*

Nor had I come to the last word when the light made a center of its middle, and spun round like a rapid millstone. Then answered the love that was therein, "A divine light is directed on me, penetrating through this wherein I embosom myself, the virtue of which, conjoined with my vision, lifts me above myself so far that I see the Supreme Essence from which it is drawn. From this comes the joy with which I am aflame, for to my sight, in the measure of its clearness, I match the clearness of my flame. But that soul in heaven which is most enlightened, that Seraph who has his eye most fixed on God, could not satisfy your question; for that which you ask lies so deep within the abyss of the eternal statute that it is cut off from every created vision. And when you return to the mortal world, carry this back, so that it may no longer presume to move its feet toward so great a goal. The mind, which shines here, on earth is smoky, and therefore think how it can do below that which it cannot do, though heaven raise it to itself."

His words so restrained me that I left the question and drew me back to ask it humbly who it was. "Between the two shores of Italy, and not very far from your native land, rise crags so high that the thunders sound far lower down;

e fanno un gibbo che si chiama Catria,
   di sotto al quale è consecrato un ermo,
   che suole esser disposto a sola latria."   *111*
Così ricominciommi il terzo sermo;
   e poi, continüando, disse: "Quivi
   al servigio di Dio mi fe' sì fermo,   *114*
che pur con cibi di liquor d'ulivi
   lievemente passava caldi e geli,
   contento ne' pensier contemplativi.   *117*
Render solea quel chiostro a questi cieli
   fertilemente; e ora è fatto vano,
   sì che tosto convien che si riveli.   *120*
In quel loco fu' io Pietro Damiano,
   e Pietro Peccator fu' ne la casa
   di Nostra Donna in sul lito adriano.   *123*
Poca vita mortal m'era rimasa,
   quando fui chiesto e tratto a quel cappello,
   che pur di male in peggio si travasa.   *126*
Venne Cefàs e venne il gran vasello
   de lo Spirito Santo, magri e scalzi,
   prendendo il cibo da qualunque ostello.   *129*
Or voglion quinci e quindi chi rincalzi
   li moderni pastori e chi li meni,
   tanto son gravi, e chi di rietro li alzi.   *132*
Cuopron d'i manti loro i palafreni,
   sì che due bestie van sott' una pelle:
   oh pazïenza che tanto sostieni!"   *135*
A questa voce vid' io più fiammelle
   di grado in grado scendere e girarsi,
   e ogne giro le facea più belle.   *138*

and they make a hump whose name is Catria, beneath which a hermitage is consecrated, which once was wholly given to worship." Thus it began again to me with its third speech; then continued, "There in the service of God I became so steadfast that with food seasoned only with olive-juice I passed easily through heats and frosts, content in contemplative thoughts. That cloister used to yield abundant harvest to these heavens, and now it is become so barren that soon it needs must be revealed. In that place was I Peter Damian, and in the House of Our Lady on the Adriatic shore I was Peter the Sinner. Little of mortal life was left to me when I was sought for and dragged to that hat which ever passes down from bad to worse. Cephas came, and the great vessel of the Holy Spirit came, lean and barefoot, taking their food at whatsoever inn. Now the modern pastors require one to prop them up on this side and one on that, and one to lead them, so heavy are they, and one to hold up their trains behind. They cover their palfreys with their mantles, so that two beasts go under one hide. O patience, that do endure so much!"

At these words I saw more flamelets from step to step descending, and whirling; and every whirl made them more beautiful.

Dintorno a questa vennero e fermarsi,
 e fero un grido di sì alto suono,
 che non potrebbe qui assomigliarsi;
né io lo 'ntesi, sì mi vinse il tuono.   *142*

Round about this one they came, and stopped, and uttered a cry of such deep sound that nothing here could be likened to it; nor did I understand it, so did the thunder overcome me.

PARADISO

OPPRESSO DI stupore, a la mia guida
mi volsi, come parvol che ricorre
sempre colà dove più si confida;
e quella, come madre che soccorre
sùbito al figlio palido e anelo
con la sua voce, che 'l suol ben disporre,
mi disse: "Non sai tu che tu se' in cielo?
e non sai tu che 'l cielo è tutto santo,
e ciò che ci si fa vien da buon zelo?
Come t'avrebbe trasmutato il canto,
e io ridendo, mo pensar lo puoi,
poscia che 'l grido t'ha mosso cotanto;
nel qual, se 'nteso avessi i prieghi suoi,
già ti sarebbe nota la vendetta
che tu vedrai innanzi che tu muoi.
La spada di qua sù non taglia in fretta
né tardo, ma' ch'al parer di colui
che disïando o temendo l'aspetta.

3

6

9

12

15

18

CANTO XXII

Overwhelmed with amazement, I turned
to my guide, like a little child who always
runs back to where it has most confidence;
and she, like a mother who quickly comforts
her pale and gasping son with her voice
which is wont to reassure him, said to me,
"Do you not know that you are in heaven, do
you not know that heaven is all holy, and
that whatever is done here comes of righteous
zeal? How the song, and I by smiling, would
have transmuted you, you can now conceive,
since this cry has so much moved you; where-
in, had you understood their prayers, already
would be known to you the vengeance which
you shall see before you die. The sword of
here on high cuts not in haste nor tardily,
save to his deeming who in longing or in fear
awaits it.

Ma rivolgiti omai inverso altrui;
  ch'assai illustri spiriti vedrai,
  se com' io dico l'aspetto redui." *21*
Come a lei piacque, li occhi ritornai,
  e vidi cento sperule che 'nsieme
  più s'abbellivan con mutüi rai. *24*
Io stava come quei che 'n sé repreme
  la punta del disio, e non s'attenta
  di domandar, sì del troppo si teme; *27*
e la maggiore e la più luculenta
  di quelle margherite innanzi fessi,
  per far di sé la mia voglia contenta. *30*
Poi dentro a lei udi': "Se tu vedessi
  com' io la carità che tra noi arde,
  li tuoi concetti sarebbero espressi. *33*
Ma perché tu, aspettando, non tarde
  a l'alto fine, io ti farò risposta
  pur al pensier, da che sì ti riguarde. *36*
Quel monte a cui Cassino è ne la costa
  fu frequentato già in su la cima
  da la gente ingannata e mal disposta; *39*
e quel son io che sù vi portai prima
  lo nome di colui che 'n terra addusse
  la verità che tanto ci soblima; *42*
e tanta grazia sopra me relusse,
  ch'io ritrassi le ville circunstanti
  da l'empio cólto che 'l mondo sedusse. *45*
Questi altri fuochi tutti contemplanti
  uomini fuoro, accesi di quel caldo
  che fa nascere i fiori e ' frutti santi. *48*

But turn now to the others, for you shall see many illustrious spirits, if you direct your sight as I say."

As was her pleasure, I turned my eyes, and I saw a hundred little spheres which together were making themselves beautiful with their mutual rays. I was standing as one who within himself represses the prick of his desire, who does not make bold to ask, he so fears to exceed. And the greatest and most shining of those pearls came forward to satisfy my desire concerning itself. Then within it I heard, "If you could see, as I do, the charity which burns among us, you would have uttered your thoughts; but lest you, by waiting, be delayed in your lofty aim, I will make answer to the thought itself about which you are so circumspect.

"That mountain on whose slope Cassino lies was of old frequented on its summit by the folk deceived and perverse, and I am he who first bore up there His name who brought to earth that truth which so uplifts us; and such grace shone upon me that I drew away the surrounding towns from the impious worship that seduced the world. These other fires were all contemplative men, kindled by that warmth which gives birth to holy flowers and fruits.

Qui è Maccario, qui è Romoaldo,
  qui son li frati miei che dentro ai chiostri
  fermar li piedi e tennero il cor saldo."   *51*
E io a lui: "L'affetto che dimostri
  meco parlando, e la buona sembianza
  ch'io veggio e noto in tutti li ardor vostri,   *54*
così m'ha dilatata mia fidanza,
  come 'l sol fa la rosa quando aperta
  tanto divien quant' ell' ha di possanza.   *57*
Però ti priego, e tu, padre, m'accerta
  s'io posso prender tanta grazia, ch'io
  ti veggia con imagine scoverta."   *60*
Ond' elli: "Frate, il tuo alto disio
  s'adempierà in su l'ultima spera,
  ove s'adempion tutti li altri e 'l mio.   *63*
Ivi è perfetta, matura e intera
  ciascuna disïanza; in quella sola
  è ogne parte là ove sempr' era,   *66*
perché non è in loco e non s'impola;
  e nostra scala infino ad essa varca,
  onde così dal viso ti s'invola.   *69*
Infin là sù la vide il patriarca
  Iacobbe porger la superna parte,
  quando li apparve d'angeli sì carca.   *72*
Ma, per salirla, mo nessun diparte
  da terra i piedi, e la regola mia
  rimasa è per danno de le carte.   *75*
Le mura che solieno esser badia
  fatte sono spelonche, e le cocolle
  sacca son piene di farina ria.   *78*

Here is Macarius, here is Romualdus, here are my brethren who stayed their feet within the cloisters and kept a steadfast heart."

And I to him, "The affection you show in speaking with me, and the good semblance which I see and note in all your ardors, have expanded my confidence as the sun does the rose when it opens to its fullest bloom. Therefore I pray you—and do you, father, assure me if I am capable of receiving so great a grace, that I may behold you in your uncovered shape."

Whereon he, "Brother, your high desire shall be fulfilled up in the last sphere, where are fulfilled all others and my own. There every desire is perfect, mature, and whole. In that alone is every part there where it always was, for it is not in space, nor has it poles; and our ladder reaches up to it, wherefore it steals itself from your sight. All the way thither the patriarch Jacob saw it stretch its upper part, when it appeared to him so laden with Angels. But no one now lifts his foot from earth to ascend it, and my Rule remains for waste of paper. The walls, which used to be an abbey, have become dens, and the cowls are sacks full of foul meal.

Ma grave usura tanto non si tolle
   contra 'l piacer di Dio, quanto quel frutto
   che fa il cor de' monaci sì folle;   *81*
ché quantunque la Chiesa guarda, tutto
   è de la gente che per Dio dimanda;
   non di parenti né d'altro più brutto.   *84*
La carne d'i mortali è tanto blanda,
   che giù non basta buon cominciamento
   dal nascer de la quercia al far la ghianda.   *87*
Pier cominciò sanz' oro e sanz' argento,
   e io con orazione e con digiuno,
   e Francesco umilmente il suo convento;   *90*
e se guardi 'l principio di ciascuno,
   poscia riguardi là dov' è trascorso,
   tu vederai del bianco fatto bruno.   *93*
Veramente Iordan vòlto retrorso
   più fu, e 'l mar fuggir, quando Dio volse,
   mirabile a veder che qui 'l soccorso."   *96*
Così mi disse, e indi si raccolse
   al suo collegio, e 'l collegio si strinse;
   poi, come turbo, in sù tutto s'avvolse.   *99*
La dolce donna dietro a lor mi pinse
   con un sol cenno su per quella scala,
   sì sua virtù la mia natura vinse;   *102*
né mai qua giù dove si monta e cala
   naturalmente, fu sì ratto moto
   ch'agguagliar si potesse a la mia ala.   *105*
S'io torni mai, lettore, a quel divoto
   trïunfo per lo quale io piango spesso
   le mie peccata e 'l petto mi percuoto,   *108*

But heavy usury is not exacted so counter to
God's pleasure as that fruit which makes the
heart of monks so mad; for whatsoever the
Church has in keeping is all for the folk that
ask it in God's name, not for kindred, or for
other filthier thing. The flesh of mortals is so
soft that on earth a good beginning does not
last from the springing of the oak to the
bearing of the acorn. Peter began his fellow-
ship without gold or silver, and I mine with
prayer and with fasting, and Francis his with
humility; and if you look at the beginning
of each, and then look again whither it has
strayed, you will see the white changed to
dark. Nevertheless, Jordan driven back, and
the sea fleeing when God willed, were sights
more wondrous than the succor here."

Thus he spoke to me, then drew back to
his company, and the company closed to-
gether; then like a whirlwind all were gath-
ered upward. My sweet lady, with only a sign,
thrust me up after them by that ladder, so did
her power overcome my nature; nor ever here
below, where we mount and descend by na-
ture's law, was motion so swift as might
match my flight. So may I return, reader, to
that devout triumph for the sake of which I
often bewail my sins and beat my breast,

tu non avresti in tanto tratto e messo
   nel foco il dito, in quant' io vidi 'l segno
   che segue il Tauro e fui dentro da esso.   *111*
O glorïose stelle, o lume pregno
   di gran virtù, dal quale io riconosco
   tutto, qual che si sia, il mio ingegno,   *114*
con voi nasceva e s'ascondeva vosco
   quelli ch'è padre d'ogne mortal vita,
   quand' io senti' di prima l'aere tosco;   *117*
e poi, quando mi fu grazia largita
   d'entrar ne l'alta rota che vi gira,
   la vostra regïon mi fu sortita.   *120*
A voi divotamente ora sospira
   l'anima mia, per acquistar virtute
   al passo forte che a sé la tira.   *123*
"Tu se' sì presso a l'ultima salute,"
   cominciò Bëatrice, "che tu dei
   aver le luci tue chiare e acute;   *126*
e però, prima che tu più t'inlei,
   rimira in giù, e vedi quanto mondo
   sotto li piedi già esser ti fei;   *129*
sì che 'l tuo cor, quantunque può, giocondo
   s'appresenti a la turba trïunfante
   che lieta vien per questo etera tondo."   *132*
Col viso ritornai per tutte quante
   le sette spere, e vidi questo globo
   tal, ch'io sorrisi del suo vil sembiante;   *135*
e quel consiglio per migliore approbo
   che l'ha per meno; e chi ad altro pensa
   chiamar si puote veramente probo.   *138*

you would not have drawn out and put your finger into the fire so quickly as I saw the sign which follows the Bull, and was within it.

O glorious stars, O light impregnated with mighty power, from which I derive all my genius, whatsoever it may be, with you was rising and with you was hiding himself he who is father of every mortal life when I first felt the air of Tuscany; and then, when the grace was bestowed on me to enter the lofty wheel that bears you round, your region was assigned to me! To you my soul now devoutly sighs, that it may acquire virtue for the hard pass which draws it to itself.

"You are so near to the final blessedness," Beatrice began, "that you must have your eyes clear and keen. And therefore, before you enter farther into it, look back downward and behold how great a world I have already set beneath your feet, in order that your heart may present itself, joyous to its utmost, to the triumphant throng which comes glad through this round ether."

With my sight I returned through all and each of the seven spheres, and saw this globe such that I smiled at its paltry semblance; and that counsel I approve as best which holds it for least, and he whose thought is turned elsewhere may be called truly upright.

Vidi la figlia di Latona incensa
    sanza quell' ombra che mi fu cagione
    per che già la credetti rara e densa.   *141*
L'aspetto del tuo nato, Iperïone,
    quivi sostenni, e vidi com' si move
    circa e vicino a lui Maia e Dïone.   *144*
Quindi m'apparve il temperar di Giove
    tra 'l padre e 'l figlio; e quindi mi fu chiaro
    il varïar che fanno di lor dove;   *147*
e tutti e sette mi si dimostraro
    quanto son grandi e quanto son veloci
    e come sono in distante riparo.   *150*
L'aiuola che ci fa tanto feroci,
    volgendom' io con li etterni Gemelli,
    tutta m'apparve da' colli a le foci;
poscia rivolsi li occhi a li occhi belli.   *154*

I saw the daughter of Latona glowing without that shade for which I once believed her rare and dense. The aspect of your son, Hyperion, I there endured, and saw how Maia and Dione move around and near him. Then appeared to me the tempering of Jove between his father and his son, and then was clear to me the varying they make in their position. And all the seven were displayed to me, how great they are and swift, and how distant each from other in location. The little threshing-floor which makes us so fierce was all revealed to me from hills to river-mouths, as I circled with the eternal Twins. Then to the beauteous eyes I turned my eyes again.

PARADISO

Come l'augello, intra l'amate fronde,
     posato al nido de' suoi dolci nati
     la notte che le cose ci nasconde,   3
che, per veder li aspetti disïati
     e per trovar lo cibo onde li pasca,
     in che gravi labor li sono aggrati,   6
previene il tempo in su aperta frasca,
     e con ardente affetto il sole aspetta,
     fiso guardando pur che l'alba nasca;   9
così la donna mïa stava eretta
     e attenta, rivolta inver' la plaga
     sotto la quale il sol mostra men fretta: 12
sì che, veggendola io sospesa e vaga,
     fecimi qual è quei che disïando
     altro vorria, e sperando s'appaga.   15
Ma poco fu tra uno e altro quando,
     del mio attender, dico, e del vedere
     lo ciel venir più e più rischiarando;   18
e Bëatrice disse: "Ecco le schiere
     del trïunfo di Cristo e tutto 'l frutto
     ricolto del girar di queste spere!"   21

CANTO XXIII

As the bird, among the beloved leaves, having sat on the nest of her sweet brood through the night which hides things from us, who, in order to look upon their longed-for aspect and to find the food wherewith to feed them, wherein her heavy toils are pleasing to her, forerums the time, upon the open bough, and with glowing love awaits the sun, fixedly gazing for the dawn to break; so was my lady standing, erect and eager, turned toward the region beneath which the sun shows less haste. I, therefore, seeing her in suspense and longing, became as he who in desire would fain have something else, and in hope is satisfied. But short was the time between the one and the other *when*, of my waiting, I mean, and of my seeing the heavens become more and more resplendent. And Beatrice said, "Behold the hosts of Christ's triumph and all the fruit garnered from the circling of these spheres!"

Pariemi che 'l suo viso ardesse tutto,
  e li occhi avea di letizia sì pieni,
  che passarmen convien sanza costrutto.   *24*
Quale ne' plenilünïi sereni
  Trivïa ride tra le ninfe etterne
  che dipingon lo ciel per tutti i seni,   *27*
vid' i' sopra migliaia di lucerne
  un sol che tutte quante l'accendea,
  come fa 'l nostro le viste superne;   *30*
e per la viva luce trasparea
  la lucente sustanza tanto chiara
  nel viso mio, che non la sostenea.   *33*
Oh Bëatrice, dolce guida e cara!
  Ella mi disse: "Quel che ti sobranza
  è virtù da cui nulla si ripara.   *36*
Quivi è la sapïenza e la possanza
  ch'aprì le strade tra 'l cielo e la terra,
  onde fu già sì lunga disïanza."   *39*
Come foco di nube si diserra
  per dilatarsi sì che non vi cape,
  e fuor di sua natura in giù s'atterra,   *42*
la mente mia così, tra quelle dape
  fatta più grande, di sé stessa uscìo,
  e che si fesse rimembrar non sape.   *45*
"Apri li occhi e riguarda qual son io;
  tu hai vedute cose, che possente
  se' fatto a sostener lo riso mio."   *48*
Io era come quei che si risente
  di visïone oblita e che s'ingegna
  indarno di ridurlasi a la mente,   *51*

It seemed to me her face was all aflame, and her eyes were so full of joy that I must needs pass it by undescribed.

As in the clear skies at the full moon Trivia smiles among the eternal nymphs that deck heaven through all its depths, I saw, above thousands of lamps, a Sun which kindled each one of them as does our own the things we see above; and through its living light the lucent Substance outglowed so bright upon my vision that it endured it not.

O Beatrice, sweet guide and dear! She said to me, "That which overcomes you is power against which naught defends itself. Therein are the wisdom and the power that opened the roads between Heaven and earth, for which of old there was such long desire."

Even as fire breaks from a cloud, because it dilates so that it has not room there, and contrary to its own nature, falls down to earth, so my mind, becoming greater amid those feasts, issued from itself, and of what it became has no remembrance.

"Open your eyes and look on what I am; you have seen things such that you are become able to sustain my smile." I was as one that wakes from a forgotten dream, and who strives in vain to bring it back to mind,

quand' io udi' questa proferta, degna
　　di tanto grato, che mai non si stingue
　　del libro che 'l preterito rassegna.　　　　　*54*
Se mo sonasser tutte quelle lingue
　　che Polimnïa con le suore fero
　　del latte lor dolcissimo più pingue,　　　　　*57*
per aiutarmi, al millesmo del vero
　　non si verria, cantando il santo riso
　　e quanto il santo aspetto facea mero;　　　　*60*
e così, figurando il paradiso,
　　convien saltar lo sacrato poema,
　　come chi trova suo cammin riciso.　　　　　*63*
Ma chi pensasse il ponderoso tema
　　e l'omero mortal che se ne carca,
　　nol biasmerebbe se sott' esso trema:　　　　*66*
non è pareggio da picciola barca
　　quel che fendendo va l'ardita prora,
　　né da nocchier ch'a sé medesmo parca.　　　*69*
"Perché la faccia mia sì t'innamora,
　　che tu non ti rivolgi al bel giardino
　　che sotto i raggi di Cristo s'infiora?　　　　*72*
Quivi è la rosa in che 'l verbo divino
　　carne si fece; quivi son li gigli
　　al cui odor si prese il buon cammino."　　　*75*
Così Beatrice; e io, che a' suoi consigli
　　tutto era pronto, ancora mi rendei
　　a la battaglia de' debili cigli.　　　　　　　*78*
Come a raggio di sol, che puro mei
　　per fratta nube, già prato di fiori
　　vider, coverti d'ombra, li occhi miei;　　　　*81*

when I heard this proffer, worthy of such gratitude that it can never be effaced from the book which records the past.

Though all those tongues which Poly-hymnia and her sisters made most rich with their sweetest milk should sound now to aid me, it would not come to a thousandth part of the truth, in singing the holy smile, and how it lit up the holy aspect; and so, depicting Paradise, the sacred poem must needs make a leap, even as one who finds his way cut off. But whoso thinks of the ponderous theme and of the mortal shoulder which is laden therewith, will not blame it if it trem-ble beneath the load. It is no voyage for a little bark, this which my daring prow cleaves as it goes, nor for a pilot who would spare himself.

"Why does my face so enamor you that you turn not to the fair garden which blossoms beneath the rays of Christ? Here is the Rose wherein the Divine Word became flesh; here are the lilies by whose odor the good way was taken."

Thus Beatrice; and I who to her counsels was all eager, again gave myself up to the battle of the feeble brows.

As under the sun's ray, which streams pure through a broken cloud, ere now my eyes, sheltered by shade, have seen a meadow of flowers,

vid' io così più turbe di splendori,
    folgorate di sù da raggi ardenti,
    sanza veder principio di folgóri.   *84*
O benigna vertù che sì li 'mprenti,
    sù t'essaltasti per largirmi loco
    a li occhi lì che non t'eran possenti.   *87*
Il nome del bel fior ch'io sempre invoco
    e mane e sera, tutto mi ristrinse
    l'animo ad avvisar lo maggior foco;   *90*
e come ambo le luci mi dipinse
    il quale e il quanto de la viva stella
    che là sù vince come qua giù vinse,   *93*
per entro il cielo scese una facella,
    formata in cerchio a guisa di corona,
    e cinsela e girossi intorno ad ella.   *96*
Qualunque melodia più dolce suona
    qua giù e più a sé l'anima tira,
    parrebbe nube che squarciata tona,   *99*
comparata al sonar di quella lira
    onde si coronava il bel zaffiro
    del quale il ciel più chiaro s'inzaffira.   *102*
"Io sono amore angelico, che giro
    l'alta letizia che spira del ventre
    che fu albergo del nostro disiro;   *105*
e girerommi, donna del ciel, mentre
    che seguirai tuo figlio, e farai dia
    più la spera supprema perché li entre."   *108*
Così la circulata melodia
    si sigillava, e tutti li altri lumi
    facean sonare il nome di Maria.   *111*

so saw I many hosts of splendors glowed on
from above by ardent rays, though I saw not
whence came the glowings. O benign Power,
which doth so imprint them, Thou didst as-
cend so as to yield place there for the eyes
that were powerless before Thee!

The name of the fair flower which I ever
invoke, both morning and evening, absorbed
all my mind as I gazed on the greatest flame.
And when on both of my eyes had been de-
picted the quality and the greatness of the liv-
ing star which conquers up there even as
down here it conquered, there descended
through the heaven a torch which formed a
circle in the likeness of a crown that girt her
and wheeled about her. Whatever melody
sounds sweetest here below and most draws
to itself the soul, would seem a cloud which,
being rent, thunders, compared with the
sound of that lyre wherewith was crowned
the beauteous sapphire by which the brightest
heaven is ensapphired.

"I am angelic love, who circle the supreme
joy that breathes from out the womb which
was the hostelry of our Desire; and I shall
circle, Lady of Heaven, until thou shalt follow
thy Son, and make the supreme sphere more
divine by entering it." Thus the circling mel-
ody sealed itself, and all the other lights made
Mary's name resound.

263

Lo real manto di tutti i volumi
  del mondo, che più ferve e più s'avviva
  ne l'alito di Dio e nei costumi,   *114*
avea sopra di noi l'interna riva
  tanto distante, che la sua parvenza,
  là dov' io era, ancor non appariva: *117*
però non ebber li occhi miei potenza
  di seguitar la coronata fiamma
  che si levò appresso sua semenza.   *120*
E come fantolin che 'nver' la mamma
  tende le braccia, poi che 'l latte prese,
  per l'animo che 'nfin di fuor s'infiamma;   *123*
ciascun di quei candori in sù si stese
  con la sua cima, sì che l'alto affetto
  ch'elli avieno a Maria mi fu palese.   *126*
Indi rimaser lì nel mio cospetto,
  "Regina celi" cantando sì dolce,
  che mai da me non si partì 'l diletto.   *129*
Oh quanta è l'ubertà che si soffolce
  in quelle arche ricchissime che fuoro
  a seminar qua giù buone bobolce!   *132*
Quivi si vive e gode del tesoro
  che s'acquistò piangendo ne lo essilio
  di Babillòn, ove si lasciò l'oro.   *135*
Quivi trïunfa, sotto l'alto Filio
  di Dio e di Maria, di sua vittoria,
  e con l'antico e col novo concilio,
colui che tien le chiavi di tal gloria.   *139*

The royal mantle of all the world's revolving spheres, which most burns and is most quickened in the breath of God and in His workings, had, above us, its inner shore so distant that sight of it, there where I was, was not yet possible to me. Therefore my eyes had not power to follow the crowned flame which mounted upward after her offspring. And as an infant which, when it has taken the milk, stretches its arms toward its mother, its affection glowing forth, each of these splendors stretched upward with its peak, so that the deep love they had for Mary was made plain to me. Then they remained there in my sight, singing *Regina celi* so sweetly that never has the delight departed from me. Oh, how great is the abundance which is heaped up in those rich coffers, who were good sowers here below! Here they live and rejoice in the treasure which was gained with tears in the exile of Babylon, where gold was scorned. Here, under the exalted Son of God and Mary, together with both the ancient and the new council, he triumphs in his victory who holds the keys of such glory.

PARADISO

"O SODALIZIO ELETTO a la gran cena
del benedetto Agnello, il qual vi ciba
sì, che la vostra voglia è sempre piena,   3
se per grazia di Dio questi preliba
di quel che cade de la vostra mensa,
prima che morte tempo li prescriba,   6
ponete mente a l'affezione immensa
e roratelo alquanto: voi bevete
sempre del fonte onde vien quel ch'ei pensa."   9
Così Beatrice; e quelle anime liete
si fero spere sopra fissi poli,
fiammando, volte, a guisa di comete.   12
E come cerchi in tempra d'orïuoli
si giran sì, che 'l primo a chi pon mente
quïeto pare, e l'ultimo che voli;   15
così quelle carole, differente-
mente danzando, de la sua ricchezza
mi facieno stimar, veloci e lente.   18

CANTO XXIV

"O FELLOWSHIP elect to the great supper of the blessed Lamb, who feeds you so that your desire is ever satisfied, since by the grace of God this man foretastes of that which falls from your table before death appoint his time to him, give heed to his immense longing and bedew him somewhat: you drink ever of the fountain whence flows that which he thinks." Thus Beatrice; and those glad souls made themselves spheres upon fixed poles, flaming like comets, as they whirled. And as wheels within the fittings of clocks revolve, so that to one who gives heed the first seems quiet and the last to fly, so did those carols, dancing severally fast and slow, make me judge of their riches.

Di quella ch'io notai di più carezza
  vid' ïo uscire un foco sì felice,
  che nullo vi lasciò di più chiarezza;   *21*
e tre fïate intorno di Beatrice
  si volse con un canto tanto divo,
  che la mia fantasia nol mi ridice.   *24*
Però salta la penna e non lo scrivo:
  chè l'imagine nostra a cotai pieghe,
  non che 'l parlare, è troppo color vivo.   *27*
"O santa suora mia che sì ne prieghe
  divota, per lo tuo ardente affetto
  da quella bella spera mi disleghe."   *30*
Poscia fermato, il foco benedetto
  a la mia donna dirizzò lo spiro,
  che favellò così com' i' ho detto.   *33*
Ed ella: "O luce etterna del gran viro
  a cui Nostro Segnor lasciò le chiavi,
  ch'ei portò giù, di questo gaudio miro,   *36*
tenta costui di punti lievi e gravi,
  come ti piace, intorno de la fede,
  per la qual tu su per lo mare andavi.   *39*
S'elli ama bene e bene spera e crede,
  non t'è occulto, perché 'l viso hai quivi
  dov' ogne cosa dipinta si vede;   *42*
ma perché questo regno ha fatto civi
  per la verace fede, a glorïarla,
  di lei parlare è ben ch'a lui arrivi."   *45*
Sì come il baccialier s'arma e non parla
  fin che 'l maestro la question propone,
  per approvarla, non per terminarla,   *48*

From the one I noted as the richest I saw
issue a fire so joyful that it left there none
of greater brightness; and it revolved three
times round Beatrice with a song so divine
that my phantasy does not repeat it to me;
wherefore my pen leaps and I do not write it,
for our imagination, not to say our speech, is
of too vivid color for such folds.

"O holy sister mine, who do so devoutly
pray to us, by your ardent affection you loose
me from that fair sphere"; after it had
stopped, the blessed fire breathed forth these
words to my lady as I have told them.

And she, "O eternal light of the great man
with whom our Lord left the keys, which He
bore below, of this marvelous joy, test this
man on points light and grave, as pleases you,
concerning the Faith by which you did walk
upon the sea. Whether he loves rightly and
rightly hopes and believes is not hidden from
you, for you have your vision where every-
thing is seen depicted. But since this kingdom
has made its citizens by the true faith, it
rightly falls to him to speak of it, that he
may glorify it."

Even as the bachelor arms himself—and
does not speak until the master propounds
the question—in order to adduce the proof,
not to decide it,

così m'armava io d'ogne ragione
mentre ch'ella dicea, per esser presto
a tal querente e a tal professione.   *51*
"Dì, buon Cristiano, fatti manifesto:
fede che è?" Ond' io levai la fronte
in quella luce onde spirava questo;   *54*
poi mi volsi a Beatrice, ed essa pronte
sembianze femmi perch' ïo spandessi
l'acqua di fuor del mio interno fonte.   *57*
"La Grazia che mi dà ch'io mi confessi,"
comincia' io, "da l'alto primipilo,
faccia li miei concetti bene espressi."   *60*
E seguitai: "Come 'l verace stilo
ne scrisse, padre, del tuo caro frate
che mise teco Roma nel buon filo,   *63*
fede è sustanza di cose sperate
e argomento de le non parventi;
e questa pare a me sua quiditate."   *66*
Allora udi': "Dirittamente senti,
se bene intendi perché la ripuose
tra le sustanze, e poi tra li argomenti."   *69*
E io appresso: "Le profonde cose
che mi largiscon qui la lor parvenza,
a li occhi di là giù son sì ascose,   *72*
che l'esser loro v'è in sola credenza,
sopra la qual si fonda l'alta spene;
e però di sustanza prende intenza.   *75*
E da questa credenza ci convene
silogizzar, sanz' avere altra vista:
però intenza d'argomento tene."   *78*

so, while she was speaking, I was arming my-
self with every reason, to be ready for such a
questioner and for such a profession.

"Speak, good Christian, and declare your-
self: Faith, what is it?" Whereon I raised my
brow to that light whence this was breathed
forth, then I turned to Beatrice, who prompt-
ly signaled to me that I should pour the water
forth from my inward fountain.

"May the grace that grants me to confess to
the Chief Centurion," I began, "cause my
conceptions to be well expressed." And I went
on, "As the veracious pen of your dear brother
wrote of it, who with you, father, put Rome
on the good path, Faith is the substance of
things hoped for and the evidence of things
not seen; and this I take to be its quiddity."

Then I heard, "Rightly do you deem, if you
understand well why he placed it among the
substances and then among the evidences."

And I thereon, "The deep things which
grant to me here the sight of themselves are
so hidden to eyes below that there their exist-
ence is in belief alone, upon which the lofty
hope is founded; and therefore it takes the
designation of substance. And from this belief
needs must we reason, without seeing more:
therefore it receives the designation of evi-
dence."

271

Allora udi': "Se quantunque s'acquista
　giù per dottrina, fosse così 'nteso,
　non li avria loco ingegno di sofista."　　　　　*81*
Così spirò di quello amore acceso;
　indi soggiunse: "Assai bene è trascorsa
　d'esta moneta già la lega e 'l peso;　　　　　*84*
ma dimmi se tu l'hai ne la tua borsa."
　Ond' io: "Sì ho, sì lucida e sì tonda,
　che nel suo conio nulla mi s'inforsa."　　　　　*87*
Appresso uscì de la luce profonda
　che lì splendeva: "Questa cara gioia
　sopra la quale ogne virtù si fonda,　　　　　*90*
onde ti venne?" E io: "La larga ploia
　de lo Spirito Santo, ch'è diffusa
　in su le vecchie e 'n su le nuove cuoia,　　　　　*93*
è silogismo che la m'ha conchiusa
　acutamente sì, che 'nverso d'ella
　ogne dimostrazion mi pare ottusa."　　　　　*96*
Io udi' poi: "L'antica e la novella
　proposizion che così ti conchiude,
　perché l'hai tu per divina favella?"　　　　　*99*
E io: "La prova che 'l ver mi dischiude,
　son l'opere seguite, a che natura
　non scalda ferro mai né batte incude."　　　　　*102*
Risposto fummi: "Dì, chi t'assicura
　che quell' opere fosser? Quel medesmo
　che vuol provarsi, non altri, il ti giura."　　　　　*105*
"Se 'l mondo si rivolse al cristianesmo,"
　diss' io, "sanza miracoli, quest' uno
　è tal, che li altri non sono il centesmo:　　　　　*108*

Then I heard, "If all that is acquired below
for doctrine were thus understood, the wit of
sophist would have no place there." These
words were breathed forth from that en-
kindled love; and it continued, "Now the
alloy and the weight of this coin have been
well enough examined; but tell me if you
have it in your purse?" And I, "Yes, I have
it so shining and so round that in its stamp
nothing is doubtful to me."

Then issued from the deep light that was
shining there, "This precious jewel whereon
every virtue is founded, whence did it come
to you?"

And I, "The plenteous rain of the Holy
Spirit which is poured over the old and over
the new parchments is a syllogism that has
proved it to me so acutely that, in comparison
with this, every demonstration seems obtuse
to me."

Then I heard, "That old and that new
proposition which are so conclusive to you,
why do you hold them for divine discourse?"

And I, "The proof which discloses the truth
to me are the works that followed, for which
nature never heats iron nor beats anvil."

"Tell me," came the reply, "who assures
you that these works ever were? The very
thing itself which requires to be proved, and
naught else, affirms them to you."

"If the world turned to Christianity with-
out miracles," I said, "that one is such that
the rest are not the hundredth part;

ché tu intrasti povero e digiuno
  in campo, a seminar la buona pianta
  che fu già vite e ora è fatta pruno."   *111*

Finito questo, l'alta corte santa
  risonò per le spere un "Dio laudamo"
  ne la melode che là sù si canta.   *114*

E quel baron che sì di ramo in ramo,
  essaminando, già tratto m'avea,
  che a l'ultime fronde appressavamo,   *117*

ricominciò: "La Grazia, che donnea
  con la tua mente, la bocca t'aperse
  infino a qui come aprir si dovea,   *120*

sì ch'io approvo ciò che fuori emerse;
  ma or convien espremer quel che credi,
  e onde a la credenza tua s'offerse."   *123*

"O santo padre, e spirito che vedi
  ciò che credesti sì, che tu vincesti
  ver' lo sepulcro più giovani piedi,"   *126*

comincia' io, "tu vuo' ch'io manifesti
  la forma qui del pronto creder mio,
  e anche la cagion di lui chiedesti.   *129*

E io rispondo: Io credo in uno Dio
  solo ed etterno, che tutto 'l ciel move,
  non moto, con amore e con disio;   *132*

e a tal creder non ho io pur prove
  fisice e metafisice, ma dalmi
  anche la verità che quinci piove   *135*

per Moïsè, per profeti e per salmi,
  per l'Evangelio e per voi che scriveste
  poi che l'ardente Spirto vi fé almi;   *138*

for you entered the field poor and hungry, to sow the good plant which was once a vine and is now become a thorn."

This ended, the high and holy court resounded a *"Te Deum laudamus"* through the spheres, in the melody which up there is sung.

And that Baron who, thus from branch to branch examining, had now drawn me on so that we were approaching the last leaves, began again, "The Grace that holds amorous discourse with your mind, till now has opened your lips aright, so that I approve what has come from them; but now you must declare what you believe and whence it was offered to your belief."

"O holy father, spirit who see that which you did so believe that you, toward the sepulchre, did outdo younger feet," I began, "you would have me declare here the form of my ready belief, and also you have asked the cause of it. And I reply: I believe in one God, sole and eternal, who, unmoved, moves all the heavens with love and with desire; and for this belief I have not only proofs physical and metaphysical, but it is given to me also in the truth that rains down hence through Moses and the Prophets and the Psalms, through the Gospel, and through you who wrote when the fiery Spirit had made you holy.

e credo in tre persone etterne, e queste
  credo una essenza sì una e sì trina,
  che soffera congiunto 'sono' ed 'este.'   *141*
De la profonda condizion divina
  ch'io tocco mo, la mente mi sigilla
  più volte l'evangelica dottrina.   *144*
Quest' è 'l principio, quest' è la favilla
  che si dilata in fiamma poi vivace,
  e come stella in cielo in me scintilla."   *147*
Come 'l segnor ch'ascolta quel che i piace,
  da indi abbraccia il servo, gratulando
  per la novella, tosto ch'el si tace;   *150*
così, benedicendomi cantando,
  tre volte cinse me, sì com' io tacqui,
  l'appostolico lume al cui comando
io avea detto: sì nel dir li piacqui!   *154*

And I believe in three Eternal Persons, and these I believe to be one essence, so one and so threefold as to comport at once with *are* and *is*. With the profound divine state whereof I now speak, the evangelic doctrine many times sets the seal upon my mind. This is the beginning, this is the spark which then dilates to a living flame and like a star in heaven shines within me."

Even as the master who listens to that which pleases him, then embraces his servant, rejoicing in his news, as soon as he is silent; so, singing benedictions on me, the apostolic light at whose bidding I had spoken encircled me three times when I was silent, I so pleased him by my speech.

PARADISO

Se mai continga che 'l poema sacro
  al quale ha posto mano e cielo e terra,
  sì che m'ha fatto per molti anni macro,   *3*
vinca la crudeltà che fuor mi serra
  del bello ovile ov' io dormi' agnello,
  nimico ai lupi che li danno guerra;   *6*
con altra voce omai, con altro vello
  ritornerò poeta, e in sul fonte
  del mio battesmo prenderò 'l cappello;   *9*
però che ne la fede, che fa conte
  l'anime a Dio, quivi intra' io, e poi
  Pietro per lei sì mi girò la fronte.   *12*
Indi si mosse un lume verso noi
  di quella spera ond' uscì la primizia
  che lasciò Cristo d'i vicari suoi;   *15*
e la mia donna, piena di letizia,
  mi disse: "Mira, mira: ecco il barone
  per cui là giù si vicita Galizia."   *18*
Sì come quando il colombo si pone
  presso al compagno, l'uno a l'altro pande,
  girando e mormorando, l'affezione;   *21*

CANTO XXV

IF EVER it come to pass that the sacred poem to which heaven and earth have so set hand that it has made me lean for many years should overcome the cruelty which bars me from the fair sheepfold where I slept as a lamb, an enemy to the wolves which war on it, with changed voice now and with changed fleece a poet will I return, and at the font of my baptism will I take the crown; because there I entered into the Faith that makes souls known to God; and afterward Peter, for its sake, thus encircled my brow.

Then a light moved towards us from that circle whence had issued the first-fruit which Christ left of His vicars; and my lady, full of gladness, said to me, "Look! look! Behold the Baron for whose sake, down below, folk visit Galicia."

As when the dove alights beside its mate, and the one lavishes its affection on the other, circling it and cooing,

così vid' ïo l'un da l'altro grande
  principe glorïoso essere accolto,
  laudando il cibo che là sù li prande.   *24*
Ma poi che 'l gratular si fu assolto,
  tacito *coram me* ciascun s'affisse,
  ignito sì che vincëa 'l mio volto.   *27*
Ridendo allora Bëatrice disse:
  "Inclita vita per cui la larghezza
  de la nostra basilica si scrisse,   *30*
fa risonar la spene in questa altezza:
  tu sai, che tante fiate la figuri,
  quante Iesù ai tre fé più carezza."   *33*
"Leva la testa e fa che t'assicuri:
  ché ciò che vien qua sù del mortal mondo,
  convien ch'ai nostri raggi si maturi."   *36*
Questo conforto del foco secondo
  mi venne; ond' io levä li occhi a' monti
  che li 'ncurvaron pria col troppo pondo.   *39*
"Poi che per grazia vuol che tu t'affronti
  lo nostro Imperadore, anzi la morte,
  ne l'aula più secreta co' suoi conti,   *42*
sì che, veduto il ver di questa corte,
  la spene, che là giù bene innamora,
  in te e in altrui di ciò conforte,   *45*
dì quel ch'ell' è, dì come se ne 'nfiora
  la mente tua, e dì onde a te venne."
  Così seguì 'l secondo lume ancora.   *48*
E quella pïa che guidò le penne
  de le mie ali a così alto volo,
  a la risposta così mi prevenne: *51*

so did I see the one great and glorious prince received by the other, praising the food which feeds them thereabove. But when the joyful greeting was completed, each stopped silent *coram me*, so aflame that it overcame my sight. Then Beatrice, smiling, said, "Illustrious life, by whom the bounty of our Court was chronicled, make hope resound in this height; you can, who did figure it all those times when Jesus showed most favor to the three."

"Lift up your head and see that you reassure yourself, for that which comes up here from the mortal world must be ripened in our beams." This assurance came to me from the second fire; whereon I lifted up my eyes unto the hills which had bent them down before with excess of weight.

"Since, of His grace, our Emperor wills that you, before your death, come face to face with His Counts in His most secret hall, so that, having seen the truth of this Court, you may strengthen in yourself and others the Hope which there below rightly enamors, say what it is, and how your mind blossoms with it, and say whence it came to you." Thus the second light continued further.

And that compassionate one, who had guided the feathers of my wings to such lofty flight, anticipated my reply thus,

"La Chiesa militante alcun figliuolo
 non ha con più speranza, com' è scritto
 nel Sol che raggia tutto nostro stuolo: *54*
però li è conceduto che d'Egitto
 vegna in Ierusalemme per vedere,
 anzi che 'l militar li sia prescritto.   *57*
Li altri due punti, che non per sapere
 son dimandati, ma perch' ei rapporti
 quanto questa virtù t'è in piacere,   *60*
a lui lasc' io, ché non li saran forti
 né di iattanza; ed elli a ciò risponda,
 e la grazia di Dio ciò li comporti."   *63*
Come discente ch'a dottor seconda
 pronto e libente in quel ch'elli è esperto,
 perché la sua bontà si disasconda,   *66*
"Spene," diss' io, "è uno attender certo
 de la gloria futura, il qual produce
 grazia divina e precedente merto.   *69*
Da molte stelle mi vien questa luce;
 ma quei la distillò nel mio cor pria
 che fu sommo cantor del sommo duce.   *72*
'Sperino in te,' ne la sua tëodia
 dice, 'color che sanno il nome tuo':
 e chi nol sa, s'elli ha la fede mia?   *75*
Tu mi stillasti, con lo stillar suo,
 ne la pistola poi; sì ch'io son pieno,
 e in altrui vostra pioggia repluo."   *78*
Mentr' io diceva, dentro al vivo seno
 di quello incendio tremolava un lampo
 sùbito e spesso a guisa di baleno.   *81*

"The Church Militant has not any child
possessed of more hope, as is written in the
Sun which irradiates all our host; therefore
is it granted him to come from Egypt to
Jerusalem, that he may see, before his term of
warfare is completed. The other two points
which are asked, not for sake of knowing, but
that he may report how greatly this virtue is
pleasing to you, I leave to him, for they will
not be difficult to him, nor of vainglory; and
let him answer thereto, and may the grace of
God concede this to him."

As the pupil who answers the teacher,
ready and eager in that wherein he is expert,
so that his worth may be disclosed, "Hope," I
said, "is a sure expectation of future glory,
which divine grace produces, and preceding
merit. From many stars this light comes to
me, but he first instilled it into my heart who
was the supreme singer of the Supreme
Leader. 'Let them hope in Thee who know
Thy name,' he says in his divine song, and
who knows it not, if he have my faith. You
afterwards in your Epistle did instill it into
me, together with his instilling, so that I am
full, and pour again your shower upon
others."

While I was speaking, within the living
bosom of that fire trembled a flash, sudden
and frequent, like lightning;

Indi spirò: "L'amore ond' ïo avvampo
  ancor ver' la virtù che mi seguette
  infin la palma e a l'uscir del campo,   *84*
vuol ch'io respiri a te che ti dilette
  di lei; ed emmi a grato che tu diche
  quello che la speranza ti 'mpromette."   *87*
E io: "Le nove e le scritture antiche
  pongon lo segno, ed esso lo mi addita,
  de l'anime che Dio s'ha fatte amiche.   *90*
Dice Isaia che ciascuna vestita
  ne la sua terra fia di doppia vesta:
  e la sua terra è questa dolce vita;   *93*
e 'l tuo fratello assai vie più digesta,
  là dove tratta de le bianche stole,
  questa revelazion ci manifesta."   *96*
E prima, appresso al fin d'este parole,
  "Sperent in te" di sopr' a noi s'udì;
  a che rispuoser tutte le carole.   *99*
Poscia tra esse un lume si schiarì
  sì che, se 'l Cancro avesse un tal cristallo,
  l'inverno avrebbe un mese d'un sol dì.   *102*
E come surge e va ed entra in ballo
  vergine lieta, sol per fare onore
  a la novizia, non per alcun fallo,   *105*
così vid' io lo schiarato splendore
  venire a' due che si volgieno a nota
  qual conveniesi al loro ardente amore.   *108*
Misesi lì nel canto e ne la rota;
  e la mia donna in lor tenea l'aspetto,
  pur come sposa tacita e immota.   *111*

then it breathed forth, "The love whereof I am still aflame toward that virtue which followed me even to the palm and the departure from the field wills that I breathe again to you, who do delight in it; and it is my pleasure that you tell that which Hope promises to you."

And I, "The new and the old Scriptures set up the token of the souls that God has made His friends, and this points it out to me. Isaiah says that each one shall be clothed in his own land with a double garment, and his own land is this sweet life; and your brother, where he treats of the white robes, makes manifest this revelation to us far more expressly."

At first, close on the end of these words, *"Sperent in te"* was heard above us, to which all the carols made answer; then one light among them shone out so bright that if the Crab had one such crystal, winter would have a month of one unbroken day. And as a glad maiden rises and goes and enters into the dance, only to do honor to the bride, not for any failing, so did I see the brightened splendor approach the two who were wheeling to such a song as befitted their burning love. It joined there in the singing and the wheeling, and my lady kept her gaze upon them, even as a bride silent and motionless.

"Questi è colui che giacque sopra 'l petto
  del nostro pellicano, e questi fue
  di su la croce al grande officio eletto."   *114*
La donna mia così; né però piùe
  mosser la vista sua di stare attenta
  poscia che prima le parole sue.   *117*
Qual è colui ch'adocchia e s'argomenta
  di vedere eclissar lo sole un poco,
  che, per veder, non vedente diventa;   *120*
tal mi fec' ïo a quell' ultimo foco
  mentre che detto fu: "Perché t'abbagli
  per veder cosa che qui non ha loco?   *123*
In terra è terra il mio corpo, e saragli
  tanto con li altri, che 'l numero nostro
  con l'etterno proposito s'agguagli.   *126*
Con le due stole nel beato chiostro
  son le due luci sole che saliro;
  e questo apporterai nel mondo vostro."   *129*
A questa voce l'infiammato giro
  si quïetò con esso il dolce mischio
  che si facea nel suon del trino spiro,   *132*
sì come, per cessar fatica o rischio,
  li remi, pria ne l'acqua ripercossi,
  tutti si posano al sonar d'un fischio.   *135*
Ahi quanto ne la mente mi commossi,
  quando mi volsi per veder Beatrice,
  per non poter veder, benché io fossi
presso di lei, e nel mondo felice!   *139*

"This is he who lay upon the breast of our Pelican, and this is he who was chosen from upon the Cross for the great office." Thus my lady; but no more after than before her words did she move her gaze from its fixed attention.

As is he who gazes and strains to see the sun a little eclipsed, and who through seeing becomes sightless, so did I become in respect to that last fire, till it was said, "Why do you dazzle yourself in order to see that which has here no place? On earth my body is earth, and there it shall be with the rest, until our number equals the eternal purpose. With the two robes in the blessed cloister are those two lights only which ascended; and this you shall carry back into your world."

At these words the flaming circle fell silent, together with the sweet mingling made within the sound of the trinal breath, even as, to avoid fatigue or danger, oars till then struck through the water, stop all at once at the sound of a whistle.

Ah! how greatly was I stirred in my mind when I turned to see Beatrice, at not being able to see, although I was near her, and in the world of bliss.

PARADISO

Mentr' io dubbiava per lo viso spento,
de la fulgida fiamma che lo spense
uscì un spiro che mi fece attento,   *3*
dicendo: "Intanto che tu ti risense
de la vista che haï in me consunta,
ben è che ragionando la compense.   *6*
Comincia dunque; e dì ove s'appunta
l'anima tua, e fa ragion che sia
la vista in te smarrita e non defunta: *9*
perché la donna che per questa dia
regïon ti conduce, ha ne lo sguardo
la virtù ch'ebbe la man d'Anania."   *12*
Io dissi: "Al suo piacere e tosto e tardo
vegna remedio a li occhi, che fuor porte
quand' ella entrò col foco ond' io sempr' ardo.   *15*
Lo ben che fa contenta questa corte,
Alfa e O è di quanta scrittura
mi legge Amore o lievemente o forte."   *18*

CANTO XXVI

While i was apprehensive because of my quenched sight, there issued forth from the effulgent flame that quenched it a breath that made me attentive, and it said, "Until you have again the sense of sight which you have consumed in me, it is well that you compensate it by discourse. Begin then, and say on what aim your soul is set; and be assured that your sight in you is confounded, not destroyed; for the lady who guides you through this divine region has in her look the power which the hand of Ananias had."

And I said, "At her good pleasure, soon or late, let succor come to the eyes which were the doors when she did enter with the fire wherewith I ever burn. The good which satisfies this Court is Alpha and Omega of all the scripture which Love reads to me, either low or loud."

Quella medesma voce che paura
   tolta m'avea del sùbito abbarbaglio,
   di ragionare ancor mi mise in cura;   *21*
e disse: "Certo a più angusto vaglio
   ti conviene schiarar: dicer convienti
   chi drizzò l'arco tuo a tal berzaglio."   *24*
E io: "Per filosofici argomenti
   e per autorità che quinci scende
   cotale amor convien che in me si 'mprenti: *27*
ché 'l bene, in quanto ben, come s'intende,
   così accende amore, e tanto maggio
   quanto più di bontate in sé comprende.   *30*
Dunque a l'essenza ov' è tanto avvantaggio,
   che ciascun ben che fuor di lei si trova
   altro non è ch'un lume di suo raggio,   *33*
più che in altra convien che si mova
   la mente, amando, di ciascun che cerne
   il vero in che si fonda questa prova.   *36*
Tal vero a l'intelletto mïo sterne
   colui che mi dimostra il primo amore
   di tutte le sustanze sempiterne.   *39*
Sternel la voce del verace autore,
   che dice a Moïsè, di sé parlando:
   'Io ti farò vedere ogne valore.'   *42*
Sternilmi tu ancora, incominciando
   l'alto preconio che grida l'arcano
   di qui là giù sovra ogne altro bando."   *45*
E io udi': "Per intelletto umano
   e per autoritadi a lui concorde
   d'i tuoi amori a Dio guarda il sovrano.   *48*

The same voice that had delivered me from my fear at the sudden dazzlement gave me concern to speak again; and it said, "Assuredly you must sift with a finer sieve: you must tell who directed your bow to such a target."

And I, "By philosophic arguments, and by authority that descends from here, such love must needs imprint itself on me; for the good, inasmuch as it is good, kindles love in proportion as it is understood, and so much the more the more of good it contains in itself. Therefore, to that Essence wherein is such supremacy that whatsoever good be found outside of It is naught else save a beam of Its own radiance, more than to any other must the mind be moved, in love, of whoever discerns the truth on which this proof is founded. Such a truth he makes plain to my intelligence who demonstrates to me the first love of all the eternal substances. The voice of the veracious Author makes it plain where, speaking of Himself, He says to Moses, 'I will make you see all goodness.' You also set it forth to me in the beginning of your sublime proclamation, which more than any other heralding, declares below the mystery of this place on high."

And I heard, "On the ground of human reason and of the authorities concordant with it, the highest of all your loves looks to God;

Ma dì ancor se tu senti altre corde
  tirarti verso lui, sì che tu suone
  con quanti denti questo amor ti morde."   *51*
Non fu latente la santa intenzione
  de l'aguglia di Cristo, anzi m'accorsi
  dove volea menar mia professione.   *54*
Però ricominciai: "Tutti quei morsi
  che posson far lo cor volgere a Dio,
  a la mia caritate son concorsi: *57*
ché l'essere del mondo e l'esser mio,
  la morte ch'el sostenne perch' io viva,
  e quel che spera ogne fedel com' io,   *60*
con la predetta conoscenza viva,
  tratto m'hanno del mar de l'amor torto,
  e del diritto m'han posto a la riva.   *63*
Le fronde onde s'infronda tutto l'orto
  de l'ortolano etterno, am' io cotanto
  quanto da lui a lor di bene è porto."   *66*
Sì com' io tacqui, un dolcissimo canto
  risonò per lo cielo, e la mia donna
  dicea con li altri: "Santo, santo, santo!"   *69*
E come a lume acuto si disonna
  per lo spirto visivo che ricorre
  a lo splendor che va di gonna in gonna,   *72*
e lo svegliato ciò che vede aborre,
  sì nescïa è la sùbita vigilia
  fin che la stimativa non soccorre;   *75*
così de li occhi miei ogne quisquilia
  fugò Beatrice col raggio d'i suoi,
  che rifulgea da più di mille milia: *78*

but tell me also if you feel other cords draw
you toward Him, so that you declare with
how many teeth this love grips you."

The holy intention of the Eagle of Christ
was not hidden, indeed it was plain to me
whither he would direct my profession.
Therefore I began again, "All those things
whose bite can make the heart turn to God
have wrought together in my love; for the
being of the world and my own being, the
death that He sustained that I might live, and
that which every believer hopes, as do I, with
the living assurance of which I spoke, have
drawn me from the sea of perverse love and
placed me on the shore of right love. The
leaves wherewith all the garden of the Eternal
Gardener is enleaved I love in measure of the
good borne unto them from Him."

As soon as I was silent a most sweet song
resounded through the heaven, and my lady
sang with the rest, "Holy, Holy, Holy!" And
as sleep is broken by a piercing light when
the visual spirit runs to meet the splendor that
goes from tunic to tunic, and he who awakens
shrinks from what he sees, so ignorant is his
sudden wakening, until his judgment comes
to his aid; thus Beatrice chased away every
mote from my eyes with the radiance of her
own, which shone more than a thousand
miles;

onde mei che dinanzi vidi poi;
   e quasi stupefatto domandai
   d'un quarto lume ch'io vidi tra noi.   *81*
E la mia donna: "Dentro da quei rai
   vagheggia il suo fattor l'anima prima
   che la prima virtù creasse mai."   *84*
Come la fronda che flette la cima
   nel transito del vento, e poi si leva
   per la propria virtù che la soblima,   *87*
fec' io in tanto in quant' ella diceva,
   stupendo, e poi mi rifece sicuro
   un disio di parlare ond' ïo ardeva.   *90*
E cominciai: "O pomo che maturo
   solo prodotto fosti, o padre antico
   a cui ciascuna sposa è figlia e nuro,   *93*
divoto quanto posso a te supplìco
   perché mi parli: tu vedi mia voglia,
   e per udirti tosto non la dico."   *96*
Talvolta un animal coverto broglia,
   sì che l'affetto convien che si paia
   per lo seguir che face a lui la 'nvoglia;   *99*
e similmente l'anima primaia
   mi facea trasparer per la coverta
   quant' ella a compiacermi venìa gaia.   *102*
Indi spirò: "Sanz' essermi proferta
   da te, la voglia tua discerno meglio
   che tu qualunque cosa t'è più certa;   *105*
perch' io la veggio nel verace speglio
   che fa di sé pareglio a l'altre cose,
   e nulla face lui di sé pareglio.   *108*

so that I then saw better than before; and as one amazed I asked concerning a fourth light which I saw with us. And my lady, "Within those rays the first soul which the First Power ever created gazes with love upon its Maker."

As the bough which bends its top at passing of the wind, and then uplifts itself by its own virtue which raises it, so did I, in amazement, while she was speaking, and then a desire to speak, wherewith I was burning, gave me assurance again, and I began, "O fruit that were alone produced mature, O ancient father of whom every bride is daughter and daughter-in-law, devoutly as I can, I implore you that you speak to me: you see my wish, and that I may hear you sooner I do not tell it."

Sometimes an animal that is covered so stirs that its impulse must needs be apparent, since what envelops it follows its movements: in like manner that first soul showed me, through its covering, how joyously it came to do me pleasure. Then it breathed forth, "Without its being told to me by you, I discern your wish better than you whatever is most certain to you, for I see it in the truthful Mirror which makes of Itself a reflection of all else, while of It nothing makes itself the reflection.

Tu vuogli udir quant' è che Dio mi puose
  ne l'eccelso giardino, ove costei
  a così lunga scala ti dispuose,   *111*
e quanto fu diletto a li occhi miei,
  e la propria cagion del gran disdegno,
  e l'idïoma ch'usai e che fei.   *114*
Or, figliuol mio, non il gustar del legno
  fu per sé la cagion di tanto essilio,
  ma solamente il trapassar del segno.   *117*
Quindi onde mosse tua donna Virgilio,
  quattromilia trecento e due volumi
  di sol desiderai questo concilio;   *120*
e vidi lui tornare a tutt' i lumi
  de la sua strada novecento trenta
  fïate, mentre ch'ïo in terra fu'mi.   *123*
La lingua ch'io parlai fu tutta spenta
  innanzi che a l'ovra inconsummabile
  fosse la gente di Nembròt attenta: *126*
ché nullo effetto mai razïonabile,
  per lo piacere uman che rinovella
  seguèndo il cielo, sempre fu durabile.   *129*
Opera naturale è ch'uom favella;
  ma così o così, natura lascia
  poi fare a voi secondo che v'abbella.   *132*
Pria ch'i' scendessi a l'infernale ambascia,
  I s'appellava in terra il sommo bene
  onde vien la letizia che mi fascia;   *135*
e *El* si chiamò poi: e ciò convene,
  ché l'uso d'i mortali è come fronda
  in ramo, che sen va e altra vene.   *138*

You wish to know how long it is since God placed me in the lofty garden wherein this lady prepared you for so long a stair; and how long it was a delight to my eyes; and the true cause of the great wrath; and the idiom which I used and shaped. Now know, my son, that the tasting of the tree was not in itself the cause of so long an exile, but solely the overpassing of the bound. In the place whence your lady dispatched Virgil, I longed for this assembly during four thousand three hundred and two revolutions of the sun; and while I was on earth I saw him return to all the lights of his path nine hundred and thirty times. The tongue which I spoke was all extinct before the people of Nimrod attempted their unaccomplishable work; for never was any product of reason durable forever, because of human liking, which alters, following the heavens. That man should speak is nature's doing, but whether thus or thus, nature then leaves you to follow your own pleasure. Before I descended to the anguish of Hell the Supreme Good from whom comes the joy that swathes me was named *I* on earth; and later He was called *El*: and that must needs be, for the usage of mortals is as a leaf on a branch, which goes away and another comes.

Nel monte che si leva più da l'onda,
　　fu' io, con vita pura e disonesta,
　　da la prim' ora a quella che seconda,
　　come 'l sol muta quadra, l'ora sesta." 　　*142*

On the mountain which rises highest from
the sea I lived pure, then guilty, from the first
hour to that which follows, when the sun
changes quadrant, next upon the sixth.

PARADISO

"Al Padre, al Figlio, a lo Spirito Santo,"
  cominciò, "gloria!" tutto 'l paradiso,
  sì che m'inebrïava il dolce canto.   *3*
Ciò ch'io vedeva mi sembiava un riso
  de l'universo; per che mia ebbrezza
  intrava per l'udire e per lo viso.   *6*
Oh gioia! oh ineffabile allegrezza!
  oh vita intègra d'amore e di pace!
  oh sanza brama sicura ricchezza!   *9*
Dinanzi a li occhi miei le quattro face
  stavano accese, e quella che pria venne
  incominciò a farsi più vivace,   *12*
e tal ne la sembianza sua divenne,
  qual diverrebbe Iove, s'elli e Marte
  fossero augelli e cambiassersi penne.   *15*
La provedenza, che quivi comparte
  vice e officio, nel beato coro
  silenzio posto avea da ogne parte,   *18*

CANTO XXVII

"Glory be to the Father, to the Son, and to the Holy Spirit!" all Paradise began, so that the sweet song held me rapt. What I saw seemed to me a smile of the universe, so that my rapture entered both by hearing and by sight. O joy! O ineffable gladness! O life entire of love and of peace! O wealth secure without longing!

Before my eyes the four torches stood enkindled, and that which had come first began to make itself more vivid, and in its aspect became as would Jupiter if he and Mars were birds and should exchange plumage. The Providence which there assigns turn and office had imposed silence on the blessed choir on every side,

quand' ïo udi': "Se io mi trascoloro,
   non ti maravigliar, ché, dicend' io,
   vedrai trascolorar tutti costoro.   *21*
Quelli ch'usurpa in terra il luogo mio,
   il luogo mio, il luogo mio che vaca
   ne la presenza del Figliuol di Dio,   *24*
fatt' ha del cimitero mio cloaca
   del sangue e de la puzza; onde 'l perverso
   che cadde di qua sù, là giù si placa."   *27*
Di quel color che per lo sole avverso
   nube dipigne da sera e da mane,
   vid' ïo allora tutto 'l ciel cosperso.   *30*
E come donna onesta che permane
   di sé sicura, e per l'altrui fallanza,
   pur ascoltando, timida si fane,   *33*
così Beatrice trasmutò sembianza;
   e tale eclissi credo che 'n ciel fue
   quando patì la suprema possanza.   *36*
Poi procedetter le parole sue
   con voce tanto da sé trasmutata,
   che la sembianza non si mutò piùe: *39*
"Non fu la sposa di Cristo allevata
   del sangue mio, di Lin, di quel di Cleto,
   per essere ad acquisto d'oro usata;   *42*
ma per acquisto d'esto viver lieto
   e Sisto e Pïo e Calisto e Urbano
   sparser lo sangue dopo molto fleto.   *45*
Non fu nostra intenzion ch'a destra mano
   d'i nostri successor parte sedesse,
   parte da l'altra del popol cristiano;   *48*

when I heard, "If I change color, marvel not, for, as I speak, you shall see all these change color. He who on earth usurps my place, my place, my place, which in the sight of the Son of God is vacant, has made my burial-ground a sewer of blood and of stench, so that the Perverse One who fell from here above takes comfort there below."

With that color which, by reason of the opposite sun, paints the cloud at evening and at morning, I then saw the whole heaven overspread. And as a chaste lady who is sure of herself, and at another's fault, only hearing of it, becomes timid, so did Beatrice change her semblance; and such, I believe, was the eclipse in heaven when the Supreme Power suffered.

Then his words continued, in a voice so altered from itself that his looks were not more changed, "The spouse of Christ was not nurtured on my blood and that of Linus and of Clerus, to be employed for gain of gold; but for gain of this happy life Sixtus and Pius and Calixtus and Urban shed their blood after much weeping. It was not our purpose that one part of the Christian people should sit on the right of our successors, and one part on the left;

né che le chiavi che mi fuor concesse,
   divenisser signaculo in vessillo
   che contra battezzati combattesse;   *51*
né ch'io fossi figura di sigillo
   a privilegi venduti e mendaci,
   ond' io sovente arrosso e disfavillo.   *54*
In vesta di pastor lupi rapaci
   si veggion di qua sù per tutti i paschi:
   o difesa di Dio, perché pur giaci?   *57*
Del sangue nostro Caorsini e Guaschi
   s'apparecchian di bere: o buon principio,
   a che vil fine convien che tu caschi!   *60*
Ma l'alta provedenza, che con Scipio
   difese a Roma la gloria del mondo,
   soccorrà tosto, sì com' io concipio;   *63*
e tu, figliuol, che per lo mortal pondo
   ancor giù tornerai, apri la bocca,
   e non asconder quel ch'io non ascondo."   *66*
Sì come di vapor gelati fiocca
   in giuso l'aere nostro, quando 'l corno
   de la capra del ciel col sol si tocca,   *69*
in sù vid' io così l'etera addorno
   farsi e fioccar di vapor trïunfanti
   che fatto avien con noi quivi soggiorno.   *72*
Lo viso mio seguiva i suoi sembianti,
   e seguì fin che 'l mezzo, per lo molto,
   li tolse il trapassar del più avanti.   *75*
Onde la donna, che mi vide assolto
   de l'attendere in sù, mi disse: "Adima
   il viso e guarda come tu se' vòlto."   *78*

nor that the keys which were committed to me should become the ensign on a banner for warfare on the baptized; nor that I should be made a figure on a seal to sold and lying privileges, whereat I often blush and flash. Rapacious wolves, in shepherd's garb, are seen from here above in all the pastures: O defense of God, wherefore dost thou yet lie still? Cahorsines and Gascons make ready to drink our blood. O good beginning, to what vile ending must you fall! But the high Providence, which with Scipio defended for Rome the glory of the world, will succor speedily, as I conceive. And you, my son, who, because of your mortal weight will again return below, open your mouth and do not hide what I hide not."

Even as our air, when the horn of the heavenly Goat is touched by the sun, flakes down frozen vapors, so I saw the ether thus adorned, flaking upwards triumphal vapors which had made sojourn with us there. My sight was following their semblances, and followed, till the intermediate space became so great that it took from it the power of passing farther onward. Whereon my lady, who saw me freed from gazing upwards, said to me, "Cast your sight down and see how far you have revolved."

Da l'ora ch'ïo avea guardato prima
  i' vidi mosso me per tutto l'arco
  che fa dal mezzo al fine il primo clima;   *81*
sì ch'io vedea di là da Gade il varco
  folle d'Ulisse, e di qua presso il lito
  nel qual si fece Europa dolce carco.   *84*
E più mi fora discoverto il sito
  di questa aiuola; ma 'l sol procedea
  sotto i mie' piedi un segno e più partito.   *87*
La mente innamorata, che donnea
  con la mia donna sempre, di ridure
  ad essa li occhi più che mai ardea;   *90*
e se natura o arte fé pasture
  da pigliare occhi, per aver la mente,
  in carne umana o ne le sue pitture,   *93*
tutte adunate, parrebber nïente
  ver' lo piacer divin che mi refulse,
  quando mi volsi al suo viso ridente.   *96*
E la virtù che lo sguardo m'indulse,
  del bel nido di Leda mi divelse
  e nel ciel velocissimo m'impulse.   *99*
Le parti sue vivissime ed eccelse
  sì uniforme son, ch'i' non so dire
  qual Bëatrice per loco mi scelse.   *102*
Ma ella, che vedëa 'l mio disire,
  incominciò, ridendo tanto lieta,
  che Dio parea nel suo volto gioire: *105*
"La natura del mondo, che quïeta
  il mezzo e tutto l'altro intorno move,
  quinci comincia come da sua meta;   *108*

306

From the time when I had looked before, I saw that I had moved through the whole arc which the first climate makes from its middle to its end; so that, on the one hand, beyond Cadiz, I saw the mad track of Ulysses, and on the other nearly to the shore where Europa made herself a sweet burden; and more of the space of this little threshing-floor would have been disclosed to me, but the sun was proceeding beneath my feet and was a sign and more away.

My enamored mind, which ever pays court to my lady, was more than ever burning to bring back my eyes to her; and if nature or art ever made baits to take the eye so as to possess the mind, in human flesh or in its portraiture, all these together would seem as nothing beside the divine delight that glowed upon me when I turned to her smiling face. And the power which her look granted me drew me forth from the fair nest of Leda and thrust me into the swiftest of the heavens.

Its parts, most living and exalted, are so uniform that I cannot tell which of them Beatrice chose as a place for me. But she, who saw my longing, began, smiling so glad that God seemed to rejoice in her countenance, "The nature of the universe which holds the center quiet and moves all the rest around it, begins here as from its starting-point.

e questo cielo non ha altro dove
   che la mente divina, in che s'accende
   l'amor che 'l volge e la virtù ch'ei piove.   *111*
Luce e amor d'un cerchio lui comprende,
   sì come questo li altri; e quel precinto
   colui che 'l cinge solamente intende.   *114*
Non è suo moto per altro distinto,
   ma li altri son mensurati da questo,
   sì come diece da mezzo e da quinto;   *117*
e come il tempo tegna in cotal testo
   le sue radici e ne li altri le fronde,
   omai a te può esser manifesto.   *120*
Oh cupidigia, che i mortali affonde
   sì sotto te, che nessuno ha podere
   di trarre li occhi fuor de le tue onde!   *123*
Ben fiorisce ne li uomini il volere;
   ma la pioggia continüa converte
   in bozzacchioni le sosine vere.   *126*
Fede e innocenza son reperte
   solo ne' parvoletti; poi ciascuna
   pria fugge che le guance sian coperte.   *129*
Tale, balbuzïendo ancor, digiuna,
   che poi divora, con la lingua sciolta,
   qualunque cibo per qualunque luna;   *132*
e tal, balbuzïendo, ama e ascolta
   la madre sua, che, con loquela intera,
   disïa poi di vederla sepolta.   *135*
Così si fa la pelle bianca nera
   nel primo aspetto de la bella figlia
   di quel ch'apporta mane e lascia sera.   *138*

And this heaven has no other *Where* than the divine mind, wherein is kindled the love that revolves it, and the virtue which it rains down. Light and love enclose it in a circle, as it does the others, and this engirdment He alone who girds it understands. Its motion is not determined by another's, but the others are measured by this, just as ten by its half and its fifth. And how time should have its roots in such a flower-pot, and in the others its leaves, may now be manifest to you.

"O greed, who do so plunge mortals in your depths that none has power to lift his eyes from your waves! The will blossoms well in men, but the continual rain turns the sound plums into blighted fruit. Faith and innocence are found only in little children; then each flies away before the cheeks are covered. One, so long as he lisps, keeps the fasts, who afterward, when his tongue is free, devours any food through any month; and one, while he lisps, loves his mother and listens to her, who afterward, when his speech is full, longs to see her buried. Thus the white skin turns black at the first sight of the fair daughter of him that brings morning and leaves evening.

Tu, perché non ti facci maraviglia,
   pensa che 'n terra non è chi governi;
   onde si svïa l'umana famiglia.   *141*
Ma prima che gennaio tutto si sverni
   per la centesma ch'è là giù negletta,
   raggeran sì questi cerchi superni,   *144*
che la fortuna che tanto s'aspetta,
   le poppe volgerà u' son le prore,
   sì che la classe correrà diretta;
e vero frutto verrà dopo 'l fiore."   *148*

That you marvel not at this, consider that on earth there is no one to govern, wherefore the human family goes thus astray. But before January be all unwintered, because of the hundredth part that is neglected below, these lofty circles shall so shine forth that the storm which has been so long awaited shall turn round the sterns to where the prows are, so that the fleet shall run straight; and good fruit shall follow on the flower."

PARADISO

Poscia che 'ncontro a la vita presente
   d'i miseri mortali aperse 'l vero
   quella che 'mparadisa la mia mente,   *3*
come in lo specchio fiamma di doppiero
   vede colui che se n'alluma retro,
   prima che l'abbia in vista o in pensiero,   *6*
e sé rivolge per veder se 'l vetro
   li dice il vero, e vede ch'el s'accorda
   con esso come nota con suo metro;   *9*
così la mia memoria si ricorda
   ch'io feci riguardando ne' belli occhi
   onde a pigliarmi fece Amor la corda.   *12*
E com' io mi rivolsi e furon tocchi
   li miei da ciò che pare in quel volume,
   quandunque nel suo giro ben s'adocchi,   *15*
un punto vidi che raggiava lume
   acuto sì, che 'l viso ch'elli affoca
   chiuder conviensi per lo forte acume;   *18*
e quale stella par quinci più poca,
   parrebbe luna, locata con esso
   come stella con stella si collòca.   *21*

CANTO XXVIII

AFTER SHE who imparadises my mind had declared the truth counter to the present life of wretched mortals, as one who sees in a mirror the flame of a torch which is lighted behind him before he has it in sight or in thought, and turns round to see if the glass tells him the truth, and sees that it accords with it as a song with its measure, so my memory recalls that I did, gazing into the beautiful eyes wherewith Love made the cord to capture me. And when I turned and my own were met by what appears in that revolving sphere whenever one gazes intently on its circling, I saw a point which radiated a light so keen that the eye on which it blazes needs must close because of its great keenness; and whatever star seems smallest from here would seem a moon if placed beside it like a star with neighboring star.

Forse cotanto quanto pare appresso
 alo cigner la luce che 'l dipigne
 quando 'l vapor che 'l porta più è spesso, *24*
distante intorno al punto un cerchio d'igne
 si girava sì ratto, ch'avria vinto
 quel moto che più tosto il mondo cigne; *27*
e questo era d'un altro circumcinto,
 e quel dal terzo, e 'l terzo poi dal quarto,
 dal quinto il quarto, e poi dal sesto il quinto. *30*
Sopra seguiva il settimo sì sparto
 già di larghezza, che 'l messo di Iuno
 intero a contenerlo sarebbe arto. *33*
Così l'ottavo e 'l nono; e ciascheduno
 più tardo si movea, secondo ch'era
 in numero distante più da l'uno; *36*
e quello avea la fiamma più sincera
 cui men distava la favilla pura,
 credo, però che più di lei s'invera. *39*
La donna mia, che mi vedëa in cura
 forte sospeso, disse: "Da quel punto
 depende il cielo e tutta la natura. *42*
Mira quel cerchio che più li è congiunto;
 e sappi che 'l suo muovere è sì tosto
 per l'affocato amore ond' elli è punto." *45*
E io a lei: "Se 'l mondo fosse posto
 con l'ordine ch'io veggio in quelle rote,
 sazio m'avrebbe ciò che m'è proposto; *48*
ma nel mondo sensibile si puote
 veder le volte tanto più divine,
 quant' elle son dal centro più remote. *51*

Perhaps as near as a halo seems to girdle
the light which paints it, when the vapor that
bears it is most dense, at such distance around
the point a circle of fire was whirling so
rapidly that it would have surpassed that mo-
tion which most swiftly girds the universe;
and this was girt around by another, and that
by a third, and the third by a fourth, by a fifth
the fourth, then by a sixth the fifth. Thereon
the seventh followed, now spread so wide that
the messenger of Juno entire would be too
narrow to contain it. So the eighth and the
ninth; and each was moving more slowly ac-
cording as it was in number more distant
from the unit. And that one had the clearest
flame from which the pure spark was least
distant, because, I believe, it partakes more of
its truth.

My lady, who saw me eager and in great
suspense, said, "On that point the heavens and
all nature are dependent. Look on that circle
which is most conjoined to it, and know that
its motion is so swift because of the burning
love whereby it is spurred."

And I to her, "If the universe were disposed
in the order which I see in those wheels, that
which is set before me would have satisfied
me. But in the world of sense the revolutions
may be seen so much the more divine as they
are more remote from the center.

Onde, se 'l mio disir dee aver fine
   in questo miro e angelico templo
   che solo amore e luce ha per confine,   *54*
udir convienmi ancor come l'essemplo
   e l'essemplare non vanno d'un modo,
   ché io per me indarno a ciò contemplo."   *57*
"Se li tuoi diti non sono a tal nodo
   sufficïenti, non è maraviglia:
   tanto, per non tentare, è fatto sodo!"   *60*
Così la donna mia; poi disse: "Piglia
   quel ch'io ti dicerò, se vuo' saziarti;
   e intorno da esso t'assottiglia.   *63*
Li cerchi corporai sono ampi e arti
   secondo il più e 'l men de la virtute
   che si distende per tutte lor parti.   *66*
Maggior bontà vuol far maggior salute;
   maggior salute maggior corpo cape,
   s'elli ha le parti igualmente compiute.   *69*
Dunque costui che tutto quanto rape
   l'altro universo seco, corrisponde
   al cerchio che più ama e che più sape: *72*
per che, se tu a la virtù circonde
   la tua misura, non a la parvenza
   de le sustanze che t'appaion tonde,   *75*
tu vederai mirabil consequenza
   di maggio a più e di minore a meno,
   in ciascun cielo, a süa intelligenza."   *78*
Come rimane splendido e sereno
   l'emisperio de l'aere, quando soffia
   Borea da quella guancia ond' è più leno,   *81*

Wherefore if my desire is to attain to its end in this wondrous and angelic temple which has only love and light for its confine, needs must I further hear why the model and the copy go not in one fashion, for by myself I contemplate this in vain."

"If your fingers are insufficient for such a knot, it is no wonder, so hard has it become by not being tried." So said my lady, then she continued, "Take that which I shall tell you, if you would be satisfied, and sharpen your wits about it. The material spheres are wide or narrow according to the more or less of virtue which is diffused through all their parts. Greater goodness must needs work greater weal; and the greater body, if it has its parts equally complete, contains the greater weal. Hence this sphere, which sweeps along with it all the rest of the universe, corresponds to the circle which loves most and knows most. Wherefore, if you draw your measure round the virtue, not the semblance, of the substances which appear to you in circles, you will see a wondrous correspondence of greater to more and of smaller to less, in each heaven with respect to its Intelligence."

As the hemisphere of the air remains splendid and serene when Boreas blows from his milder cheek,

per che si purga e risolve la roffia
   che pria turbava, sì che 'l ciel ne ride
   con le bellezze d'ogne sua paroffia;   *84*
così fec'ïo, poi che mi provide
   la donna mia del suo risponder chiaro,
   e come stella in cielo il ver si vide.   *87*
E poi che le parole sue restaro,
   non altrimenti ferro disfavilla
   che bolle, come i cerchi sfavillaro.   *90*
L'incendio suo seguiva ogne scintilla;
   ed eran tante, che 'l numero loro
   più che 'l doppiar de li scacchi s'inmilla.   *93*
Io sentiva osannar di coro in coro
   al punto fisso che li tiene a li *ubi*,
   e terrà sempre, ne' quai sempre fuoro.   *96*
E quella che vedëa i pensier dubi
   ne la mia mente, disse: "I cerchi primi
   t'hanno mostrato Serafi e Cherubi.   *99*
Così veloci seguono i suoi vimi,
   per somigliarsi al punto quanto ponno;
   e posson quanto a veder son soblimi.   *102*
Quelli altri amori che 'ntorno li vonno,
   si chiaman Troni del divino aspetto,
   per che 'l primo ternaro terminonno;   *105*
e dei saper che tutti hanno diletto
   quanto la sua veduta si profonda
   nel vero in che si queta ogne intelletto.   *108*
Quinci si può veder come si fonda
   l'esser beato ne l'atto che vede,
   non in quel ch'ama, che poscia seconda;   *111*

whereby the obscuring mist is cleared and dis-
solved, so that the heaven smiles to us with
the beauties of its every region, so I became
after my lady had provided me with her clear
answer, and like a star in heaven the truth
was seen.

And when she had paused in her speech,
not otherwise does molten iron throw out
sparks than the circles sparkled. Each spark
kept to its fiery ring, and they were so many
that their number stretches to more thousands
than the doubling of the chessboard. I heard
Hosannah sung from choir to choir to the
fixed point that holds them, and will forever
hold them at the *Ubi* in which they have ever
been. And she, who saw the questioning
thoughts within my mind, said, "The first
circles have shown to you the Seraphim and
the Cherubim. Thus swiftly they follow their
bonds, in order to liken themselves to the
point as most they can, and they can in pro-
portion as they are exalted in vision. Those
other loves who go round them are called
Thrones of the divine aspect, because they
terminated the first triad. And you should
know that all have delight in the measure of
the depth to which their sight penetrates the
Truth in which every intellect finds rest;
from which it may be seen that the state of
blessedness is founded on the act of vision,
not on that which loves, which follows after;

e del vedere è misura mercede,
  che grazia partorisce e buona voglia:
  così di grado in grado si procede.   *114*

L'altro ternaro, che così germoglia
  in questa primavera sempiterna
  che notturno Arïete non dispoglia,   *117*

perpetüalemente *'Osanna'* sberna
  con tre melode, che suonano in tree
  ordini di letizia onde s'interna.   *120*

In essa gerarcia son l'altre dee:
  prima Dominazioni, e poi Virtudi;
  l'ordine terzo di Podestadi èe.   *123*

Poscia ne' due penultimi tripudi
  Principati e Arcangeli si girano;
  l'ultimo è tutto d'Angelici ludi.   *126*

Questi ordini di sù tutti s'ammirano,
  e di giù vincon sì, che verso Dio
  tutti tirati sono e tutti tirano.   *129*

E Dïonisio con tanto disio
  a contemplar questi ordini si mise,
  che li nomò e distinse com' io.   *132*

Ma Gregorio da lui poi si divise;
  onde, sì tosto come li occhi aperse
  in questo ciel, di sé medesmo rise.   *135*

E se tanto secreto ver proferse
  mortale in terra, non voglio ch'ammiri:
  ché chi 'l vide qua sù gliel discoperse
con altro assai del ver di questi giri."   *139*

and the merit, to which grace and good will give birth, is the measure of their vision; thus, from grade to grade the progression goes.

"The next triad that thus flowers in this eternal spring which nightly Aries does not despoil perpetually sings Hosannah with three melodies which sound in the three orders of bliss that form the triad. In this hierarchy are the next divinities, first Dominions, then Virtues; and the third are Powers. Then in the two penultimate dances, the Principalities and Archangels circle; the last is wholly of Angelic sports. These orders all gaze upward and prevail downward, so that toward God all are drawn, and all do draw. And Dionysius with such great desire set himself to contemplate these orders that he named and distinguished them, as I: but Gregory afterward differed from him, wherefore, as soon as he opened his eyes in this heaven, he smiled at himself. And if a mortal declared on earth so much of secret truth, I would not have you wonder, for he who saw it here on high disclosed it to him, with much else of the truth about these circles."

PARADISO

Q<small>UANDO</small> <small>AMBEDUE</small> li figli di Latona,
  coperti del Montone e de la Libra,
  fanno de l'orizzonte insieme zona,   *3*
quant' è dal punto che 'l cenìt inlibra
  infin che l'uno e l'altro da quel cinto,
  cambiando l'emisperio, si dilibra,   *6*
tanto, col volto di riso dipinto,
  si tacque Bëatrice, riguardando
  fiso nel punto che m'avëa vinto.   *9*
Poi cominciò: "Io dico, e non dimando,
  quel che tu vuoli udir, perch' io l'ho visto
  là 've s'appunta ogne *ubi* e ogne *quando*.   *12*
Non per aver a sé di bene acquisto,
  ch'esser non può, ma perché suo splendore
  potesse, risplendendo, dir '*Subsisto*,'   *15*
in sua etternità di tempo fore,
  fuor d'ogne altro comprender, come i piacque,
  s'aperse in nuovi amor l'etterno amore.   *18*

322

CANTO XXIX

When the two children of Latona, covered by the Ram and by the Scales, make the horizon their belt at one same moment, as long as from the instant when the zenith holds them balanced till the one and the other, changing hemispheres, are unbalanced from that belt, for so long, her face illumined with a smile, was Beatrice silent, looking fixedly at the point which had overcome me. Then she began, "I tell, not ask, what you wish to hear, for I have seen it there where every *ubi* and every *quando* is centered. Not for gain of good unto Himself, which cannot be, but that His splendor might, in resplendence, say, *'Subsisto'*—in His eternity beyond time, beyond every other bound, as it pleased Him, the Eternal Love opened into new loves.

323

Né prima quasi torpente si giacque;
    ché né prima né poscia procedette
    lo discorrer di Dio sovra quest' acque.   *21*
Forma e materia, congiunte e purette,
    usciro ad esser che non avia fallo,
    come d'arco tricordo tre saette.   *24*
E come in vetro, in ambra o in cristallo
    raggio resplende sì, che dal venire
    a l'esser tutto non è intervallo,   *27*
così 'l triforme effetto del suo sire
    ne l'esser suo raggiò insieme tutto
    sanza distinzïone in essordire.   *30*
Concreato fu ordine e costrutto
    a le sustanze; e quelle furon cima
    nel mondo in che puro atto fu produtto;   *33*
pura potenza tenne la parte ima;
    nel mezzo strinse potenza con atto
    tal vime, che già mai non si divima.   *36*
Ieronimo vi scrisse lungo tratto
    di secoli de li angeli creati
    anzi che l'altro mondo fosse fatto;   *39*
ma questo vero è scritto in molti lati
    da li scrittor de lo Spirito Santo,
    e tu te n'avvedrai se bene agguati;   *42*
e anche la ragione il vede alquanto,
    che non concederebbe che ' motori
    sanza sua perfezion fosser cotanto.   *45*
Or sai tu dove e quando questi amori
    furon creati e come: sì che spenti
    nel tuo disïo già son tre ardori.   *48*

Nor before, as if inert, did He lie, for neither before nor after did the moving of God upon these waters proceed. Form and matter, conjoined and simple, came into being which had no defect, as three arrows from a three-stringed bow; and as in glass, in amber, or in crystal, a ray shines so that there is no interval between its coming and its pervading all, so did the triform effect ray forth from its Lord into its being, all at once, without distinction of beginning. Therewith order was created and ordained for the substances; and those in whom pure act was produced were the summit of the universe. Pure potentiality held the lowest place; in the middle such a bond tied up potentiality with act that it is never unbound. Jerome wrote for you of the angels as being created a long stretch of ages before aught else of the universe was made; but the truth I tell is written on many a page of the scribes of the Holy Spirit, and you shall be aware of it if you look well; and also reason sees it somewhat, which would not admit that the movers could be so long without their perfection. Now you know where and when these Loves were created, and how; so that three flames of your desire are already quenched.

Né giugneriesi, numerando, al venti
   sì tosto, come de li angeli parte
   turbò il suggetto d'i vostri alimenti.   *51*
L'altra rimase, e cominciò quest' arte
   che tu discerni, con tanto diletto,
   che mai da circüir non si diparte.   *54*
Principio del cader fu il maladetto
   superbir di colui che tu vedesti
   da tutti i pesi del mondo costretto.   *57*
Quelli che vedi qui furon modesti
   a riconoscer sé da la bontate
   che li avea fatti a tanto intender presti: *60*
per che le viste lor furo essaltate
   con grazia illuminante e con lor merto,
   sì c'hanno ferma e piena volontate;   *63*
e non voglio che dubbi, ma sia certo,
   che ricever la grazia è meritorio
   secondo che l'affetto l'è aperto.   *66*
Omai dintorno a questo consistorio
   puoi contemplare assai, se le parole
   mie son ricolte, sanz' altro aiutorio.   *69*
Ma perché 'n terra per le vostre scole
   si legge che l'angelica natura
   è tal, che 'ntende e si ricorda e vole,   *72*
ancor dirò, perché tu veggi pura
   la verità che là giù si confonde,
   equivocando in sì fatta lettura.   *75*
Queste sustanze, poi che fur gioconde
   de la faccia di Dio, non volser viso
   da essa, da cui nulla si nasconde: *78*

Then, sooner than one might count to
twenty, a part of the Angels disturbed the
substrate of your elements. The rest remained
and with such great delight began this art
which you behold that they never cease from
circling. The origin of the fall was the ac-
cursed pride of him whom you have seen con-
strained by all the weights of the universe.
Those whom you see here were modest to
recognize their being as from the Goodness
which had made them apt for intelligence so
great: wherefore their vision was exalted with
illuminating grace and with their merit, so
that they have their will full and established.
And I would not have you doubt, but be as-
sured that to receive grace is meritorious, in
proportion as the affection is open to it.

"By now, if you have taken in my words,
you may contemplate much in regard to this
consistory without more help. But since it is
taught in your schools on earth that the an-
gelic nature is such that it understands and
remembers and wills, I will speak further, in
order that you may see in purity the truth
that down there is confounded by the equivo-
cation in such like teaching. These substances,
since first they were gladdened by the face of
God, have never turned their eyes from It,
wherefrom nothing is concealed;

però non hanno vedere interciso
  da novo obietto, e però non bisogna
  rememorar per concetto diviso;   *81*
sì che là giù, non dormendo, si sogna,
  credendo e non credendo dicer vero;
  ma ne l'uno è più colpa e più vergogna.   *84*
Voi non andate giù per un sentiero
  filosofando: tanto vi trasporta
  l'amor de l'apparenza e 'l suo pensiero!   *87*
E ancor questo qua sù si comporta
  con men disdegno che quando è posposta
  la divina Scrittura o quando è torta.   *90*
Non vi si pensa quanto sangue costa
  seminarla nel mondo e quanto piace
  chi umilmente con essa s'accosta.   *93*
Per apparer ciascun s'ingegna e face
  sue invenzioni; e quelle son trascorse
  da' predicanti e 'l Vangelio si tace.   *96*
Un dice che la luna si ritorse
  ne la passion di Cristo e s'interpuose,
  per che 'l lume del sol giù non si porse;   *99*
e mente, ché la luce si nascose
  da sé: però a li Spani e a l'Indi
  come a' Giudei tale eclissi rispuose.   *102*
Non ha Fiorenza tanti Lapi e Bindi
  quante sì fatte favole per anno
  in pergamo si gridan quinci e quindi: *105*
sì che le pecorelle, che non sanno,
  tornan del pasco pasciute di vento,
  e non le scusa non veder lo danno.   *108*

so that their sight is never intercepted by a
new object, and therefore they have no need
to remember by reason of interrupted concept.
Thus down there men dream while awake,
believing or not believing that they speak
truth—but in the one case is the greater blame
and shame. You mortals do not proceed along
one same path in philosophizing, so much
does the love of show and the thought of it
carry you away; and even this is borne with
less anger up here than when the Divine
Scripture is set aside or when it is perverted.
They think not there how much blood it costs
to sow it in the world, nor how much he
pleases who humbly keeps close to it. Each one
strives for display and makes his own inven
tions, and these are treated of by the preachers,
and the Gospel is silent. One says that at
Christ's passion the moon turned back and in-
terposed itself, so that the light of the sun did
not reach below—and he lies, for the light it-
self hid itself, so that this eclipse took place for
the Spaniards and the Indians, as well as for the
Jews. Florence has not so many Lapos and
Bindos as fables such as these that are shouted
the year long from the pulpits on every side;
so that the poor sheep, who know naught, re-
turn from the pasture fed with wind—and
not seeing the harm does not excuse them.

Non disse Cristo al suo primo convento:
  'Andate, e predicate al mondo ciance';
  ma diede lor verace fondamento;   *111*
e quel tanto sonò ne le sue guance,
  sì ch'a pugnar per accender la fede
  de l'Evangelio fero scudo e lance.   *114*
Ora si va con motti e con iscede
  a predicare, e pur che ben si rida,
  gonfia il cappuccio e più non si richiede.   *117*
Ma tale uccel nel becchetto s'annida,
  che se 'l vulgo il vedesse, vederebbe
  la perdonanza di ch'el si confida: *120*
per cui tanta stoltezza in terra crebbe,
  che, sanza prova d'alcun testimonio,
  ad ogne promession si correrebbe.   *123*
Di questo ingrassa il porco sant' Antonio,
  e altri assai che sono ancor più porci,
  pagando di moneta sanza conio.   *126*
Ma perché siam digressi assai, ritorci
  li occhi oramai verso la dritta strada,
  sì che la via col tempo si raccorci.   *129*
Questa natura sì oltre s'ingrada
  in numero, che mai non fu loquela
  né concetto mortal che tanto vada;   *132*
e se tu guardi quel che si revela
  per Danïel, vedrai che 'n sue migliaia
  determinato numero si cela.   *135*
La prima luce, che tutta la raia,
  per tanti modi in essa si recepe,
  quanti son li splendori a chi s'appaia.   *138*

Christ did not say to his first company, 'Go and preach idle stories to the world,' but he gave to them the true foundation; and that alone sounded on their lips, so that to fight for kindling of the faith they made shield and lance of the Gospel. Now men go forth to preach with jests and with buffooneries, and so there be only a good laugh, the cowl puffs up and nothing more is asked. But such a bird nests in the hood's tail that if the people saw it, they would see what pardons they are trusting in; from which such folly has grown on earth that without proof of any testimony they would flock to every promise. On this the pig of St. Anthony fattens, and others also, who are far more pigs, paying with money that has no stamp of coinage.

"But since we have digressed enough, turn back your eyes now to the true path, so that the way be shortened with the time. This nature extends so exceedingly in number that never was there speech or mortal concept that might advance so far; and if you look at that which is revealed by Daniel, you will see that in his thousands no definite number is to be found. The Primal Light that irradiates them all is received by them in as many ways as are the splendors to which It joins Itself.

Onde, però che a l'atto che concepe
    segue l'affetto, d'amar la dolcezza
    diversamente in essa ferve e tepe.   *141*
Vedi l'eccelso omai e la larghezza
    de l'etterno valor, poscia che tanti
    speculi fatti s'ha in che si spezza,
uno manendo in sé come davanti."   *145*

Wherefore, since the affection follows upon the act of conceiving, the sweetness of love glows variously in them, more and less. Behold now the height and breadth of the Eternal Goodness, since it has made itself so many mirrors wherein it is reflected, remaining in itself One as before."

PARADISO

Forse semilia miglia di lontano
  ci ferve l'ora sesta, e questo mondo
  china già l'ombra quasi al letto piano,   *3*
quando 'l mezzo del cielo, a noi profondo,
  comincia a farsi tal, ch'alcuna stella
  perde il parere infino a questo fondo;   *6*
e come vien la chiarissima ancella
  del sol più oltre, così 'l ciel si chiude
  di vista in vista infino a la più bella.   *9*
Non altrimenti il trïunfo che lude
  sempre dintorno al punto che mi vinse,
  parendo inchiuso da quel ch'elli 'nchiude,   *12*
a poco a poco al mio veder si stinse:
  per che tornar con li occhi a Bëatrice
  nulla vedere e amor mi costrinse.   *15*
Se quanto infino a qui di lei si dice
  fosse conchiuso tutto in una loda,
  poca sarebbe a fornir questa vice.   *18*

CANTO XXX

THE SIXTH hour is glowing perhaps six thousand miles away, and this world already slopes its shadow almost to a level bed, when the midst of heaven deep above us begins to grow such that a star here and there is lost to sight at this depth; and as the brightest handmaid of the sun advances, the heaven then shuts off its lights one by one, till the fairest is gone; not otherwise the triumph that plays forever round the Point which overcame me, seeming enclosed by that which it encloses, was gradually extinguished to my sight, wherefore seeing nothing and love constrained me to return with my eyes to Beatrice. If what has been said of her so far as here were all included in a single praise, it would be too slight to serve this present turn.

La bellezza ch'io vidi si trasmoda
   non pur di là da noi, ma certo io credo
   che solo il suo fattor tutta la goda.   *21*
Da questo passo vinto mi concedo
   più che già mai da punto di suo tema
   soprato fosse comico o tragedo: *24*
ché, come sole in viso che più trema,
   così lo rimembrar del dolce riso
   la mente mia da me medesmo scema.   *27*
Dal primo giorno ch'i' vidi il suo viso
   in questa vita, infino a questa vista,
   non m'è il seguire al mio cantar preciso;   *30*
ma or convien che mio seguir desista
   più dietro a sua bellezza, poetando,
   come a l'ultimo suo ciascuno artista.   *33*
Cotal qual io la lascio a maggior bando
   che quel de la mia tuba, che deduce
   l'ardüa sua matera terminando,   *36*
con atto e voce di spedito duce
   ricominciò: "Noi siamo usciti fore
   del maggior corpo al ciel ch'è pura luce: *39*
luce intellettüal, piena d'amore;
   amor di vero ben, pien di letizia;
   letizia che trascende ogne dolzore.   *42*
Qui vederai l'una e l'altra milizia
   di paradiso, e l'una in quelli aspetti
   che tu vedrai a l'ultima giustizia."   *45*
Come sùbito lampo che discetti
   li spiriti visivi, sì che priva
   da l'atto l'occhio di più forti obietti,   *48*

The beauty I beheld transcends measure not only beyond our reach, but I truly believe that He alone who made it can enjoy it all. At this pass I concede myself defeated more than ever comic or tragic poet was defeated by a point in his theme; for, as the sun does to the sight which trembles most, even so remembrance of the sweet smile shears my memory of its very self. From the first day when in this life I saw her face, until this sight, the continuing of my song has not been cut off, but now my pursuit must desist from following her beauty further in my verses, as at his utmost reach must every artist.

Such as I leave her to a greater heralding than that of my trumpet, which draws its arduous subject to a close, with the act and voice of a leader whose task is accomplished she began again, "We have issued forth from the greatest body to the heaven which is pure light: light intellectual full of love, love of true good full of joy, joy that transcends every sweetness. Here you shall see the one and the other soldiery of Paradise, and the one in those aspects which you shall see at the last judgment."

As a sudden flash of lightning which scatters the visual spirits so that it robs the eye of the sight of the clearest objects,

337

così mi circunfulse luce viva,
e lasciommi fasciato di tal velo
del suo fulgor, che nulla m'appariva.   *51*
"Sempre l'amor che queta questo cielo
accoglie in sé con sì fatta salute,
per far disposto a sua fiamma il candelo."   *54*
Non fur più tosto dentro a me venute
queste parole brievi, ch'io compresi
me sormontar di sopr' a mia virtute;   *57*
e di novella vista mi raccesi
tale, che nulla luce è tanto mera,
che li occhi miei non si fosser difesi;   *60*
e vidi lume in forma di rivera
fulvido di fulgore, intra due rive
dipinte di mirabil primavera.   *63*
Di tal fiumana uscian faville vive,
e d'ogne parte si mettien ne' fiori,
quasi rubin che oro circunscrive;   *66*
poi, come inebrïate da li odori,
riprofondavan sé nel miro gurge,
e s'una intrava, un'altra n'uscia fori.   *69*
"L'alto disio che mo t'infiamma e urge,
d'aver notizia di ciò che tu vei,
tanto mi piace più quanto più turge;   *72*
ma di quest' acqua convien che tu bei
prima che tanta sete in te si sazi":
così mi disse il sol de li occhi miei.   *75*
Anche soggiunse: "Il fiume e li topazi
ch'entrano ed escono e 'l rider de l'erbe
son di lor vero umbriferi prefazi.   *78*

so round about me there shone a vivid light and left me so swathed in the veil of its effulgence that nothing was visible to me.

"Ever does the love which quiets this heaven receive into itself with such like salutation, in order to prepare the candle for its flame." No sooner had these brief words come within me than I comprehended that I was surmounting beyond my own power, and such new vision was kindled in me that there is no light so bright that my eyes could not have withstood it. And I saw a light in form of a river glowing tawny between two banks painted with marvelous spring. From out this river issued living sparks and dropped on every side into the blossoms, like rubies set in gold. Then, as if inebriated by the odors, they plunged again into the wondrous flood, and as one was entering another was issuing forth.

"The high desire which now inflames and urges you to have knowledge concerning that which you see pleases me the more the more it swells; but first you must needs drink of this water before so great a thirst in you be slaked." So spoke the sun of my eyes to me, then added, "The stream and the topazes which enter and issue, and the smiling of the grasses, are the shadowy prefaces of their truth;

Non che da sé sian queste cose acerbe;
   ma è difetto da la parte tua,
   che non hai viste ancor tanto superbe."   *81*
Non è fantin che sì sùbito rua
   col volto verso il latte, se si svegli
   molto tardato da l'usanza sua,   *84*
come fec' io, per far migliori spegli
   ancor de li occhi, chinandomi a l'onda
   che si deriva perché vi s'immegli;   *87*
e sì come di lei bevve la gronda
   de le palpebre mie, così mi parve
   di sua lunghezza divenuta tonda.   *90*
Poi, come gente stata sotto larve,
   che pare altro che prima, se si sveste
   la sembianza non süa in che disparve,   *93*
così mi si cambiaro in maggior feste
   li fiori e le faville, sì ch'io vidi
   ambo le corti del ciel manifeste.   *96*
O isplendor di Dio, per cu' io vidi
   l'alto trïunfo del regno verace,
   dammi virtù a dir com' ïo il vidi!   *99*
Lume è là sù che visibile face
   lo creatore a quella creatura
   che solo in lui vedere ha la sua pace.   *102*
E' si distende in circular figura,
   in tanto che la sua circunferenza
   sarebbe al sol troppo larga cintura.   *105*
Fassi di raggio tutta sua parvenza
   reflesso al sommo del mobile primo,
   che prende quindi vivere e potenza.   *108*

not that these things are defective in themselves, but on your side is the defect, in that you do not yet have vision so exalted."

No infant, on waking far after its hour, so suddenly rushes with face toward the milk, as then did I, to make yet better mirrors of my eyes, stooping to the wave which flows there that we may be bettered in it. And even as the eaves of my eyelids drank of it, so it seemed to me out of its length to have become round. Then, as folk who have been under masks seem other than before, if they do off the semblances not their own wherein they were hid, so into greater festival the flowers and the sparks did change before me that I saw both the courts of Heaven made manifest. O splendor of God whereby I saw the high triumph of the true kingdom, give to me power to tell how I beheld it!

A Light is thereabove which makes the Creator visible to every creature that has his peace only in beholding Him. It spreads so wide a circle that the circumference would be too large a girdle for the sun. Its whole expanse is made by a ray reflected from the summit of the Primum Mobile, which therefrom takes its life and potency;

E come clivo in acqua di suo imo
   si specchia, quasi per vedersi addorno,
   quando è nel verde e ne' fioretti opimo,   *111*
sì, soprastando al lume intorno intorno,
   vidi specchiarsi in più di mille soglie
   quanto di noi là sù fatto ha ritorno.   *114*
E se l'infimo grado in sé raccoglie
   sì grande lume, quanta è la larghezza
   di questa rosa ne l'estreme foglie!   *117*
La vista mia ne l'ampio e ne l'altezza
   non si smarriva, ma tutto prendeva
   il quanto e 'l quale di quella allegrezza.   *120*
Presso e lontano, lì, né pon né leva:
   ché dove Dio sanza mezzo governa,
   la legge natural nulla rileva.   *123*
Nel giallo de la rosa sempiterna,
   che si digrada e dilata e redole
   odor di lode al sol che sempre verna,   *126*
qual è colui che tace e dicer vole,
   mi trasse Bëatrice, e disse: "Mira
   quanto è 'l convento de le bianche stole!   *129*
Vedi nostra città quant' ella gira;
   vedi li nostri scanni sì ripieni,
   che poca gente più ci si disira.   *132*
E 'n quel gran seggio a che tu li occhi tieni
   per la corona che già v'è sù posta,
   prima che tu a queste nozze ceni,   *135*
sederà l'alma, che fia giù agosta,
   de l'alto Arrigo, ch'a drizzare Italia
   verrà in prima ch'ella sia disposta.   *138*

and as a hillside mirrors itself in water at its base, as if to look upon its own adornment when it is rich in grasses and in flowers, so above the light round and round about in more than a thousand tiers I saw all that of us have won return up there. And if the lowest rank encloses within itself so great a light, how vast is the spread of this rose in its outermost leaves! My sight lost not itself in the breadth and in the height, but took in all the extent and quality of that joy. There, near and far neither add not take away, for where God governs without intermediary, the law of nature in no way prevails.

Into the yellow of the eternal Rose, which rises in ranks and expands and breathes forth odor of praise unto the Sun which makes perpetual spring, Beatrice drew me as one who is silent and wishes to speak, and she said, "Behold how great the assembly of the white robes! See our city, how wide is its circuit! See our seats so filled that few souls are now wanted there!

"And in that great chair whereon you fix your eyes because of the crown that already is set above it, before you sup at these nuptials shall sit the soul, which on earth will be imperial, of the lofty Henry, who will come to set Italy straight before she is ready.

La cieca cupidigia che v'ammalia
  simili fatti v'ha al fantolino
  che muor per fame e caccia via la balia.   *141*
E fia prefetto nel foro divino
  allora tal, che palese e coverto
  non anderà con lui per un cammino.   *144*
Ma poco poi sarà da Dio sofferto
  nel santo officio: ch'el sarà detruso
  là dove Simon mago è per suo merto,
e farà quel d'Alagna intrar più giuso."   *148*

The blind cupidity which bewitches you has
made you like the little child who dies of
hunger and drives away his nurse. And such
a one will then be prefect in the divine forum
who openly and secretly will not go with him
along one same road. But not for long shall
God then suffer him in the holy office; for he
shall be thrust down where Simon Magus is
for his deserts, and shall make him of Alagna
go deeper still."

PARADISO

IN FORMA dunque di candida rosa
  mi si mostrava la milizia santa
  che nel suo sangue Cristo fece sposa;   *3*
ma l'altra, che volando vede e canta
  la gloria di colui che la 'nnamora
  e la bontà che la fece cotanta,   *6*
sì come schiera d'ape che s'infiora
  una fïata e una si ritorna
  là dove suo laboro s'insapora,   *9*
nel gran fior discendeva che s'addorna
  di tante foglie, e quindi risaliva
  là dove 'l süo amor sempre soggiorna.   *12*
Le facce tutte avean di fiamma viva
  e l'ali d'oro, e l'altro tanto bianco,
  che nulla neve a quel termine arriva.   *15*
Quando scendean nel fior, di banco in banco
  porgevan de la pace e de l'ardore
  ch'elli acquistavan ventilando il fianco.   *18*

CANTO XXXI

In form then of a pure white rose the saintly host was shown to me, which with His own blood Christ made His bride. But the other host—who, as it flies, sees and sings His glory who enamors it and the goodness which made it so great—like a swarm of bees which one moment enflower themselves, and the next return to where their work acquires savor—was descending into the great flower which is adorned with so many petals, and thence reascending to where its love abides forever. They had their faces all of living flame, and their wings of gold, and the rest so white that no snow reaches such a limit. When they descended into the flower, from rank to rank they proffered of the peace and the ardor which they had acquired as they fanned their sides.

Né l'interporsi tra 'l disopra e 'l fiore
di tanta moltitudine volante
impediva la vista e lo splendore: *21*
ché la luce divina è penetrante
per l'universo secondo ch'è degno,
sì che nulla le puote essere ostante. *24*
Questo sicuro e gaudïoso regno,
frequente in gente antica e in novella,
viso e amore avea tutto ad un segno. *27*
Oh trina luce che 'n unica stella
scintillando a lor vista, sì li appaga!
guarda qua giuso a la nostra procella! *30*
Se i barbari, venendo da tal plaga
che ciascun giorno d'Elice si cuopra,
rotante col suo figlio ond' ella è vaga, *33*
veggendo Roma e l'ardüa sua opra,
stupefaciensi, quando Laterano
a le cose mortali andò di sopra; *36*
ïo, che al divino da l'umano,
a l'etterno dal tempo era venuto,
e di Fiorenza in popol giusto e sano, *39*
di che stupor dovea esser compiuto!
Certo tra esso e 'l gaudio mi facea
libito non udire e starmi muto. *42*
E quasi peregrin che si ricrea
nel tempio del suo voto riguardando,
e spera già ridir com' ello stea, *45*
su per la viva luce passeggiando,
menava ïo li occhi per li gradi,
mo sù, mo giù e mo recirculando. *48*

Nor did the interposing of so great a flying plenitude, between what was above and the flower, impede the vision or the splendor; for the divine light so penetrates through the universe, in measure of its worthiness, that naught can be an obstacle to it. This secure and joyful kingdom, thronged with ancient and with modern folk, had look and love all directed on one mark.

O threefold Light, which, in a single star sparkling on their sight, dost so satisfy them, look down upon our tempest here below!

If the Barbarians, coming from such region as is covered every day by Helice, wheeling with her son whom she delights in, when they beheld Rome and her mighty work, when Lateran rose above all mortal things, were wonder-struck, I, who to the divine from the human, to the eternal from time had come, and from Florence to a people just and sane, with what amazement must I have been full! Truly, what with it and with the joy, I was content to hear naught and to stand mute. And as a pilgrim who is refreshed within the temple of his vow as he looks around, and already hopes to tell again how it was, so, taking my way upwards through the living light, I led my eyes along the ranks, now up, now down, and now circling about.

Vedëa visi a carità süadi,
  d'altrui lume fregiati e di suo riso,
  e atti ornati di tutte onestadi.   *51*
La forma general di paradiso
  già tutta mïo sguardo avea compresa,
  in nulla parte ancor fermato fiso;   *54*
e volgeami con voglia rïaccesa
  per domandar la mia donna di cose
  di che la mente mia era sospesa.   *57*
Uno intendëa, e altro mi rispuose:
  credea veder Beatrice e vidi un sene
  vestito con le genti glorïose.   *60*
Diffuso era per li occhi e per le gene
  di benigna letizia, in atto pio
  quale a tenero padre si convene.   *63*
E "Ov' è ella?" sùbito diss' io.
  Ond' elli: "A terminar lo tuo disiro
  mosse Beatrice me del loco mio;   *66*
e se riguardi sù nel terzo giro
  dal sommo grado, tu la rivedrai
  nel trono che suoi merti le sortiro."   *69*
Sanza risponder, li occhi sù levai,
  e vidi lei che si facea corona
  reflettendo da sé li etterni rai.   *72*
Da quella regïon che più sù tona
  occhio mortale alcun tanto non dista,
  qualunque in mare più giù s'abbandona,   *75*
quanto lì da Beatrice la mia vista;
  ma nulla mi facea, ché süa effige
  non discendëa a me per mezzo mista.   *78*

I saw faces all given to love, adorned by the light of Another, and by their own smile, and movements graced with every dignity.

My look had now taken in the general form of Paradise as a whole, and on no part as yet had my sight paused; and I turned with re-kindled will to ask my lady about things as to which my mind was in suspense. One thing I purposed, and another answered me: I thought to see Beatrice, and I saw an elder, clad like the folk in glory. His eyes and cheeks were suffused with benign gladness, his mien kindly such as befits a tender father. And, "Where is she?" I said at once; whereon he, "To terminate your desire Beatrice urged me from my place; and if you look up to the circle which is third from the highest tier, you will see her again, in the throne her merits have allotted to her."

Without answering I lifted up my eyes and saw her where she made for herself a crown as she reflected the eternal rays. From the region which thunders most high no mortal eye is so far distant, were it plunged most deep within the sea, as there from Beatrice was my sight. But to me it made no differ-ence, for her image came down to me un-blurred by aught between.

"O donna in cui la mia speranza vige,
  e che soffristi per la mia salute
  in inferno lasciar le tue vestige,   *81*
di tante cose quant' i' ho vedute,
  dal tuo podere e da la tua bontate
  riconosco la grazia e la virtute.   *84*
Tu m'hai di servo tratto a libertate
  per tutte quelle vie, per tutt' i modi
  che di ciò fare avei la potestate.   *87*
La tua magnificenza in me custodi,
  sì che l'anima mia, che fatt' hai sana,
  piacente a te dal corpo si disnodi."   *90*
Così orai; e quella, sì lontana
  come parea, sorrise e riguardommi;
  poi si tornò a l'etterna fontana.   *93*
E 'l santo sene: "Acciò che tu assommi
  perfettamente," disse, "il tuo cammino,
  a che priego e amor santo mandommi,   *96*
vola con li occhi per questo giardino;
  ché veder lui t'acconcerà lo sguardo
  più al montar per lo raggio divino.   *99*
E la regina del cielo, ond' ïo ardo
  tutto d'amor, ne farà ogne grazia,
  però ch'i' sono il suo fedel Bernardo."   *102*
Qual è colui che forse di Croazia
  viene a veder la Veronica nostra,
  che per l'antica fame non sen sazia,   *105*
ma dice nel pensier, fin che si mostra:
  "Segnor mio Iesù Cristo, Dio verace,
  or fu sì fatta la sembianza vostra?";   *108*

"O lady, in whom my hope is strong, and who for my salvation did endure to leave in Hell your footprints, of all those things which I have seen I acknowledge the grace and the virtue to be from your power and your excellence. It is you who have drawn me from bondage into liberty by all those paths, by all those means by which you had the power so to do. Preserve in me your great munificence, so that my soul, which you have made whole, may be loosed from the body, pleasing unto you." So did I pray; and she, so distant as she seemed, smiled and looked on me, then turned again to the eternal fountain.

And the holy elder said, "In order that you may consummate your journey perfectly, whereto prayer and holy love dispatched me, fly with your eyes throughout this garden; for gazing on it will better prepare your sight to mount through the divine ray. And the Queen of Heaven, for whom I am all afire with love, will grant us every grace, since I am her faithful Bernard."

As is he who comes perchance from Croatia to look on our Veronica, and whose old hunger is not sated, but says in thought so long as it is shown, "My Lord Jesus Christ, true God, was then your semblance like to this?"

tal era io mirando la vivace
   carità di colui che 'n questo mondo,
   contemplando, gustò di quella pace.   *111*
"Figliuol di grazia, quest' esser giocondo,"
   cominciò elli, "non ti sarà noto,
   tenendo li occhi pur qua giù al fondo;   *114*
ma guarda i cerchi infino al più remoto,
   tanto che veggi seder la regina
   cui questo regno è suddito e devoto."   *117*
Io levai li occhi; e come da mattina
   la parte oriëntal de l'orizzonte
   soverchia quella dove 'l sol declina,   *120*
così, quasi di valle andando a monte
   con li occhi, vidi parte ne lo stremo
   vincer di lume tutta l'altra fronte.   *123*
E come quivi ove s'aspetta il temo
   che mal guidò Fetonte, più s'infiamma,
   e quinci e quindi il lume si fa scemo,   *126*
così quella pacifica oriafiamma
   nel mezzo s'avvivava, e d'ogne parte
   per igual modo allentava la fiamma;   *129*
e a quel mezzo, con le penne sparte,
   vid' io più di mille angeli festanti,
   ciascun distinto di fulgore e d'arte.   *132*
Vidi a lor giochi quivi e a lor canti
   ridere una bellezza, che letizia
   era ne li occhi a tutti li altri santi;   *135*
e s'io avessi in dir tanta divizia
   quanta ad imaginar, non ardirei
   lo minimo tentar di sua delizia.   *138*

such was I, gazing on the living charity of him who, in this world, in contemplation tasted of that peace.

"Son of grace, this joyous being," he began, "will not be known to you if you hold your eyes only down here at the base; but look upon the circles, even to the most remote, until you see upon her seat the Queen to whom this realm is subject and devoted."

I lifted up my eyes; and as at morning the eastern parts of the horizon outshine that where the sun declines, so, as if going with my eyes from valley to mountain-top I saw a part on the extreme verge surpass with its light all the rest of the rim. And as the point where we await the pole that Phaethon misguided is most aglow, and on this side and on that the light diminishes, so was that pacific oriflamme quickened in the middle, on either side in equal measure tempering its flame. And at the midpoint, with outstretched wings, I saw more than a thousand Angels making festival, each one distinct in effulgence and in ministry. I saw there, smiling to their sports and to their songs, a beauty which was gladness in the eyes of all the other saints. And had I equal wealth in speech as in conception, yet would I not dare to attempt the least of her delightfulness.

Bernardo, come vide li occhi miei
   nel caldo suo caler fissi e attenti,
   li suoi con tanto affetto volse a lei,
che ' miei di rimirar fé più ardenti.   *142*

Bernard, when he saw my eyes fixed and intent on the object of his own burning glow, turned his own with such affection to her, that he made mine more ardent in their gazing.

PARADISO

Affetto al suo piacer, quel contemplante
  libero officio di dottore assunse,
  e cominciò queste parole sante: 3
"La piaga che Maria richiuse e unse,
  quella ch'è tanto bella da' suoi piedi
  è colei che l'aperse e che la punse.   6
Ne l'ordine che fanno i terzi sedi,
  siede Rachel di sotto da costei
  con Bëatrice, sì come tu vedi.   9
Sarra e Rebecca, Iudìt e colei
  che fu bisava al cantor che per doglia
  del fallo disse 'Miserere mei,'   12
puoi tu veder così di soglia in soglia
  giù digradar, com' io ch'a proprio nome
  vo per la rosa giù di foglia in foglia.   15
E dal settimo grado in giù, sì come
  infino ad esso, succedono Ebree,
  dirimendo del fior tutte le chiome;   18

CANTO XXXII

Wɪᴛʜ ʜɪs love fixed on his Delight, that contemplator freely assumed the office of a teacher, and began these holy words, "The wound which Mary closed and anointed, that one who is so beautiful at her feet is she who opened it and pierced it. Below her, in the order which the third seats make, sits Rachel with Beatrice, as you see. Sarah, Rebecca, Judith, and she who was great-grandmother of the singer who, through sorrow for his sin, cried '*Miserere mei*,' you may see, thus from rank to rank in gradation downward, as with the name of each I go downward through the rose from petal to petal. And from the seventh row downwards, even as down to it, Hebrew women follow in succession, dividing all the tresses of the flower;

perché, secondo lo sguardo che fée
   la fede in Cristo, queste sono il muro
   a che si parton le sacre scalee.   *21*
Da questa parte onde 'l fiore è maturo
   di tutte le sue foglie, sono assisi
   quei che credettero in Cristo venturo;   *24*
da l'altra parte onde sono intercisi
   di vòti i semicirculi, si stanno
   quei ch'a Cristo venuto ebber li visi.   *27*
E come quinci il glorïoso scanno
   de la donna del cielo e li altri scanni
   di sotto lui cotanta cerna fanno,   *30*
così di contra quel del gran Giovanni,
   che sempre santo 'l diserto e 'l martiro
   sofferse, e poi l'inferno da due anni;   *33*
e sotto lui così cerner sortiro
   Francesco, Benedetto e Augustino
   e altri fin qua giù di giro in giro.   *36*
Or mira l'alto proveder divino:
   ché l'uno e l'altro aspetto de la fede
   igualmente empierà questo giardino.   *39*
E sappi che dal grado in giù che fiede
   a mezzo il tratto le due discrezioni,
   per nullo proprio merito si siede,   *42*
ma per l'altrui, con certe condizioni:
   ché tutti questi son spiriti asciolti
   prima ch'avesser vere elezïoni.   *45*
Ben te ne puoi accorger per li volti
   e anche per le voci püerili,
   se tu li guardi bene e se li ascolti.   *48*

because, according to the look which their faith turned to Christ, these are the wall by which the sacred stairway is divided. On this side, wherein the flower is mature in all its petals, are seated those who believed in Christ yet to come. On the other side, where the half-circles are broken by vacant places, sit those who turned their faces toward Christ already come. And as on this side the glorious seat of the Lady of Heaven, and the other seats below it, make so great a partition, thus, opposite, does the seat of the great John who, ever holy, endured the desert and martyrdom, and then Hell for two years; and beneath him, Francis and Benedict and Augustine and others were allotted thus to divide, as far down as here, from circle to circle. Now behold the depth of the divine foresight, for one and the other aspect of the faith shall fill this garden equally. And know that, downward from the row which cleaves midway the two dividing lines, they are seated for no merit of their own, but for that of others, under certain conditions; for all these are spirits absolved before they had true power of choice. Well can you perceive it by their faces and by their childish voices, if you look well upon them and if you listen to them.

Or dubbi tu e dubitando sili;
    ma io discioglierò 'l forte legame
    in che ti stringon li pensier sottili.   *51*
Dentro a l'ampiezza di questo reame
    casüal punto non puote aver sito,
    se non come tristizia o sete o fame: *54*
ché per etterna legge è stabilito
    quantunque vedi, sì che giustamente
    ci si risponde da l'anello al dito;   *57*
e però questa festinata gente
    a vera vita non è *sine causa*
    intra sé qui più e meno eccellente.   *60*
Lo rege per cui questo regno pausa
    in tanto amore e in tanto diletto,
    che nulla volontà è di più ausa,   *63*
le menti tutte nel suo lieto aspetto
    creando, a suo piacer di grazia dota
    diversamente; e qui basti l'effetto.   *66*
E ciò espresso e chiaro vi si nota
    ne la Scrittura santa in quei gemelli
    che ne la madre ebber l'ira commota.   *69*
Però, secondo il color d'i capelli,
    di cotal grazia l'altissimo lume
    degnamente convien che s'incappelli.   *72*
Dunque, sanza mercé di lor costume,
    locati son per gradi differenti,
    sol differendo nel primiero acume.   *75*
Bastavasi ne' secoli recenti
    con l'innocenza, per aver salute,
    solamente la fede d'i parenti;   *78*

"Now you are perplexed, and in perplexity are silent; but I will loose the hard knot wherein your subtle thoughts are binding you. Within the amplitude of this realm a casual point can have no place, any more than can sorrow, or thirst, or hunger; for whatever you see is established by eternal law, so that the correspondence is exact between the ring and finger. And therefore this company, hastened to true life, is not *sine causa* more or less excellent here among themselves. The King, through whom this realm reposes in such great love and in such great delight that no will dares for more, creating all the minds in His glad sight, at His own pleasure endows with grace diversely—and here let the fact suffice. And this is clearly and expressly noted for you in Holy Scripture in those twins whose anger was stirred within their mother's womb. Therefore, according to the color of the locks, of such grace needs must the lofty light crown them according to their worth. Wherefore, without merit of their own works, they are placed in different ranks, differing only in the primal keenness of vision. In the early ages, their parents' faith alone, with their own innocence, sufficed for their salvation;

poi che le prime etadi fuor compiute,
   convenne ai maschi a l'innocenti penne
   per circuncidere acquistar virtute;   *81*
ma poi che 'l tempo de la grazia venne,
   sanza battesmo perfetto di Cristo
   tale innocenza là giù si ritenne.   *84*
Riguarda omai ne la faccia che a Cristo
   più si somiglia, ché la sua chiarezza
   sola ti può disporre a veder Cristo."   *87*
Io vidi sopra lei tanta allegrezza
   piover, portata ne le menti sante
   create a trasvolar per quella altezza,   *90*
che quantunque io avea visto davante,
   di tanta ammirazion non mi sospese,
   né mi mostrò di Dio tanto sembiante;   *93*
e quello amor che primo lì discese,
   cantando "*Ave, Maria, gratïa plena,*"
   dinanzi a lei le sue ali distese.   *96*
Rispuose a la divina cantilena
   da tutte parti la beata corte,
   sì ch'ogne vista sen fé più serena.   *99*
"O santo padre, che per me comporte
   l'esser qua giù, lasciando il dolce loco
   nel qual tu siedi per etterna sorte,   *102*
qual è quell' angel che con tanto gioco
   guarda ne li occhi la nostra regina,
   innamorato sì che par di foco?"   *105*
Così ricorsi ancora a la dottrina
   di colui ch'abbelliva di Maria,
   come del sole stella mattutina.   *108*

After those first ages were complete, it was needful for males, through circumcision, to acquire power for their innocent wings; but after the time of grace had come, without perfect baptism in Christ such innocence was held there below.

"Look now upon the face which most resembles Christ, for only its brightness can prepare you to see Christ."

I saw such gladness rain down upon her, borne in the holy minds created to fly through that height, that all I had seen before had not held me in suspense of such great marveling, nor showed me such likeness to God. And that Love which first descended there, singing *Ave Maria, gratia plena,* now spread his wings before her. On all sides the blessed Court responded to the divine song, so that every face became the brighter therefor.

"O holy father, who for my sake endure to be here below, leaving the sweet place in which by eternal lot you have your seat, who is that angel who with such joy looks into the eyes of our Queen, so enamored that he seems afire?" Thus did I again recur to the teaching of him who drew beauty from Mary, as the morning star from the sun.

Ed elli a me: "Baldezza e leggiadria
   quant' esser puote in angelo e in alma,
   tutta è in lui; e sì volem che sia,   *111*
perch' elli è quelli che portò la palma
   giuso a Maria, quando 'l Figliuol di Dio
   carcar si volse de la nostra salma.   *114*
Ma vieni omai con li occhi sì com' io
   andrò parlando, e nota i gran patrici
   di questo imperio giustissimo e pio.   *117*
Quei due che seggon là sù più felici
   per esser propinquissimi ad Agusta,
   son d'esta rosa quasi due radici: *120*
colui che da sinistra le s'aggiusta
   è 'l padre per lo cui ardito gusto
   l'umana specie tanto amaro gusta;   *123*
dal destro vedi quel padre vetusto
   di Santa Chiesa a cui Cristo le chiavi
   raccomandò di questo fior venusto.   *126*
E quei che vide tutti i tempi gravi,
   pria che morisse, de la bella sposa
   che s'acquistò con la lancia e coi clavi,   *129*
siede lungh' esso, e lungo l'altro posa
   quel duca sotto cui visse di manna
   la gente ingrata, mobile e retrosa.   *132*
Di contr' a Pietro vedi sedere Anna,
   tanto contenta di mirar sua figlia,
   che non move occhio per cantare osanna;   *135*
e contro al maggior padre di famiglia
   siede Lucia, che mosse la tua donna
   quando chinavi, a rovinar, le ciglia.   *138*

And he to me, "Confidence and grace, as much as there can be in angel and in soul, are all in him, and we would have it so, for it is he who bore the palm down to Mary, when the Son of God willed to load Himself with the burden of our flesh.

"But come now with your eyes, as I proceed in speaking, and note the great patricians of this most just and pious empire. Those two who sit there above, most happy for being nearest to the Empress, are, as it were, two roots of this rose: he who is beside her upon the left is that Father because of whose audacious tasting the human race tastes such bitterness. On the right you see that ancient Father of Holy Church to whom Christ entrusted the keys of this beauteous flower. And he who saw, before he died, all the grievous times of the fair Bride who was won with the spear and the nails sits at his side; and beside the other rests that leader, under whom the thankless, fickle, and stubborn people lived on manna. Opposite Peter you see Anna sitting, so content to gaze upon her daughter that she moves not her eyes as she sings Hosannah. And opposite the greatest father of a family sits Lucy, who moved your lady when you were bending your brows downward to your ruin.

Ma perché 'l tempo fugge che t'assonna,
  qui farem punto, come buon sartore
  che com' elli ha del panno fa la gonna;   *141*
e drizzeremo li occhi al primo amore,
  sì che, guardando verso lui, penètri
  quant' è possibil per lo suo fulgore.   *144*
Veramente, *ne* forse tu t'arretri
  movendo l'ali tue, credendo oltrarti,
  orando grazia conven che s'impetri   *147*
grazia da quella che puote aiutarti;
  e tu mi seguirai con l'affezione,
  sì che dal dicer mio lo cor non parti."
E cominciò questa santa orazione: *151*

"But because the time flies that brings sleep upon you, we will stop here, like a good tailor that cuts the garment according to his cloth, and we will turn our eyes to the Primal Love, so that, gazing toward Him, you may penetrate, as far as that can be, into His effulgence. But lest, perchance, you fall back, moving your wings and thinking to advance, grace must be obtained by prayer, grace from her who has power to aid you; and do you follow me with your affection so that your heart depart not from my words."

And he began this holy prayer:

PARADISO

"Vergine Madre, figlia del tuo figlio,
    umile e alta più che creatura,
    termine fisso d'etterno consiglio,   3
tu se' colei che l'umana natura
    nobilitasti sì, che 'l suo fattore
    non disdegnò di farsi sua fattura.   6
Nel ventre tuo si raccese l'amore,
    per lo cui caldo ne l'etterna pace
    così è germinato questo fiore.   9
Qui se' a noi meridïana face
    di caritate, e giuso, intra ' mortali,
    se' di speranza fontana vivace.   12
Donna, se' tanto grande e tanto vali,
    che qual vuol grazia e a te non ricorre,
    sua disïanza vuol volar sanz' ali.   15
La tua benignità non pur soccorre
    a chi domanda, ma molte fiate
    liberamente al dimandar precorre.   18

CANTO XXXIII

"Virgin mother, daughter of thy Son, humble and exalted more than any creature, fixed goal of the eternal counsel, thou art she who didst so enoble human nature that its Maker did not disdain to become its creature. In thy womb was rekindled the Love under whose warmth this flower in the eternal peace has thus unfolded. Here thou art for us the noonday torch of charity, and below among mortals thou art the living fount of hope. Lady, thou art so great and so availest, that whoso would have grace and has not recourse to thee, his desire seeks to fly without wings. Thy loving-kindness not only succors him who asks, but oftentimes freely foreruns the asking.

In te misericordia, in te pietate,
   in te magnificenza, in te s'aduna
   quantunque in creatura è di bontate.   *21*
Or questi, che da l'infima lacuna
   de l'universo infin qui ha vedute
   le vite spiritali ad una ad una,   *24*
supplica a te, per grazia, di virtute
   tanto, che possa con li occhi levarsi
   più alto verso l'ultima salute.   *27*
E io, che mai per mio veder non arsi
   più ch'i' fo per lo suo, tutti miei prieghi
   ti porgo, e priego che non sieno scarsi,   *30*
perché tu ogne nube li disleghi
   di sua mortalità co' prieghi tuoi,
   sì che 'l sommo piacer li si dispieghi.   *33*
Ancor ti priego, regina, che puoi
   ciò che tu vuoli, che conservi sani,
   dopo tanto veder, li affetti suoi.   *36*
Vinca tua guardia i movimenti umani:
   vedi Beatrice con quanti beati
   per li miei prieghi ti chiudon le mani!"　 *39*
Li occhi da Dio diletti e venerati,
   fissi ne l'orator, ne dimostraro
   quanto i devoti prieghi le son grati;   *42*
indi a l'etterno lume s'addrizzaro,
   nel qual non si dee creder che s'invii
   per creatura l'occhio tanto chiaro.   *45*
E io ch'al fine di tutt' i disii
   appropinquava, sì com' io dovea,
   l'ardor del desiderio in me finii.   *48*

In thee is mercy, in thee pity, in thee munifi-
cence, in thee is found whatever of goodness
is in any creature. Now this man, who from
the lowest pit of the universe even to here
has seen one by one the spiritual lives, im-
plores thee of thy grace for power such that
he may be able with his eyes to rise still
higher toward the last salvation. And I, who
never for my own vision burned more than
I do for his, proffer to thee all my prayers,
and pray that they be not scant, that with thy
prayers thou wouldst dispel for him every
cloud of his mortality, so that the Supreme
Pleasure may be disclosed to him. Further I
pray thee, Queen, who canst do whatsoever
thou wilt, that thou preserve sound for him
his affections, after so great a vision. Let thy
protection vanquish human impulses. Be-
hold Beatrice, with how many saints, for my
prayers clasping their hands to thee."

The eyes beloved and reverenced by God,
fixed upon him who prayed, showed us how
greatly devout prayers do please her; then
they were turned to the Eternal Light,
wherein we may not believe that any crea-
ture's eye finds its way so clear.

And I, who was drawing near to the end
of all desires, raised to its utmost, even as I
ought, the ardor of my longing.

Bernardo m'accennava, e sorridea,
    perch' io guardassi suso; ma io era
    già per me stesso tal qual ei volea: *51*
ché la mia vista, venendo sincera,
    e più e più intrava per lo raggio
    de l'alta luce che da sé è vera.   *54*
Da quinci innanzi il mio veder fu maggio
    che 'l parlar mostra, ch'a tal vista cede,
    e cede la memoria a tanto oltraggio.   *57*
Qual è colüi che sognando vede,
    che dopo 'l sogno la passione impressa
    rimane, e l'altro a la mente non riede,   *60*
cotal son io, ché quasi tutta cessa
    mia visïone, e ancor mi distilla
    nel core il dolce che nacque da essa.   *63*
Così la neve al sol si disigilla;
    così al vento ne le foglie levi
    si perdea la sentenza di Sibilla.   *66*
O somma luce che tanto ti levi
    da' concetti mortali, a la mia mente
    ripresta un poco di quel che parevi,   *69*
e fa la lingua mia tanto possente,
    ch'una favilla sol de la tua gloria
    possa lasciare a la futura gente;   *72*
ché, per tornare alquanto a mia memoria
    e per sonare un poco in questi versi,
    più si conceperà di tua vittoria.   *75*
Io credo, per l'acume ch'io soffersi
    del vivo raggio, ch'i' sarei smarrito,
    se li occhi miei da lui fossero aversi.   *78*

Bernard was signing to me with a smile to look upward, but I was already of myself such as he wished; for my sight, becoming pure, was entering more and more through the beam of the lofty Light which in Itself is true.

Thenceforward my vision was greater than speech can show, which fails at such a sight, and at such excess memory fails. As is he who dreaming sees, and after the dream the passion remains imprinted and the rest returns not to the mind; such am I, for my vision almost wholly fades away, yet does the sweetness that was born of it still drop within my heart. Thus is the snow unsealed by the sun; thus in the wind, on the light leaves, the Sibyl's oracle was lost.

O Light Supreme that art so far uplifted above mortal conceiving, relend to my mind a little of what Thou didst appear, and give my tongue such power that it may leave only a single spark of Thy glory for the folk to come; for, by returning somewhat to my memory and by sounding a little in these lines, more of Thy victory shall be conceived.

I believe that, because of the keenness of the living ray which I endured, I should have been lost if my eyes had been turned from it.

E' mi ricorda ch'io fui più ardito
   per questo a sostener, tanto ch'i' giunsi
   l'aspetto mio col valore infinito.   *81*
Oh abbondante grazia ond' io presunsi
   ficcar lo viso per la luce etterna,
   tanto che la veduta vi consunsi!   *84*
Nel suo profondo vidi che s'interna,
   legato con amore in un volume,
   ciò che per l'universo si squaderna: *87*
sustanze e accidenti e lor costume
   quasi conflati insieme, per tal modo
   che ciò ch'i' dico è un semplice lume.   *90*
La forma universal di questo nodo
   credo ch'i' vidi, perché più di largo,
   dicendo questo, mi sento ch'i' godo.   *93*
Un punto solo m'è maggior letargo
   che venticinque secoli a la 'mpresa
   che fé Nettuno ammirar l'ombra d'Argo.   *96*
Così la mente mia, tutta sospesa,
   mirava fissa, immobile e attenta,
   e sempre di mirar faceasi accesa.   *99*
A quella luce cotal si diventa,
   che volgersi da lei per altro aspetto
   è impossibil che mai si consenta;   *102*
però che 'l ben, ch'è del volere obietto,
   tutto s'accoglie in lei, e fuor di quella
   è defettivo ciò ch'è lì perfetto.   *105*
Omai sarà più corta mia favella,
   pur a quel ch'io ricordo, che d'un fante
   che bagni ancor la lingua a la mammella.   *108*

I remember that on this account I was the bolder to sustain it, until I united my gaze with the Infinite Goodness.

O abounding grace whereby I presumed to fix my look through the Eternal Light so far that all my sight was spent therein.

In its depth I saw ingathered, bound by love in one single volume, that which is dispersed in leaves throughout the universe: substances and accidents and their relations, as though fused together in such a way that what I tell is but a simple light. The universal form of this knot I believe that I saw, because, in telling this, I feel my joy increase.

A single moment makes for me greater oblivion than five and twenty centuries have wrought upon the enterprise that made Neptune wonder at the shadow of the Argo. Thus my mind, all rapt, was gazing, fixed, motionless and intent, ever enkindled by its gazing. In that Light one becomes such that it is impossible he should ever consent to turn himself from it for other sight; for the good, which is the object of the will, is all gathered in it, and outside of it that is defective which is perfect there.

Now will my speech fall more short, even in respect to that which I remember, than that of an infant who still bathes his tongue at the breast.

Non perché più ch'un semplice sembiante
  fosse nel vivo lume ch'io mirava,
    che tal è sempre qual s'era davante;   *111*
ma per la vista che s'avvalorava
  in me guardando, una sola parvenza,
    mutandom' io, a me si travagliava.   *114*
Ne la profonda e chiara sussistenza
  de l'alto lume parvermi tre giri
    di tre colori e d'una contenenza;   *117*
e l'un da l'altro come iri da iri
  parea reflesso, e 'l terzo parea foco
    che quinci e quindi igualmente si spiri.   *120*
Oh quanto è corto il dire e come fioco
  al mio concetto! e questo, a quel ch'i' vidi,
    è tanto, che non basta a dicer "poco."   *123*
O luce etterna che sola in te sidi,
  sola t'intendi, e da te intelletta
    e intendente te ami e arridi!   *126*
Quella circulazion che sì concetta
  pareva in te come lume reflesso,
    da li occhi miei alquanto circunspetta,   *129*
dentro da sé, del suo colore stesso,
  mi parve pinta de la nostra effige:
    per che 'l mio viso in lei tutto era messo.   *132*
Qual è 'l geomètra che tutto s'affige
  per misurar lo cerchio, e non ritrova,
    pensando, quel principio ond' elli indige,   *135*
tal era io a quella vista nova:
  veder voleva come si convenne
    l'imago al cerchio e come vi s'indova;   *138*

Not because more than one simple semblance was in the Living Light wherein I was gazing, which ever is such as it was before; but through my sight, which was growing strong in me as I looked, one sole appearance, even as I changed, was altering itself to me.

Within the profound and shining subsistence of the lofty Light appeared to me three circles of three colors and one magnitude; and one seemed reflected by the other, as rainbow by rainbow, and the third seemed fire breathed forth equally from the one and the other.

O how scant is speech, and how feeble to my conception! and this, to what I saw, is such that it is not enough to call it little.

O Light Eternal, who alone abidest in Thyself, alone knowest Thyself, and, known to Thyself and knowing, lovest and smilest on Thyself!

That circling which, thus begotten, appeared in Thee as reflected light, when my eyes had dwelt on it for a time, seemed to me depicted with our image within itself and in its own color, wherefore my sight was entirely set upon it.

As is the geometer who wholly applies himself to measure the circle, and finds not, in pondering, the principle of which he is in need, such was I at that new sight. I wished to see how the image conformed to the circle and how it has its place therein;

ma non eran da ciò le proprie penne:
se non che la mia mente fu percossa
da un fulgore in che sua voglia venne.   *141*
A l'alta fantasia qui mancò possa;
ma già volgeva il mio disio e 'l *velle*,
sì come rota ch'igualmente è mossa,
l'amor che move il sole e l'altre stelle.   *145*

but my own wings were not sufficient for that, save that my mind was smitten by a flash wherein its wish came to it. Here power failed the lofty phantasy; but already my desire and my will were revolved, like a wheel that is evenly moved, by the Love which moves the sun and the other stars.

INDEX

This LIST includes the names of persons and places mentioned in the *Paradiso*. All names are given in their conventional English form where possible, according to the translation in this volume. Even though a name may occur more than once in a single passage or canto, only its first occurrence there is listed. Italicized numbers of cantos and verses indicate indirect reference to a person or place in the verse cited.